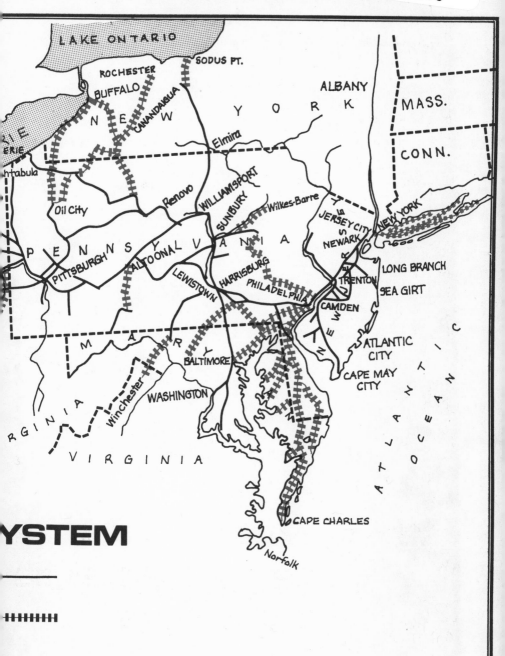

LAKE ONTARIO

ROCHESTER
BUFFALO
SODUS PT.
CANANDAIGUA

N E W   Y O R K   ALBANY   MASS.

Elmira   CONN.

Ashtabula
ERIE

Oil City   Renovo   WILLIAMSPORT   SUNBURY   Wilkes-Barre   JERSEY CITY   NEW YORK
NEWARK

P E N N S   Y   L V A N I A.
PITTSBURGH   ALTOONA   HARRISBURG   PHILADELPHIA   TRENTON   LONG BRANCH
LEWISTOWN   SEA GIRT
CAMDEN

M A R   Y
BALTIMORE   ATLANTIC CITY
Winchester   CAPE MAY CITY
WASHINGTON

RGINIA   V I R G I N I A   A T L A N T I C   O C E A N

CAPE CHARLES
Norfolk

YSTEM

++++++++

END
OF THE LINE

Alexander J. Cassatt and the
Pennsylvania Railroad

Patricia T. Davis

NEALE WATSON ACADEMIC PUBLICATIONS, INC.
NEW YORK

First published in the United States by
Neale Watson Academic Publications, Inc.
156 Fifth Avenue, New York, N.Y. 10010

© Neale Watson Academic Publications, Inc. 1978
Printed and manufactured in the U.S.A.

Library of Congress Cataloging in Publication Data

Davis, Patricia Talbot.
    End of the line.

    Bibliography: p.
    Includes index.
    1. Cassatt, Alexander Johnston, 1839-1906.
2. Businessmen--United States--Biography.
3. Pennsylvania Railroad. I. Title.
HE2754.C3D38   385'.092'4 [B]   78-977
ISBN 0-88202-181-8

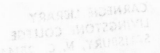

FOR

A. J. C.'s GRANDDAUGHTER,

MRS. JOHN B. THAYER

In Loving Memory

Contents

Acknowledgments

A biographer's delight is an unheralded hero, and such is Alexander Johnston Cassatt. I owe my discovery of this railroad pioneer to his granddaughter, Lois Cassatt Thayer, who urged me to read through her family letters. Without her encouragement, support, and reminiscences, this book would never have been attempted. Not only did she allow me unquestioned access to her collection of family letters and memorabilia, but she spent many hours talking about her grandfather, evoking his personality, character, and accomplishments. Her tales of travel on the Pennsylvania Railroad in the president's private car prior to the New York tunnel extension were invaluable. The dedication of this book can in no way repay my immense debt to her. A few months before publication Mrs. John B. Thayer died, assured that her grandfather's story would be told.

Other members of the Cassatt-Thayer family were helpful to me during the research. Mrs. W. West Frazier escorted me around her great-grandfather's 600 acre farm, Chesterbrook, now to become a developer's tract. John B. Thayer IV loaned books on railroad history. Charles W. Hare visited Harvard's Library to search through financial records. Mrs. J. Norman Henry offered unrestricted use of other Cassatt letters. Robert Maguire, an historian and writer, read every word of the manuscript and gave gentle but trenchant criticism. He was also of great assistance in securing permission for the reproduction of Mary Cassatt's portraits of her brother and sister-in-law, through the artist's chief cataloguer, Adelyn Breeskin.

Jacques de Spoelberch combined the talents of editor and agent, a stern taskmaster but a sympathetic listener when despair threatened to overwhelm me. Gerald Lombardi gave much needed direction in the final stages of preparation. Barbara Rex took me firmly in hand when the frustrations of revision and organization seemed insurmountable: "Let us see him," she insisted, advice of incalculable worth to a novice who often forgot that Cassatt was a stranger to many.

Thomas C. Cochran, an authority on railroad history, offered books and discussed thorny questions. I am also grateful for the loan of volumes from his railroad collection. Keith Doms, Director of the Free Library of Philadelphia, and his assistant, R. S. Rosensteel, far exceeded the responsibility of librarians in providing material and photographs. William Green, the Free Library's custodian of newspaper files, was more than cooperative. Charles Martyn and Wayne Kessler of *The Philadelphia Bulletin* library searched for and supplied the necessary newspaper accounts of the period. William Fidati of *The Bulletin* sports staff explained racing in clear terms. Authors Nicholas von Hoffman, Nancy Hale, and Nathaniel Burt were very generous. Edwin P. Roeser, an engineer, read the tunnel chapter for technical accuracy, although any mistakes must be laid to my door, not his. Bayard Roberts allowed me to read the correspondence of his grandfather, George P. Roberts, Cassatt's predecessor.

For many years the Pennsylvania Railroad shunned the efforts of historians to tell its story. Although much has been written about the history of the railroads in America, the Pennsylvania has been largely ignored. William Lashley, former vice president of the Penn Central, cooperated fully with my requests to search in the 49th Street warehouse which housed over one hundred years of Pennsylvania records. Cecil Muldoon, another Penn Central executive and long-time railroad student, provided information on the New York tunnel extension. Vincent Stamato, clerk in the president's office, was unfailing in his cheerful willingness to delve into dusty stockpiles at the warehouse. He found and supplied the Cassatt letterbooks of presidential correspondence, heretofore unexamined by historian or biographer. Armond Martorelli provided the annual reports of the Pennsylvania for the vital years.

Jacqueline Hammerschmidt and Georgiana Snyder uncomplainingly typed and retyped the manuscript. Through the three years of research and writing my husband, B. Dale Davis, and my daughters, if at times impatient with my preoccupation, proved long-suffering and understanding.

For any ommissions to this catalogue of gratitude, and there must be many, I apologize. In the long months of travail which a biographer endures in pursuit of the subject, sustenance and encouragement come from many sources. For all this aid and comfort, I am indeed thankful.

Introduction

On the drizzling morning of October 29, 1963, bulldozers, jackhammers, and a giant crane moved into New York's Pennsylvania Station to begin a ten million dollar demolition of the classical terminal. The weather matched the mood of the members of the Action Group for Better Architecture parading before the station in protest, their arms banded in black. Although urban soot and grime now darkened its once pristine pink granite walls, for fifty-six years this symbol of the great railroad's power had dominated seven acres in the heart of Manhattan. Modeled after the Roman Baths of Caracalla with a concourse longer than the nave of St. Peter's, a vaulted glass and steel ceiling one hundred and thirty feet high, and a grand staircase more than forty feet wide, the arrogant monument to train travel was doomed. "Just another job," said foreman John Rezin as he watched the crane slowly lower the first of six 5,700-pound eagles from its perch above the entrance ledge.

At the turn of the century, the $150,000,000 project that brought the Pennsylvania into New York through tunnels under the Hudson and East Rivers into the magnificent station was regarded as "the eighth wonder of the world," an engineering and architecural marvel, testifying to the dominance of the locomotive engine. In 1900 America ran on rails. Fifty years later the country moved by automobile, truck, and airplane. Wasted space was the real estate agents appraisal of Pennsylvania Station. Traffic managers, equally pragmatic, decided that the terminal did not provide efficient dispersal of people. "The handling of 200,000 passengers is much more important to me," said the Pennsylvania's New York manager. Those passengers must sacrifice the misty, romantic, if somewhat decayed, splendour of a grand gateway, which had promised to make a ceremony of every journey, to a truncated station topped by office buildings and a huge sports complex, the third Madison Square Garden.

By the spring of 1964, only the shell of the station remained, although outside the eighty-four Doric columns still masked the desecration within. By April of that year, the mellow, creamy interior walls, constructed of the same Tivoli marble used to build Rome's Colisium in the first century A.D. had disappeared. Now the grand stairway would fall beneath the wreckers' hammers. Few passengers, scurrying through the noise and confusion to catch their trains in the unchanged underground burrow, stopped to watch the crew remove the bronze statue of the man who had conceived this architectural wonder, Alexander Johnston Cassatt, seventh president of the Pennsylvania Railroad, 1899–1906. That statue, which had flanked the stairway since the station's dedication in 1910, accompanied thousands of tons of rubble to the dump heap in Hackensack meadow.

James McCrea, Cassatt's successor, in dedicating the station and the statue, had remarked, "As the years roll round the greater will be the tribute to Mr. Cassatt's genius." The years have rolled round to bring Alexander J. Cassatt and the Pennsylvania which he commanded onto the dump heap of history. America rode into the twentieth century on rails, and no one man contributed more to the growth of the nation's most vital industry than Cassatt, a man whose prominence rivalled that of the giants with whom he did business, Vanderbilt, Morgan, Carnegie, Rockefeller. Today his reputation, his Roman station, his railroad, have reached the end of the line with no return trip scheduled.

Alexander Johnston Cassatt knew how to run a railroad, whether into New York or across any of the Pennsylvania's 11,000 miles of track from Philadelphia to the Mississippi. He had learned his trade in the backwoods, clay hills of Georgia, as a humble rodman, before the Civil War. By his thirtieth birthday he had risen to be general superintendent of the Pennsylvania. In those nine years he absorbed the basic fundamentals of railroading. He ran an engine over the Horseshoe Curve in western Pennsylvania, spent hours with wrench and torch amid the smokey dank yards of Altoona investigating an air brake, correcting a faulty coupling device, experimenting with steel ties. Cassatt mastered every aspect of the steam locomotive and the tracks on which it ran, not just on the drawing board but in the yard and on the line. His command of the practical problems of railroading was exceeded only by his grasp of the ledger and the annual report. He knew what to build, how and when to built it. And he knew how to pay for it, too. He learned early to be a company man, to suspect and thwart any rival who threatened his line.

Those rivals were knowledgeable, determined, and hungry. The prize was incalcuable. More than 75,000,000 people needed the goods and services the locomotives could bring to their door. Where the horse and wagon took months to cross plains and desert, the locomotive spanned the continent in days, linking every hamlet and city to an economy which burgeoned fantastically. No single factor was more responsible for opening up America, for driving it into the industrial age, than the growth and expansion of the railroad. By rare good fortune, allied with his own ability to see and seize the opportunity, Cassatt arrived when the locomotive became the paramount engine of national prosperity.

If the Civil War had tested the new transportation giant, the decades before the century closed proved the pervading power of the iron monster which propelled America into the industrial leadership of the world. Fortunes were made and lost in the wake of railroad expansion, nurtured by a permissive political and business climate in which machines were omnipotent, men expendable. Cheap labor to build roads and man trains was always available. The horde of Irish immigrants pouring through New York eagerly fought for the low paying jobs on the railroad. Soon they were joined by Poles, Italians, Chinese, all seeking advancement by trying their fortunes to the rails. Rockefeller's oil empire, Morgan's banking trust, Carnegie's steel hegemony rested on those same rails inching across the land from the eastern marketplaces to the Pacific. By 1900 the railroad pervaded American life, altering it forever.

Few prophets foretold that a bicycle mechanic working in a Detroit back alley or two brothers experimenting with gliders on the flat salt marshes of Carolina would overturn the dictatorship of the railroad. Certainly, Cassatt saw no cloud on a future to which he had tied his own fortunes. He believed that his own carefully tended company would wheel his country into a new era of prosperity and dominance and bent every effort to that end. His railroad, every railroad, must be protected, encouraged, regulated, its property insured from the inroads of greedy exploiters whether they be venal politicians, ruthless shippers, demanding employees, or the uneducated public. The perogatives of the men who built and manned those trains came far behind expansion and development. Rights and privileges of the working man were luxuries that Cassatt and every other determined American industrialist could ill afford.

Cassatt and his fellow barons were above all "men of property," with all the virtues and vices of Galsworthy's Soames Forsythe. They were as convinced of the sanctity of property as the founding fathers who knew it to be as important as "life or liberty." We must understand, if we cannot defend, the sins committed by these adventurers in the name of property and their drive to acquire it. Free land was fast disappearing along the frontier which the railroad steadily eroded, but free profits, unhampered by government fiat or ideals of social justice, were there for the taking, and most envied the man who could seize a giant share. Cassatt yielded to no rival in his desire to bring those profits home to the Pennsylvania and its supporters.

In an arena which saw the untrammeled rise of Drew, Fiske, and Gould, Cassatt's methods were as ruthless, although he could show an unusual tolerance and compassion. Under his strong hand the Pennsylvania Railroad reached its apogee. During his years as president, the company made its greatest gains in capital expansion, in improvements, in mileage, in passenger and freight traffic. From 1899–1906, the Pennsylvania's gross income rose from $71,000,000 to $146,000,000, while his employees received a ten percent raise in wages. He increased the trackage to 11,774 miles and added 40,000 new locomotives to the road. He never feared the money lords or the dangers of financing which proved so detrimental to other railroad executives. All his reforms and innovations cost money, millions of dollars, but he recapitalized the railroad with $200,000,000 worth of gilt-edged stocks and bonds, while raising his stockholder's dividends by two percent. For his 40,000 investors Cassatt's reign meant sound returns in a company which faced the future with imagination and excitement. And those tunnels promised even more profit and prestige. No wonder Cassatt was hailed as an innovator, a manager without peer, a practical railroad man whose genius commanded respect.

He had his detractors: Andrew Carnegie, unmindful of his own relentless march from bobbin boy to steelmaster, called Cassatt a "railroad imperialist whose acts provoked admiration in his arch enemies." Carnegie wanted preferential and illegal treatment from the Pennsylvania. Pittsburgh citizens, great and small, also had no love for the Pennsylvania president who refused to let rival roads into the city. His own colleagues found Cassatt's imaginative financing too frightening to swallow. Even the press of his own city turned against him in the final months of his life. The journals of the day were quick to accuse him of arrogance, indifference to criticism and even of corruption—feathering his own nest at the expense of independent shippers.

To foes and friends alike, Cassatt offered no excuses. Neither tragedy nor triumph disturbed his outer reserve. Any attempt to penetrate his privacy he rebuffed firmly. And after his death his widow discouraged all who would defend him through an assessment of his life and work. He craved obscurity, and in the end that was his reward.

What was he really like behind that unapproachable desk in his Broad Street office? Naturally shy and reserved, when he left the yards and boardroom behind, he retired into the inviolability of his family circle. No hint of scandal ever marred his personal life. If he found need of the distractions so lustily embraced by less disciplined men, that story remains unknown and untold. Devoted to his wife and indulgent with his children, he found in his domestic circle whatever relaxation he required. Well-born, well-bred, well educated, well-endowed, Cassatt never suffered the experiences which shaped a Carnegie or a Rockefeller. He was born with a sufficiency of this world's goods and easily acquired more to satisfy the regal style in which he lived. For all his respect for property—and it was considerable—he was not greedy. He enjoyed the life of a country squire, the thoroughbred horses, the four sumptuous mansions, the yacht, the yearly trips to Europe. Yet Cassatt had few equals in the thrust and parry of the marketplace, and when he finally achieved the presidency of the Pennsylvania, at an age when most men would be content to retire, he threw himself into the demands of his position with energy and talent. He embodied, then, all the attributes so dear to Americans. Hardworking, hard-headed, inventive he pushed his railroad into the forefront of the American industrial scene, commanded attention by his sheer genius, and bequeathed the greatest transportation engine the country has ever seen.

A handsome man, of upright stature, clear complexion, piercing blue eyes, and chestnut hair turning to white, Cassatt looked every inch the aristocrat, embodying dignity and success. Striding down the streets of New York on his way to inspect his tunnel project, he conveyed, even to the casual observer, a picture of strength and discipline. Socially impeccable, financially secure, professionally renowned, Cassatt represented every attribute Philadelphia had long admired in its men of affairs. A member of every prominant club, a sportsman, a supporter of proper charitable and cultural institutions, Cassatt earned the respect of the city. But he never really became a Philadelphian, never totally embraced the sedate, parochial, proper attitudes dear to it. Always, he looked beyond Broad Street to a larger vision. He saw his railroad carrying the nation's goods and people forward into a new era. America would serve the world and profit from it, and Cassatt was convinced that the motive power of this ascendancy would be the railroad. His Pennsylvania must be the best line of all.

Romantic, his conception of his railroad and its role. Shortsighted, too, perhaps—he never realized the competition inherent in the automobile or airplane. How could another combustion machine replace what he had spent his life improving, protecting, expanding? Safe, conservative, patient in decision, slow of judgment, but capable of revolutionary action and determination to see the job done, Cassatt combined conflicting qualities of temperament and talent. His career was not without drama, even controversy, but his natural inclination subdued any flamboyance. He escaped the notoriety of his fellow "robber barons." His railroad never earned the hatred of its users while he directed its progress. The Pennsylvania, under Cassatt, earned the respect and devotion it enjoyed, a legacy of service which outlasted the man responsible.

Seventy years have passed since his death, since those innovative years when the New York tunnels and the Pennsylvania Station rose in triumph in Manhattan. His railroad merged with its rival and then disappeared entirely, sunk under a burden of mismanagement, chicanery, competition, and bankruptcy. Replacing the dignity and community of the Pennsylvania is a faceless bureaucracy, the government controlled Am Trak and Con

Rail. Like the clipper ship, the canal barge, the covered wagon, the horse and buggy, trains are vanishing. In the northeastern corridor of America and spasmodically across the land, trains still lumber along eroding tracks, but more often nostalgia rides the trains than commuters or freight. The safest, most economical, least ecologically damaging mode of transport, the locomotive, has been forced to cede its role as common carrier. Only a few romantics yearn for the revival of the train as the kingpin of transportation. The president of General Motors or Ford now represents the epitome of industrial fame. Who can name the head of an American railroad today? Alexander Johnston Cassatt evokes no memories of those days when America rode the rails. He would not be disturbed by such obscurity, but his name should not be forgotten, if only because of the lessons he taught. His problems were ours, competition, financing, labor strife, government interference, creating then as now, obstacles to efficiency and service. His expert direction enabled the railroad to rise above them all. He laid the foundations for a transportation system which could alleviate our energy crisis, move our exploding people and goods triumphantly ahead. Another transportation dilemma is upon us, but no Cassatt looms on the horizon to offer solutions and inspire progress.

Cassatt's sister, Mary, the artist upon whom the family's fame now rests, delivered the ultimate judgment: "My brother helped build the country, and in any other country he would be surrounded with respect. . . ." Not even remembrance has been his due. Alexander Cassatt deserves better.

From Pittsburgh
to Heidelberg

The seventh president of the Pennsylvania Railroad did not follow Horatio Alger's path to fame and fortune. He enjoyed the advantages which his ancestors had grasped on first coming to the New World in search of religious freedom and economic opportunity. The first of his name, Jacques, spelt it Cossart when he left Normandy for Holland in 1595, as a Huguenot refugee. His son, another Jacques, moved to Germany and then to America in 1654. By 1800 the Cossarts had settled in York, Pa., and had become Cassats with a strong Dutch strain.

Alexander's grandfather, Denis Cassat, emigrated to Pittsburgh in the early 1800s where he married a Scotch-Irish girl, Lydia Simpson. He died soon after, in Wheeling, West Virginia, leaving two children, Mary and Robert, and no money. In despair, his widow returned to her brother's house in Pittsburgh and married again. Her children grew up and married in Pittsburgh—Mary to Dr. Frank Gardner and Robert to Katherine Kelso Johnston, whose ancestors had come to western Pennsylvania in that vast migration of displaced Celts at the beginning of the eighteenth century. The Johnstons, all fervent patriots, were early and distinguished members of Chester County. Katherine Johnston Cassat was a woman of superior intelligence, highly educated with a bright and animated disposition.

The young Robert Cassats settled down in Pittsburgh after their marriage on January 22, 1835. Their first child, Katherine, was born toward the end of that year and died the same day. The following year, 1836, Robert built a new home, where another daughter, Lydia, was born in 1837. In this house, on the corner of Penn Avenue and Bay Street, a few blocks from the

Allegheny River, Alexander Johnston Cassat, was born on December 8, 1839. Of all Robert and Katherine Cassat's children, he in later years, most resembled his mother in appearance and temperament.

A year after Alexander's birth, the family moved across the river to Allegheny City, a suburb now incorporated into Pittsburgh. Robert Cassat prospered there, establishing a sound banking business and becoming mayor of the small municipality. In the years of Alexander Cassat's early boyhood, Allegheny was a booming cotton mill town of 10,000 inhabitants, profiting from the western extension of the Pennsylvania Canal, for this was the brief era of the growing waterways system spawned by the successful Erie Canal in New York. The Cassats lived near the Ohio River which was considered the most desirable residential area before the railroad spoiled the riverfront. Although flourishing as a man of business and civic prominence in Allegheny, the small town could not hold restless Robert Cassat, and within six years he had transferred his family, now increased by a daughter, Mary, born 1844, and a son, Robert, born 1842, back to Pittsburgh proper.

The Steel City did not yet enjoy the wealth which its chief citizen Andrew Carnegie would soon bring to it, but iron and glass mills were thriving, and and a nucleus of professional men like Robert Cassat were attracted by the commercial opportunities. Many of these ambitious businessmen were neighbors of the Cassats on Penn Street where they built large mansions with well-kept lawns stretching down to the Allegheny River. Occasionally, the river would overflow its banks during the spring floods, carrying lumber, boats, and sections of the gardens away in its swirling waters. The Pittsburgh waterfront offered endless delights to a small boy who could watch the red-jacketed loggers unload their timber or the heavy laden barges dock with goods from New Orleans. The river was the chief avenue of transportation for the west, since it still took several weeks for pack trains to carry goods across the mountains.

Life in Pittsburgh during the early 1840s may have been rough and free-wheeling, but it did offer certain refinements to a culture-conscious family like the Cassats. Although the city did not yet have an art museum, paintings were exhibited in hired halls. Pittsburgh's most famous artist, David G. Blythe, who was to win fame during the Civil War, moved to Uniontown in 1845, but he did paint portraits of some well-to-do civic and cultural leaders of Pittsburgh while still in his thirties. The Pittsburgh Academy of Music was established in the 1840s, and the Harmonic Society was already several decades old. Pittsburgh's most famous song writer, Stephen Collins Foster, published his first composition in 1844. There is no record that the Cassats and the Fosters were acquainted in these years, but they were to have a close connection through Alexander in the decades ahead.

Although families like the Cassats endeavored to improve Pittsburgh's cultural tone, they probably would not have endorsed the city's two most popular causes, temperance and abolition, which attracted many of the town's worthy citizens. Temperance and abolition societies abounded, drawing such distinguished supporters and lecturers to the Lyceum as Ralph Waldo Emerson, William Lloyd Garrison, Henry Ward Beecher, and Lucy Stone, all enthusiastically received by Pittsburgh's stalwart Scotch-Irish Presbyterians and German Protestants. The Cassats were Democrats and worshipped at the Episcopalian Church.

During the spring of 1846, when Alexander Cassat was just beginning to show promise in the public schools of Pittsburgh, an event of vital importance to his future and that of his native town occured in Philadelphia. Worried by the quick growth of the pioneer Baltimore and Ohio Railroad which was threatening to extend its Cumberland spur to Pittsburgh, some Philadelphia merchants incorporated the Pennsylvania Railroad under a charter passed after much foot dragging by the Harrisburg legislators. Philadelphia had decided to wrest the western trade from the competing B & O which intended to channel the lucrative commerce of the back country into the Maryland port. But not until twelve years later would the first passenger train arrive, to much jubilation, in Pittsburgh.

Before 1848 had ended, Robert Cassatt—he had added an extra "t" to the family name—decided on yet another move: He took his family 250 miles east to a county seat, Hardwicke, a mile beyond Lancaster. His inability to settle permanently in one home must have given his children a sense of insecurity, although the family circle was close and affectionate. A man of impeccable domestic habits, faithful, a good provider, cultured, Robert had an itch for adventure, a yearning for new scenery. His children learned early to be adaptable, to cloak their vulnerability with reserve, to find their pleasure in each other's company. At Hardwicke the Cassatts last child, a son, James Gardner, named for his father's brother-in-law, was born in 1849.

The Cassatt children enjoyed the rolling green hills of Lancaster County, the long walks and the farm animals, especially the horses. Years later Alexander recalled with pleasure the many rides through the countryside with his sister, Mary, "always a great favorite of mine. I suppose because our taste was a good deal alike—whenever it was a question of a walk or a ride or a gallop on horseback it didn't matter when or what the weather, Mary was always ready, so when I was at home we were together a great deal—We used to have plenty of fights, for she had a pretty quick temper, and I was not always exempt from that feeling myself, but we very soon made friends again." Aleck, too, had a quick temper, which he soon learned to control, accompanied by an extreme shyness from which he suffered all his life. If Aleck remembered the horses and rides, his sister, Mary's memories of her brother's boyhood were more prophetic. At Hardwicke he built a water wheel which Mary felt gave promise of his future career.

After two years at Hardwicke Robert Cassatt, still incurably peripatetic, moved the family again, to a newly developed residential area west of Broad

Street in Philadelphia. Alexander entered yet another school, a strict boys' academy run by an unbending headmaster. This intolerant pedagogue could not understand the ten-year old boy's inability to recite in class. Thoroughly irritated by Alexander's shyness, he wrote to Mr. Cassatt that the only cure was a good flogging. Appalled, Robert quickly removed his son from the school.

These constant interruptions of his academic life seemed to have little affect on Alexander's proficiency in his studies. He showed a real talent in technological and scientific subjects which spurred his father to consider his future education. Meanwhile, the Cassatts settled into yet another house at 496 Chestnut Street and enjoyed Hardwicke during the holidays. Mr. Cassatt established a brokerage house on Walnut Street and, again, prospered, saving enough money to plan an even more stimulating move for his family. Obviously Robert Cassatt did not consider the commercial world sufficiently challenging to contemplate devoting his life to making money, but he did intend to secure a respectable competence which would enable him to lead a comfortable existence as a leisured gentleman.

While Alexander Cassatt was a schoolboy in Philadelphia he may have visited the museum on Seventh and Chestnut, which had been sold by Franklin Peale to P. T. Barnum. One of its chief attractions was a small-scale steam locomotive which pulled two cars around a track, designed by Matthias William Baldwin in 1831. Before the end of 1831 Baldwin had produced "Old Ironsides," a steam locomotive commissioned by the Philadelphia, Germantown, and Norristown line. Alexander Cassatt may have taken the six-mile run to Germantown behind "Old Ironsides" or ridden on the Columbia Road which meandered out the Pennsylvania Main Line of Public Works toward Harrisburg.

The railroad was still called "a devilish invention" in the 1840s by many Philadelphians who preferred the horse and buggy to the jerky engines which belched smoke and cinders, burnt their clothes, and often required the passengers to embark and push the car up the primitive gradients. By the end of the decade, they were having second thoughts. Sutter's discovery of gold excited the country which soon saw the advantages in fast transportation to the gold fields on the West Coast. The Pennsylvania Railroad placed its first order for three of the new locomotives the year Alexander came east. Contracts were let for extending the road 117 miles west of Harrisburg under the superintendency of John Edgar Thomson, who would eventually become president of the line.

Robert Cassatt, aside from joining the Athenaeum, an exclusive Philadelphia establishment, took little part in the civic and social affairs of the city. He seemed to have small interest in the growing business opportunities of Philadelphia and before long decided to take his family abroad. By the fall of 1851, the Cassatts were established in the Hotel Continental in Paris, in time to witness Louis Napoleon's coup d'état, which for a few days in early

December brought barricades and mob violence to their adopted city. Mrs. Cassatt had learned French as a girl in Pittsburgh and attempted to teach it to her children. They were also enrolled immediately in a Parisian day school. Alexander attended Monsieur Gachotte's academy near the Cassatt's apartment off the Champs Élysée. Although only twelve years old he had already changed schools at least five times, and this would not be the last because Mr. Cassatt soon realized that facility in French was not all that Alexander required. He may not have been dedicated to business himself, but he was determined that Alexander should be fitted for a career commensurate with his abilities.

Two years after their arrival in Paris, the Cassatts traveled to Heidelberg where Alexander was entered in a boarding school. The move to Germany was not entirely on Alexander's account. Robbie, now eleven, had been ill even before they left America, and it was thought that a German specialist might relieve his condition. But that was not to be. His father recorded in a brief family history: "For almost five years previous . . . Robert had been afflicted with disease of the knee joint. He suffered very severely at times. He was a model of fortitude and patience."

By 1855 the Cassatts were in Darmstadt which boasted one of the finest technical universities in the world. Alexander again settled to his studies. In May of that year Robbie died from the mysterious bone ailment which had plagued him for years, and was buried at Darmstadt until his reinternment many years later in the family burial plot at Mesnil-Théribus, France. Disheartened by his death, the Cassatts returned to America, to a rented home in West Chester near Mr. Cassatt's widowed sister, Mary Gardner, leaving Alexander to complete his education at Darmstadt. Because of his extended stay abroad, Alexander became more proficient in both French and German than in his native tongue. This was to cause him some problems when he returned after five years at age 17 to America where he planned to study civil engineering.

At the Astor Hotel in New York, Alexander wrote a telegram notifying his family of his safe arrival. He headed his message Astor Haus but realized immediately that this was incorrect. Too bashful to ask for the proper spelling, he walked outside the hotel to discover the proper address from the sign. All his life Alexander Cassatt was to have trouble with double consonants, a legacy of his European education.

After a brief reunion with his family in West Chester, Alexander enrolled at Yale but soon decided that it could not offer the engineering courses he required. He left Yale and entered Rensselaer Polytechnic Institute in Troy, N. Y., the alma mater of another future president of the Pennsylvania Railroad who had graduated some years before, J. Edgar Thomson. The railroad, meanwhile, had emerged from its pioneer stages to become a major transportation force. By the time Alexander Cassatt had received his civil engineering degree (his senior thesis was entitled "Review of a Pressure

Turbine") in the summer of 1859, the first train had reached Chicago, and in the years ahead, it would span the continent, the single most important factor in the settlement of the west. Alexander Cassatt determined to play an important role in the coming Iron Age. But first he had to find a job. While waiting for a suitable position, he returned to Philadelphia, where his father had moved the family from West Chester in 1858 to a house on Olive and Fifteenth Streets near the present City Hall. During that summer Robert Cassatt took his eldest son to Washington to call on James Buchanan, a former Lancaster neighbor who was now in the White House.

By the fall of 1860, Alexander Cassatt had been hired as a surveyor, or rodman to use the railroad term, by the same Georgia road which the Pennsylvania's president, J. Edgar Thomson had developed. The Georgia experience, not an entirely happy one for a Northerner during the months preceding secession, was to prove an effective training ground for Alexander Cassatt.

Boarding the Pennsylvania

Carrying a surveyor's rod and chain through the red clay of backwoods Georgia was such tiring work, that young Alexander Cassatt considered abandoning railroading altogether. He wrote to his father from Dalton in mid-November 1860 that "anybody can build a railroad. What do you think I got paid for my three days work at surveying; work as hard as any Blacksmith's with the continual risk of falling down and breaking my neck or my Transit at least. Why five dollars."

He continued in exasperation, "Any little Pettifogging Lawyer would have charged and been paid fifty for the same amount of work, and yet I would not have been paid without a great deal of grumbling if I had charged more. And there are several men who call themselves surveyors who would have been glad to have done the work for that." For a young man, not yet twenty-one, late of Heidelberg, Darmstadt, and Rennsalaer, the lack of appreciation was galling. Dalton, Georgia could not have been too congenial for the young cosmopolite. It was a far cry from the sophisticated Astor House or the cultural amenities of Philadelphia. But Dalton had some charms. Encircled by the blue ranges of the Cohutta Mountains, planted with large shade trees whose branches arched across the broad streets, the town of less than 500 citizens had certain bucolic advantages for a young man who would always prefer the countryside to the metropolis. Dalton had none of the classic architecture associated with the Old South. It was a shipping point for the copper mined in Tennessee and hauled to Dalton by wagon. The railroad would facilitate moving the ore. Even more important, it would serve as a vital transportation terminus for Confederate troops in the coming conflict.

Alexander relished the ride out of the small town, beyond the main avenue of gabled houses and sweeping green lawns to the farms some distance from the county seat. He discovered a farmer, one Mr. Kaiser, who tended a vineyard which inspired the disgruntled engineer to think about going into the grape growing business himself. Accustomed to wine from his European days, he believed that his countrymen could be persuaded to buy the produce of the local grapes. Mr. Kaiser was selling his wine at 75 cents a bottle or $3.75 a gallon, which encouraged Alexander to think he could make his fortune in a similar vineyard.

Not that he was tired of engineering, he assured his father, but "I'm tired of doing nothing. I am afraid the prospects for engineers are not going to improve." This was his analysis during a period of the greatest railroad building the country would ever see. But conditions in the South in the fall of 1860 might have tempted even a more experienced observer than Alexander to believe America's industrial revolution and accompanying transportation expansion would be indefinitely delayed. Secession dominated the scene. Only a few weeks before, Abraham Lincoln had been elected President by a minority of the Northern voters and those of the two western states, California and Oregon. Georgia had preferred Kentucky's John C. Breckenridge who espoused the slaveowners' cause in opposition to Stephen Douglas, the Democratic candidate who reluctantly opposed them. Alexander Cassatt, in after years a staunch Democrat, expressed no views to his father about the election, but he realized that for some Southern states, secession had gone beyond the talking stage. He used the possibility of war to push his vineyard scheme.

"If there is a dissolution of the Union it will break up all the Railroad enterprise, but it will not hurt vine growing," he wrote his father, failing to realize that Southern farmlands would be the battlefield. His own future depended on the political situation: "There is no use my going further now until I hear what the South is going to do." Although he considered that he and his father might do well to embark on a joint venture of wine production, he had also made other plans: "My expenses here are small, not more than ten or twelve dollars a month, and I can afford to wait a few weeks and have money enough to go to Texas in case Major Lee calls me."

The Major Lee he mentioned must have been Robert E. Lee, then serving in the United States Army in the west. A cavalry officer in 1860, Lee had begun his army career in the engineering corps. Perhaps Alexander Cassatt thirsted for military action, the sound of bugles, the testing under fire. Certainly, he would have been an asset as an engineering officer, if not as a cavalryman, for he rode well. But he never saw a battlefield. When those brutal, bitter fights at Manassas, Gettysburg, Shiloh, and Chancellorsville decimated a whole generation, his name was not on any muster call. It was not fear that kept him from combat. Later in life he showed physical courage of a high order, but his failure to enlist in either army, Confederate or Union, is not easily understood. He had no ideological convictions against war. In fact, he admired the military life and encouraged his own son to follow that career. In a time of violent passions he stood aside and worried instead about his business prospects, his vineyard, an unattractive stance in a young man from whom gallantry and ardor were expected.

He claimed family obligations as a pressing inducement to enter wine making. Aleck reminded his father that his sister, Mary, then enrolled in the Academy of Arts in Philadelphia and not finding the instruction to her liking, would "in three years want to go to Rome to study. By that time our vineyards would be in bearing and you could afford to go and leave me here to work for you." No doubt Robert Cassatt's perspective was clearer, and he did nothing to encourage his son.

Alexander's situation as a Yankee in a state burgeoning with bellicose secessionists did not overly trouble him. There is no evidence that he held abolitionist views which would have angered his neighbors, and he appeared willing to remain in Dalton and proceed with grape growing. To tempt his father further he sent him a sample bottle of wine distilled from the local grapes. But long before Georgia left the Union on January, 19, 1861, Alexander Cassatt had abandoned both the vineyards and the rod and chain to come north. All work on the Dalton-Knoxville road was postponed indefinitely which left the Yankee surveyor jobless. Georgia, which eventually became one of the bloodiest battlegrounds, had neither time nor money for building railroads, a short-sighted policy, but understandable since Confederate resources were so limited. North of the Mason-Dixon Line, conditions were very different: Lines proliferated during the four years of the struggle, and young Cassatt would be among those profiting from the growth. His immediate concern was to find another job, and Philadelphia seemed the obvious place to launch the search.

By the spring of 1861, he had been hired as a rodman in the engineering corps by the Pennsylvania Railroad, where he worked on the construction between Frankford Junction, a few miles north of Philadelphia on the Delaware River, and the Main Line. Several years before the war, the railroad had bought from the state for $7,500,000 The Main Line of Public Works, a complicated and primitive network of railroads, locks, canals, and bridges, which carried goods and passengers west. Under J. Edgar Thomson the Main Line was gradually being replaced by 236 miles of railroad, running through a series of tunnels and over new gradients to Pittsburgh where Thomas A. Scott supervised the expanding company offices.

By 1861 Scott had been temporarily relieved of his duties as vice president, a post to which he had been promoted in the spring of 1860, to manage the arduous transport of the Union Army. As Assistant Secretary of War, he directed the movement of Northern troops with great dispatch and efficiency. It had been Scott's idea to protect Lincoln from assassination attempts on his entrance into Washington by secretly spiriting the newly elected President through Baltimore after the announcement of a different route. Scott also initiated the Secret Service by hiring the Pinkerton detectives who guarded the railroads from sabotage by Southern spies and sympathizers.

Among the young men appointed by Thomson to manage the expanding railroad in the years before the Civil War, Thomas A. Scott, of all the railroad's officers, can most justifiably be castigated by later critics as a "robber baron." An affable, handsome man of extraordinary charm, he had risen rapidly through the ranks of the railroad from his humble beginnings as a station agent in western Pennsylvania. Losing his father at age twelve, he had worked in a country store and in the toll collector's office of The Main Line of Public Works, before his discovery by Herman Haupt, the engineering genius who planned the railroad's western development. After working for some years in Pittsburgh, where he hired an ambitious young Scotsman, Andrew Carnegie, as a telegrapher, Scott moved into the front office. Adept at public relations, he managed to conciliate those irate Pittsburgh citizens who disliked the Pennsylvania for its effort to keep the Baltimore and Ohio out of the city. He persuaded the state legislature by methods which could be considered questionable, to abolish the hated "tonnage tax" on railroad freight and generally manipulated political events in favor of his employers. While Scott's chief, Thomson, was inclined to be aloof, reticent, and shy in public, the younger man entered the bitter battle for railroad supremacy with enthusiasm. Scott was energetic, convivial, and diplomatic, but something of a plunger in contrast to the cautious Thomson. In his own way each avidly pursued the expansion of the railroad.

Scott and Thomson were impressed with young Cassatt, and the president furthered his protegé's career at every opportunity. Thomson also shared his young engineer's continental interests. He had traveled to England to study that country's civil and mechanical engineering feats, applying his knowledge to the upgrading of the Philadelphia & Columbia line which served as a basis for the road west. Cassatt, in turn, respected Thomson and relied on his advice when he later considered leaving the railroad for other opportunities.

How Alexander Cassatt, a healthy young man in his early twenties, escaped being drafted into the Union Army is unknown. He may have purchased a substitute, a common practice among Northerners who did not wish to fight. Possibly, Scott secured his exemption pleading his engineering skills as a vital adjunct to the railroad and the war effort. Alexander did not remain long at his lowly rodman's job on the Frankford Junction. From a position as assistant engineer in the construction of the connecting railway linking the Pennsylvania to the Philadelphia & Trenton road, he was sent to Renovo, Pennsylvania, in 1864, as resident engineer of the middle division of the Philadelphia & Erie. With its terminus at Renovo, on the western branch of the Susquehanna, the Erie linked the state's coal fields to the eastern markets.

By 1866 young Cassatt had become superintendent of the Warren & Franklin road, headquartered in Williamsport, and was living in Irvineton, not far from Erie. Renovo and Irvineton have all but disappeared, but in those years they were growing rapidly under the impetus of oil discovery and coal mining. In Irvineton, on the northern banks of the Allegheny River, Alexander's family joined him and set up temporary housekeeping. The senior Cassatt was willing to abandon close supervision of his own commercial interests to encourage his son in what he suspected would be a career which could give the family solid security. By this time Mary had left Philadelphia for Paris, where with the reluctant permission of her father, she lived temporarily with family friends.

In brotherly fashion Alexander scoffed at Mary's desire for a serious artistic career. While still in Dalton he had informed his father that his sister must be persuaded to study geometry because "she has no sense of perspective." He later changed his mind, but in the beginning Alexander had grave doubts about Mary's talents. Condescendingly, he reported, "She thinks she can become an artist, poor child." While Aleck had doubts about his sister's realizing her artistic dreams, Mary had more foresight or more faith in her brother. In the days of their Hardwicke childhood, she had recognized his mechanical talents. She also early analyzed his temperment and hoped that "his ability and drive and rare good sense would bring him a satisfying career."

Sometime during his stay in Irvineton, Alexander met Harriett Buchanan, niece of the former President, and daughter of the Reverend and Mrs. Edward Y. Buchanan, of Oxford, a suburb of Philadelphia. Harriett, the second eldest of five daughters, was a striking beauty with luxuriant chestnut hair, sparkling dark eyes, and classic features, a lovely figure in her graceful crinolines. No wonder Alexander Cassatt, impressionable and seeking feminine companionship, was attracted to such a belle. They became engaged shortly before the close of the war, probably while she was visiting her brother, James, who was then working for an oil company in Tidionte near Irvineton. Far from Philadelphia and its cultural and social interests, Alexander would naturally be drawn to such a young woman, no matter how incompatible their temperaments. Neither Irvineton nor Tidionte offered many competitors to Harriett, and the rough railroad towns drew women of a far different type. James, writing to another sister, described Tidionte as "all built of wood and the mud is very deep. Also there is considerable conversation about oil and big wells and all that sort of thing. Take it all together I know of several places where I would rather live but of course this is confidential. We have had rain here all week and I have been desperate."

Alexander Cassatt also may have been desperate, which would promote romance. He enjoyed music, the theater, and reading, particularly Tennyson. In Tidionte the most he could expect was a checkers game with Harriett. On the surface the pair seemed ideally matched. Alexander gave every indication of a brilliant career, but his professional prospects were only one of his obvious assets. Standing well over six feet, with a virile athletic build, he was clean shaven, with vibrant dark blue eyes and thick sandy hair. His appearance alone would stir the heart of most young women. He was not only handsome but well-born, well-educated, interested in art, music, and literature, an ornament to civilized society. His eligibility as a husband was apparent.

Yet almost immediately impediments arose to thwart their union. Harriett was often ill, liable to depressions and crying spells; her indisposition went beyond the normal vapors expected of a sheltered Victorian miss of good family. Then, too, she did not really enjoy masculine society. Perhaps the attentions of a healthy, ardent young man, even one as considerate and gentlemanly as Alexander Cassatt, proved too offensive. Her upbringing in the smug, highly moral, prudish parsonage would tend to discourage passionate emotion. Psychologists might analyze her frequent retreats into illness as a reluctance to face the physical reality of conjugal life. The relationship between the engaged pair soon deteriorated.

The Reverend Buchanan and his wife did not help, believing their daughter's fiancé too worldly and irreligious. But the real difficulty lay in Harriett herself, and Alexander was not slow to see it. Later he wrote ". . . whatever hopes I had of winning Miss Harriett's hand were very slight . . . I felt this all the time and never really expected to succeed and although I allowed myself to entertain some hope, in my secret soul, I always felt it was in vain."

And in vain it was. Not too long after the engagement was announced, it ended. But the rejected suitor was not despondent for long. He quickly plunged into the work which provided him with all the challenge he needed. The attractions the lovely Harriett provided would not be wholly forgotten, however. In a year or two he would renew his acquaintance with the Buchanans and meet another daughter of the family.

Meanwhile, he continued to advance rapidly in the executive ranks of the Pennsylvania Railroad, always under the vigilant and approving eyes of Thomson and Scott. Unlike some young men raised in comfortable circumstances, young Cassatt did not scorn long hours, uncongenial surroundings, or hard work. He learned to run the cumbersome engines, understand repairs, compute a payroll, and master every facet of railroad maintenance and invention. Western Pennsylvania offered rare opportunities to the ambitious young man in the late '60s, and Cassatt was eager to take advantage of them. The Pennsylvania's revenues had quadrupled during the war years, from $5,000,000 in 1860 to $19,500,000 in 1865. Much of this stimulus came from the increase in the anthracite coal industry, which during the Civil War had risen from less than a million to over ten million tons in production per year.

Although the Pennsylvania would eventually carry more passengers than any other American road, freight was its real revenue maker, always exceeding passenger income by 150 percent which would one day would bode ill for passenger service. The railroad was founded on freight carriage, established to transport goods from the west and coal from the hills around Pittsburgh to market in Philadelphia. The passengers, who traveled in early discomfort along the 236-mile, road were of secondary concern. Now coal, the cash crop of Pennsylvania, would be augmented by steel from the Pittsburgh furnaces, which converted rapidly from iron production after Bessemer's invention of the stronger alloy in England. Coal, iron, and steel, these were the products which brought profits to the conservative Philadelphia investors who sponsored the railroad. Soon oil, under Rockefeller's aegis, added significantly to the railroad's income.

While the Pennsylvania seemed in an enviable position to take advantage of the boom in Pittsburgh, other railroad men had an eye on a share of the lucrative carriage. The B & O had been temporarily halted and rerouted to Wheeling, but the Erie Road, mismanaged and milked by a former cattle drover, Daniel Drew, and his henchmen Jim Fiske and Jay Gould, threatened the Pennsylvania's paramountcy. The Erie, a great trunk line, nearly 500 miles long, connected New York harbor and the Great Lakes, but its capital had been watered, its decrepit rolling stock and decaying road beds evidence that the owners cared little for the Erie's efficiency and much for its speculative growth. While Drew, Fiske, and Gould manipulated the Erie's stock with the venal cooperation of New York legislators, Commodore Cornelius Vanderbilt, who had earned a fortune and learned his business practices as a hard-driving steamboat captain, began his bitter fight with the Drew interests for control of the Erie.

As a result of the Erie "war," railroads and the magnates who managed them garnered a deep-seated public distrust which exists today. Vanderbilt won another fortune. He grabbed the ownership of the Erie and eventually organized the New York Central to become the Pennsylvania's largest competitor. Drew died disillusioned and penniless. Fiske committed suicide. Only Gould survived to endure the lasting social enmity of Astors and Vanderbilts, prevented by their hostility from joining the ranks of New York society, a bitter blow to his family's pretensions.

Alexander Cassatt did not meet the redoubtable Vanderbilt until 1870, but he was aware of that tycoon's efforts to manipulate stock, force lower freight rates on the Pennsylvania, and challenge Cassatt's employer, J. Edgar Thomson, on every front. Thomson, like Scott, Roberts, and Cassatt, who followed him in the presidency, was primarily a railroad man dedicated to improving his line. Even the most critical students of the railroad wars have admitted that the Pennsylvania in those days never suffered from the chicanery and speculation which reduced rival roads to mere pawns in their owner's struggles to achieve fortunes on the New York Stock Exchange. One railroad historian has conceded that the Pennsylvania, in contrast to the Erie, New York Central, Northern Pacific, and Union Pacific, "never had anything but a succession of conservative directors and able presidents, who believed in sticking to the railroad business and making it pay, by building up the road as an operating property and fighting off attempts of speculative wizards to use it as a financial football." That assessment changed dramatically after World War II.

From the professional, reticent Thomson, Alexander Cassatt learned his railroad ethics and his business acumen. He followed these standards throughout his career, often in the face of severe pressures from Congress, Presidents, stockholders, and the public. While Thomson concentrated on improving his road, replacing iron rails with steel, double tracking the Main Line, standardizing equipment, leasing subsidiary lines, he left the political infighting to his vice president, Thomas A. Scott, who was well suited to such affairs.

The Pennsylvania, and almost every other railroad, received thousands of acres of free land from state and federal governments for expansion. Cheap transportation was opening the west, and few impediments were put in the way of railroad moguls who took every advantage of government cooperation.

It was Scott who persuaded the Pennsylvania State Legislature to keep the B & O out of Pittsburgh for years. In 1864, after a vote denying the Maryland interests access to the Steel City, a member rose to ask, "Mr. Speaker, may we not now go Scott free." When Jay Gould threatened to swoop down and take the Pennsylvania's freight traffic from the west for his Erie line, Scott's bill to prevent the notorious Gould's success passed through the State House in thirty-four minutes, surely a record for Pennsylvania legislators.

By 1869 the Pennsylvania had extended its influence through leasing subsidiary lines as far west as Indianapolis and St. Louis. Among these lines was the Sudbury & Erie, renamed the Philadelphia & Erie, the line on which Alexander Cassatt would make his mark. Scott was not too busy with his public relations efforts on behalf of the railroad to keep an eye on his protegé and he liked what he saw. In April, 1866 Cassatt had been transferred to Williamsport as superintendent of motive power and machinery for the Philadelphia & Erie. One day Scott appeared in Cassatt's office to check on some items of bookkeeping. Instead of sending for the clerk in charge to look up the queried amounts, Cassatt reeled off the figures. Scott was amazed at his memory. "How do you know that?" Scott asked the young manager. "Oh, I think it's a pretty good scheme to go through the books every few days, so that if anything happened in the bookkeeping department I might not be left in the lurch," he replied.

Scott was impressed. Obviously, this was a young man to encourage. From Renovo in January, 1867, the rising young executive sent his report to the annual stockholders' meeting on the condition of the motive power of the Philadelphia & Erie, which at that time was operating at a loss to the parent line of over $250,000 a year. Cassatt had decided to alter those figures and he made a good start during his first year as superintendent. His ninety locomotives, were then running a total mileage of 1,429,110, an increase over the previous year of 400,000 miles, but he managed to decrease costs from 55 to 48 cents a mile.

He knew the stockholders looked for a healthy return on their investment, but he also believed that his road would only run at maximum efficiency if improvements and repairs were assured. He asked for a larger engine house and ten new stalls. "The expense of car repairs at this point has been largely increased by this want of adequate facilities. I would therefore respectfully urge on your consideration the importance of erecting car and paint shops during the present year." No stranger to repair shop or roundhouse, Alexander Cassatt would never hesitate to sacrifice revenues, even borrow in the millions, for proper maintenance. He had his new shops.

He did not remain in the Williamsport office long enough to see them in operation, however. In November, 1867, before his twenty-eighth birthday, Thomson appointed Cassatt superintendent of machinery and motive power for the entire Pennsylvania road. His new position transferred him to Altoona with a salary of $3,000 a year, a princely sum at a time when a trainman made less than $10 a week. Now he had the position which would enable him to support a wife in comfortable style. Harriett had failed him, but he would soon find a young woman to share his life in Altoona, that bustling, smoky, muddy railroad town perched in the midst of the Kitanning Mountains. Unfortunately, his wooing would not be as rapid, or as unencumbered by problems as his rise through the executive ranks of the railroad.

A Difficult Wooing

Vulnerable, lonely, eager for a wife, in the fall of 1867, Alexander Cassatt met Maria Lois Buchanan, younger sister of Harriet. James Buchanan had invited his sisters, Harriet and Lois, to visit him in Tidionte. James missed the companionship of his family in the Oxford parsonage and found in Alexander Cassatt a sympathetic companion. How natural to enlist his aid in entertaining his sisters. James ignored any embarrassment which might arise from Aleck's previous attachment to Harriet.

Aleck described the impact of that meeting with Lois to her in one of his first love letters: ". . . if you could be aware of the power of your charm you would not be surprised that you should have won my heart at first sight." Did that first meeting take place under Harriet's sardonic eye? With what regret or reluctance did the young railroad superintendent abandon one sister for another? Harriet must have found the courtship of her more vivacious and willing sister by her own former suitor a slight to her vanity and pride if not to her heart.

Cool, cautious, and reserved in pursuit of the railroad's concerns, in affairs of the heart Aleck rushed headlong into a passionate attachment on the strength of one meeting. Despite his Continental experience, Aleck, at twenty-eight, remained curiously naive, almost innocent—amazingly so in a young man with his opportunities. About to move to Altoona, a rough railroad town which would offer few attractions beyond advancing his career, Aleck met Lois when he was most susceptible to a winning smile and obvious admiration. Harriet's rebuff of his affection must have been a bitter blow to his self-esteem if not to his deeper emotions.

Lois herself, then twenty, a year younger than her sister, lacked the latter's outstanding beauty and dignity of manner. Perhaps the primitive photographs of the period do not show her real quality. Petite, with a wealth of auburn hair, and those curious, pale-clear blue eyes which appear diamond cold, she undoubtedly possessed charms not apparent in her portraits. She had many admirers but few with the obvious assets of Alexander Cassatt. Unlike her sister, she craved the worldly life beyond the parsonage gates, which he, a coming young man, could offer her. Lois made no secret of her social ambitions, nor of her interest in luxury. What is not so understandable is why Aleck chose Lois.

A biographer of Mary Cassatt complained that Lois was "narrow minded, prosaic and prudish." Certainly, her upbringing lacked the sophistication of the Cassatts. She did not share his appreciation of the arts and deplored his irregular church attendance. The Buchanans were a respectable family of some social pretensions but an established Philadelphian, irritated by Lois' blatant ambition, referred to her as "that little nobody, a niece of President Buchanan," a severe judgment reflecting as much upon the author of the sentiments as upon Lois. Aleck must have been introduced to several Philadelphia belles who would have found the well-born, handsome, and successful young man sufficient to satisfy the most demanding parents as well as fulfill their own romantic imaginations. But they never had the opportunity to pursue him.

While Aleck endearingly fell deeply in love with Lois, she was more cautious. Even allowing for the reticence of a proper Victorian miss, she appeared to be more calculating than enamoured. She described the courtship in her diary years later: "Mr. Alexander Cassatt was stationed at the time at Irvineton, and was superintendent of the Warren and Franklin Branch of the Pennsylvania Railroad. He was with us a great deal and we went up to Irvineton and paid a short visit to his home, where his father, mother and sister Lydia were living with him. After a delightful visit, during which we took long rides on horseback through the country, we started home, stopping on our way to Niagara Falls. Before we reached home I had become engaged to your father." Little passion lies in that laconic statement. Lois was not one to lose her head in favor of her heart, but surely such an ardent wooer as Aleck must have offered exciting possibilities. No doubt the hurried courtship was hampered by the presence of Harriet. Under her speculative eye, Aleck's pursuit of her sister must have been restrained. Once free from her uncomfortable company, he became much more ardent. Evidently, the Buchanan sisters had powerful attractions. Why else would he become entangled again after the treatment he received at Harriet's hands? Only an overwhelming desire for Lois could have made the situation endurable.

Although Lois had quickly accepted Aleck, her parents were not so amenable. They had not forgotten the earlier relationship and did not regard the new engagement with much enthusiasm. Lois later remembered that on her arrival at the Oxford parsonage "my father, thinking I was too young to be married, prevailed upon me to wait until after a promised visit to Baltimore the following winter, saying if we were then of the same mind, he would consent to our marriage."

Quite naturally, the Reverend Buchanan suspected the ardor of Alexander's devotion to Lois, following as it did so rapidly upon his former attachment to Harriet. The young man himself had no such doubts. In his first love letter to Lois from Irvineton, September 21, 1867, he wrote "the moment you entered the room, I felt that you were the dear one I have been seeking." The moment she entered the room—Aleck implies he had never met her before. But while Lois was still a school girl in Philadelphia, she had taken an unaccountable dislike to her sister's fiancé. A friend wrote to her that she could not understand Lois' objection to Harriet's choice. Perhaps they had met, and Aleck, preoccupied with Harriet, had not noticed Lois. He continues in a lighter vein, "Say, then, My Dearest Miss Lois, that you will be mine and gladden the heart of a lonely man. I am sure that we will be happy together for I think that our tastes are entirely similar. You sing divinely, I adore music, you are fond of fried tomatoes, I dote on them! So you see we agree on all important points."

They did not agree on all important points. Most notably they differed on Mary Cassatt, but such disagreements would not appear until much later in their relationship. Aleck wanted to set an early date for their marriage, but he accepted the postponement which Lois' parents insisted upon with his usual good nature and objective understanding: "I suppose the view which your father and mother take is the natural one for them under the circumstances, and I ought to be very glad it is so favorable to me, but I hope when I see them to be able to persuade them that there is no necessity for any further delay before considering the affair settled."

He endured the interminable delay writing delightful and loving letters to the capricious lady of his choice, patient under the Buchanan's demands and Lois' far from reciprocal ardor. At least, during the long year of his engagement, he was acquiring a thorough grounding in the technical business of running the railroad, experience which would gain him the respect not only of his superiors, but also of the humble trainmen on whom the Pennsylvania depended to repair and operate the trains.

About twenty years earlier the railroad's managers had chosen Altoona as the site for its principal repair shops, when it became evident that the expanding traffic demanded a more efficient method of moving passengers and freight over the mountains than the old inclined planes of the Portage Line. Company draftsmen laid out towns primarily with the needs of the railroad in mind, caring little for the aesthetic values of the company town. Although the approaches to Altoona were of rare beauty, curving through the towering mountains broken by swift, clear-running streams and small patches of cultivated land, the town itself embodied none of these rural delights.

The name Altoona was derived from the Cherokee word "allatoona," meaning "high lands of great worth," as indeed this depot of the railroad became, but not, perhaps, within the sense of the Indian description. J. Edgar Thomson had worked early in his career on the Allatoona Pass in Georgia, which may also have inspired the name of this great railroad terminus. Acting for the Pennsylvania, Archibald Wright, in 1854, had brought the 233-acre farm of an early settler, David Robeson, for $11,000 and began to lay out the shops and roundhouses so vital to servicing the locomotives which by that date were running through Altoona to Pittsburgh over the spectacular Horse Shoe Curve.

This engineering marvel, which began five miles west of Altoona, climbed the 2,200-foot summit of Kitconning Mountain by a series of planes, through twin tunnels, forming a great U-turn. In 1867 when Cassatt arrived in Altoona, the line was still single tracked. Through his efforts and under his direction, a beginning was made toward double tracking the whole route from Philadelphia to Pittsburgh, to be completed by the turn of the century.

Nearly 8,000 people lived in Altoona that year, the male adults employed by the railroad settling in the soot-blackened red brick buildings which fanned out from the depot. Their modest wooden homes, grimed by the constant smoke from the locomotives, clustered around the shops as closely as possible, so that no time would be wasted in getting to work. In contrast to the surrounding beauty of the countryside, the town itself, completely utilitarian, made no effort to hide its squalid purpose. No parks nor broad avenues relieved the tedium of the criss-crossing steel rails and smoke-belching shops.

The streets were unpaved, impassable quagmires of mud in the spring with a stream of filthy water a foot deep running down Twelfth Avenue, the main thoroughfare. Workmen carried planks to throw across the vicious mess on their way to the shops. There was no sewage system, and the waste water ran in the gutters of the four main streets which in summer were choked with weeds that rose above the sidewalks.

A few yards from the stationhouse, on the former site of the farmer's duck pond, an attempt to introduce a luxurious note had been made by the railroad in 1854 when the company built the imposing Logan House. This hostelry spread out along the tracks, a rambling 200-foot long H-shaped building of gray stone, established to serve the passengers traveling along the line rather than the town's citizens. Famous for its cuisine, Logan House was reputed to serve the best vanilla ice cream in the nation, although Alexander Cassatt did not regard the hotel's meals very highly. Its interior decoration was impressive with heavy red velvet carpeting covering the floors of the two great parlors which were filled with ornate red plush furniture. Black walnut framed the sashes and doorways, and large mirrors graced the walls. Contrasting with the mud and silt beyond its iron and stone fences were the green lawns planted in defiance of the general gray sooty aspect of most of Altoona.

Altoona was rich in churches, twelve in all, and even boasted an opera house and a few cultural societies. But the center of its activity remained the shops and thirty-six-stall roundhouse of the railroad. With the exception of a few more elaborate houses for the railroad officers, who were forced by their duties to live in the town, Altoona offered little in the way of gracious living for the leisure hours of such a young man as Alexander Cassatt, but he entered enthusiastically into whatever enjoyments were offered.

On October 11, 1867, the chief operator of the line, besieged by break-downs and obstructions on the route, received an unexpected visit from the Pennsylvania's president. Accompanying J. Edgar Thomson was "a tall, light-complexioned young man, neatly dressed and wearing a high, light colored silk hat." Mr. Thomson introduced his companion, Alexander J. Cassatt, to the operator, J. J. Hendricks, and announced he would be the new superintendent.

Hendricks, ordered to make the future superintendent familiar with the different departments of the railroad, looked dubiously at the silk hat, but soon changed his mind about its wearer. Cassatt "seemed to grasp the whole situation in a few hours, and in a day or two after he had gone over the road, he knew more about it than we did who had been there for a year." Hendricks continued in his memoir that the new superintendent had "a modest, unassuming manner and showed courtesy to all with whom he came in contact, although he was familiar with none," an attitude Cassatt cultivated throughout his life in business affairs.

The superintendent's sartorial elegance did not prevent his rolling up his sleeves and getting to work in roundhouse and engine shop. He settled down to improve the efficiency of the railroad by standardizing the motor power, for the company was then running over eight classes of engines along its tracks, a cumbersome and wasteful practice to Cassatt's mind. Shortly after assuming his duties in Altoona, a landslide occurred on the line. Cassat was in Oil City at the time, and finding that the route would be blocked for some days, he hired a steamboat that happened to be on the Allegheny River. Loading all perishable freight and the impatient stranded passengers aboard, he sent the boat safely to its destination, although the trip took twenty-four hours.

Such an improvising, take-charge attitude impressed the brakemen, fire-men, and engineers, but they were even more awed by his command of the locomotives they drove and serviced. "He seemed to have a natural talent for machinery," Hendricks recalled, "and when riding over the road he would almost invariably be found handling the machine, while the engineer rested. He was a good 'runner' and made good time." His skill as an engineer enabled him to win the respect of the under-paid, overworked, tough trainmen who overlooked the austere manner of the sophisticated easterner, their equal at the controls of any locomotive.

In the front office his command of the company's business was compassionate and effective. At a time when consideration for the employee was not encouraged by management, Cassatt believed kindness accomplished more than arrogance. Mr. Hendricks remembered one snowy bitter winter evening when he fell asleep at his dispatching key: "As soon as Mr. Cassatt came to his office that day I reported the matter to him. After learning that I had been constantly on duty for 48 hours, he told me to get an assistant at once and in the future to take regular sleep. Thus it was that all cases of reported neglect or violation of the rules, were carefully investigated, and when a verdict was given, it was invariably just." Cassatt's rapid promotion to the top echelons of the Pennsylvania's executives did not surprise these hard judges of men and machines.

In the murky, steam-filled atmosphere of the great roundhouse at Altoona, Cassatt soon became a familiar figure. A noisy grimy cavern, the roundhouse constantly echoed with riveting hammers, the popping of engines and the ringing of bells. Dim incandescent lights pierced the darkness which enveloped it day and night. Water and scale spilled onto the floor while the men worked with kerosene torches on the giant machines. Little wonder that Alexander Cassatt was eager to leave the roundhouse and offices by the Altoona tracks for the comfort of his superintendent's house, to be presided over by a young and loving wife. But that day seemed ever more distant. While he waited impatiently for the Buchanans to permit the engagement to be announced and the wedding date set, he wrote affectionate letters to his "Lodie," describing his bleak existence at Logan House, his temporary home.

In the new year, 1868, Lois traveled to Wheatlands for a visit with her uncle, President Buchanan, where Alexander joined her for a few days, seeking the head of the family's approval for the intended marriage. President Buchanan approved immediately of his niece's young man, and his endorsement carried some weight with his more sanctimonious brother. After Alexander had returned to Altoona and Lois had gone to the Johnstons in Baltimore, President Buchanan wrote to his niece about her choice: "I am glad you have communicated all to Mrs. Johnston and that she approves. I differ from her in one particular. She has always been inclined to be dilatory. I think you ought to be married without unnecessary delay. In my long life observation has taught me the danger of long engagements. You will, I believe, return home on the first of April. You can now have no disposition to make conquests for I believe you are an honest girl."

But Lois was disposed to make conquests, and was reluctant to surrender her freedom for the restrictions of marriage. Although promised to Alexander, she was not above flirting with other desirable young men who found her attractive. Her sister Henrietta confirms that Lodie had other interests when she reminds her that if she marries Alexander these attentions from beaux must cease: "Now you just have as good a time as you can and have fun with whom you please . . . not that I don't like Alek very much, but you know he has shown a decided disposition to be jealous of other men's attentions to you, and I think if you are married before next winter, you know just as well as I do that if you receive a good deal of attention it will not be as a 'young lady.' " Lois could not help dreaming of an Oxford neighbor, James Rowland, who had caught her fancy. Henrietta rebukes her for such thoughts, writing to Lois in Baltimore, "If you have made up your mind to marry Mr. Cassatt, try your best to drive from your mind all thoughts of *James,* for I think that thinking about him makes you not study Mr. C.'s character and tastes as much as you might do otherwise."

It is a wonder that Alexander did not forget the whole affair for surely he could find another young woman more willing and compatible. Added to his troubled wooing was a concern about his career. He had received an offer from the Freedom Iron Company to take over its presidency and leave the railroad. By early May, he decided to refuse the Iron Company's offer. He had discussed the position with J. Edgar Thomson who advised him to remain where he was. He also decided to ignore Lois' doubts and continued to write warmly to her. "I see you now as you sat at the table yesterday evening—your face and hair illuminated into the most beautiful color—the roses in the bouquet could not vie with the beauty of your complexion, and your eyes—the brightest in the world—never was there a more engaging picture." Lois could never complain that Alexander failed to express his love or to appreciate her.

Finally overcoming her reluctance, on July 14, 1868, Lois agreed to become properly engaged. Delighted, Alexander continued preparing the Altoona house for the reception of his bride and asked for an October wedding date. He hoped that Lois would "soon make up your mind to fix an early date for our wedding . . . I am very lonely here without you, my darling. Do not ask me to spend another winter here alone."

Lois had an interview with Aleck's mother who seems to have viewed the engagement with controlled delight. The uncomfortable relationship between Lois and her future in-laws began early, the cause unknown. Perhaps it lay in a conflict of personalities, but one is inclined to place the fault at Lois' door.

Alex took a decided and unusual interest in the wedding plans, down to the last detail. The invitations, Lois' gown, even the bridesmaids' costumes received his scrutiny. He traveled back and forth between Altoona and Philadelphia to inspect bolts of cloth for wallpaper for their home. "I had to send back the paper we selected on Saturday," he confided. "I found that the blue rubbed off so easily that your dresses would have been spoiled." Few bridegrooms have been so discerning or so meticulous. He intended to install his father's gift of a grandfather clock which had belonged to Marie Antoinette in their parlor, and a new mirror from Wheatlands would be packed by one of the railroad men for shipment from Lancaster to the

Altoona house. The wedding date was set for November 25, to be followed by a trip to New York and Boston, all the traveling arrangements on the Pennsylvania Railroad carefully arranged by the bridegroom: he had offered Lois a variety of schedules from which to choose.

Unaccountably, Lydia Cassatt, Aleck's elder sister, received no invitation to the wedding. Mary, of course, was in France, planning to paint a picture of Tennyson's Mariana of the Moated Grange, and would not be present. Fond as she was of Aleck, Mary did not regard his wedding as an occasion important enough to draw her home from France. Like Lydia, Mary never learned to like her new sister-in-law. There were faults on both sides, but one's sympathy in the conflict is more with Mary than Lois. In no way could the two women ever become compatible. Mary had no time for the petty interests which occupied Lois, and she resented the awkwardness her sister-in-law introduced into the close Cassatt circle. Of all the Cassatts, past or present, only Mary and Aleck had the rare quality and talent to lift them above the common ruck. Each appreciated the other's particular drive and power, and no one, even Lois, ever threatened their mutual admiration and respect. Nor did the senior Cassatts attend the ceremony, although they were living at 1635 Chestnut Street in Philadelphia, an easy journey to Trinity Church in Oxford. Aleck excused his mother's absence to Lodie by pleading her ill health.

Two weeks before the wedding, Aleck, in Altoona, received requests for railroad passes for the Buchanan relatives, demands which were to accelerate throughout his career until the company policy prevented their issuance. He informed Lodie of the housekeeping problems he encountered—the carpets had been cut too short and had to be returned; a cook and a housemaid had been interviewed and hired; chickens and turkeys were purchased from a local farmer to assure the couple a fresh supply of eggs and poultry. Alek went to considerable pains to supervise every detail of his new household, insisting that all be in readiness for his bride.

After the wedding trip to New York, where Lois suffered from "a headache and other maladies," the pair returned to Altoona and "found everything in readiness for our reception, my sister Henrietta and Lydia Cassatt having gone up to Altoona and prepared the house, and they also prepared a good dinner." Considering that Lydia had not been invited to the wedding, that neither she nor her parents particularly liked Lois, her gesture of welcome showed unusual magnanimity.

Quite frankly, Lois was not a likeable woman, although she had her champions. A wife of more warmth, intelligence, and tolerance would have made Aleck's path easier, but he never reproached her and remained devoted throughout their thirty-eight years of marriage. Only when he was gone, did she really understand what an exceptional man she had married: "His mind was receptive, his memory prodigious and his energy and power of achievement were marvelous. His courage, foresight and judgement were unequalled, and I can never cease to regret that my occupations with the house and children and later with society, should have caused me to overlook the opportunity I had of recording the daily life of so great a man." Even if she had grasped the opportunity, it is doubtful that Lois had the capacity to analyze the talent and spirit of her remarkable husband. Within her limitations and experience, she appreciated his rare qualities, but her restricted background, the influence of her narrow, straitlaced parents, and her own rigid temperment, prevented her from enlarging her view of the world to meet that of her husband. She did not share his enjoyment of the arts, although she embraced with enthusiasm the social prestige a patron of culture attracted. She enjoyed to the utmost the "society" to which her position as Aleck's wife entitled her, but she could not delve beneath that facade. Travel failed to broaden her interests; indeed, the hardships encountered irritated her. Paris gowns and hats invoked more excitement than Degas' paintings or the architectural marvels of Rome. With her husband's family she failed to establish any rapport, a situation Aleck managed to ignore while continuing his own affectionate and concerned relationship.

Lois Cassatt was blessed with a husband of unusual compassion, warmth, and equable disposition in the domestic circle. There was nothing of the Victorian tyrant in Alexander Cassatt. He was consistently kind, charming, and indulgent, a loving husband and father, who enjoyed family life far more than the competitive business struggles which his corporate rivals found so stimulating. Surely occasions occured in their long married life when the provincial and unimaginative aspects of his wife's interests and character must have proved irksome, but no trace of this incompatibility ever showed in his treatment of her.

Lois was not without assets. She more than did her duty toward friends and relatives less fortunate than herself. Her granddaughter, for one, found her warm and loving, hospitable, and a source of strength. She is not to be blamed that she could not look beyond the family circle to the wider world. In every way she was a typical product of her Victorian age: sheltered, submissive to her parents and husband, devoted entirely to their interests. She learned to love and respect her husband if she could not offer him that deeper companionship which would have been such a comfort as he moved onto the broader stage of the nation's industrial struggle. Living with Aleck softened her judgements and actions if it did not appreciably change her thorny character. Lois Buchanan chose well when she accepted Alexander Johnston Cassatt, and she learned to realize it.

For his part, although he never showed any desire to find companionship or affection beyond the marital bonds, he might have found more comfort with another life partner than this wife from the Oxford parsonage. In the mid-nineteenth century, incompatibility in a marriage was not recognized as a bar to the relationship. Fidelity and security meant a great deal more, and these Alexander Cassatt provided in good measure.

Moving Up The Line: From Altoona To Philadelphia

No sooner had the newly married Cassatts moved into the austere house overlooking the Altoona yards than Aleck settled down to compile his annual report. In his office, at the walnut table covered with the maroon cloth, he listed, modestly and concisely, his accomplishments of the past year, and more importantly, his hopes for the future. He stressed standarization of equipment for locomotives as essential to the growth and improvement of the Pennsylvania. Additional facilities for repairing cars would soon be needed in Altoona "to provide for the rapidly increasing business" of the lines east of Pittsburgh. Passenger service received some attention but the main focus of the report was on freight traffic, the company's bread and butter. The railroad had increased its passenger cars from 156 to 174 during the past year, but during the same period the Main Line and its branches had 2,278 freight cars in service, further evidence that carrying coal, oil, and steel were the Pennsylvania's chief concern then as today.

While Aleck attended to his job, Lois began her life as a matron, with plenty of advice from her mother. Mrs. Buchanan was determined that Lois would establish the proper spiritual atmosphere in her new home and lead her husband back into the church. "Ask him if he will not try with you to make the honor and glory of the Creator and *Savior* of your souls paramount to every other consideration in the ordering of your household." Aleck's fitful attendance at church, his spasmodic interest in religious devotions, rankled the Buchanans. For a personal account of how the young Cassatts were progressing the Buchanans sent Henrietta, "Netsie," as she was known in the family, for a visit to Altoona. Lois eagerly welcomed her favorite sister. She intended to hold her husband to his promise of allowing friends and family to visit them frequently. Lois' parents decided that the newlyweds would spend Christmas with them, although the pair had only been settled in their first home for a few weeks. Mrs. Buchanan felt aggrieved that they would only remain for a week and wrote to her daughter, "I thought, of course, that when you came home at Christmas, it would be for some considerable stay, or I expect I would have made a great deal more fuss than I did about your leaving me this winter." Obviously, the Buchanans did not share their son-in-law's opinion that the engagement had been an extended one. It would have been far better if the young Cassatts had been allowed to remain alone at home enabling Lois to adjust to marriage without the pervasive Buchanan influence.

Certainly, adjustments were necessary. All was not bliss around the domestic hearth in Altoona. Mrs. Buchanan recognized the difficulties in her letter of December 18: "Do not be too hasty, my dear Lodie, in your judgments of your husband and relatives. There may be reasons for their acting in a way that appears strange to you, that you know nothing of." Lois' mother was making a belated attempt to soothe her daughter's feelings, but whatever the cause of the discord, there is evidence that from the beginning Lois did not enjoy amicable relations with her in-laws and that Aleck may have tried to act as mediator. Whatever his early efforts or the reasons for the clash of personalities, he soon learned to ignore his wife's attitude while continuing to support his parents, sisters, and brother with his usual sympathy and warmth.

Aleck returned to Altoona from the holiday at the parsonage before his wife, stopping dutifully en route "to have a word with Caldwell's about the silver." He wrote of his arrival home to his wife, mentioning that his brother, Gard, was with him and enclosing a pass for Lois, Birdie Foster, her cousin, and one for her sister, Alice, if Mrs. Buchanan would allow the youngest daughter to accompany her sister to Altoona. For the present, Gardner Cassatt, was living with the young married pair, a situation which did not improve in-law relations and caused Mrs. Buchanan some disquiet. "I was rather glad to hear from Netsie that G. was not to board with you. . . . You should, however, be guarded by circumstances and your own good sense in this matter. If he should continue to act towards you, so as to put it in your power, you may be able to do him a great deal of good. . . ." Gard, an ebullient, friendly young man, may have chafed under such condescension but he remained attached to his brother.

Accustomed as large Victorian families were to living in one another's pockets, the young Cassatts did not find these constant visits as galling as today's generation would, but certainly they endured many family visitors. The senior Cassatts had spent Christmas with friends, but Mrs. Cassatt wrote Lois a civil, dutiful letter congratulating her on her success with domestic help, "as that is the great drawback to comfort almost everywhere in the country."

In the new year, 1868, Lois prepared to receive a visit from her younger brother, William, aged twenty, who was about to begin his short career of job hunting. She discovered during the month that she was pregnant, which brought additional advice from her mother. Mrs. Buchanan developed one of her periodic illnesses, and Lois was urged by Harriet to come home. Harriet informed her sister that she would not marry her curate in April, and "I doubt very much if it (the wedding) will ever take place." If Harriet could not accept marriage with Alexander Cassatt, she would not have endured domestic life with anyone.

Fortunately, these family disagreements did not prevent Aleck from efforts to improve the railroad. Standardization and upgrading of locomotives and roadbeds became an obsession with Cassatt. He believed that spending money for repairs and new equipment was an economy in the long run. Since the Pennsylvania had absorbed many small lines, gauges varied, and a continuing effort was made to introduce the standard gauge of four feet nine inches, the normal gauge of the Pennsylvania in the late 1860s. Cassatt was fortunate that J. Edgar Thomson also recognized the need for constant improvement in the line. With the lease of the Pittsburgh, Cincinnati, and St. Louis Railway, the Pennsylvania in 1869 extended its operation to St. Louis, and Thomson insisted that the road had no interest in going beyond the Mississippi, a statement he made to stockholders in that year which was to prove not entirely accurate. The Pennsylvania, Thomson stressed, must concentrate on building up the freight business, carrying coal, oil, and steel from the west to Philadelphia, and he promised to "cheerfully unite in any reasonable plan by which this object can be secured." In the conclusion of his annual report of 1869, Thomson congratulated Cassatt and his immediate superior, E. H. Williams, for "their careful and judicious management of the interests committed to their charge."

Cassatt, always vigilant on behalf of those interests, during 1869 introduced a revolutionary invention on the Pennsylvania locomotives which would vitally affect the performance of the trains as well as the lives of the men who ran them, the latter not often of primary importance to railroad executives. During his many trips to Pittsburgh on railroad affairs, he met a young Union Army veteran who had invented a startling device for safely braking locomotives. George Westinghouse, son of a Schenectady, New York agricultural implement manufacturer, had, at twenty-three, produced an air brake which would replace the tedious and dangerous process of tightening the brakes on each car by hand. After a series of experiments based on an article he had read about compressed air drills used in tunnel building in the Alps, Westinghouse manufactured a brake which operated by transmitting air pressure from a single tank to activate brake shoes on every car.

In April of 1869, Westinghouse, a smiling, affable young man with an enthusiastic air, persuaded Cassatt to give his air brake a trial on a daily train running the eighty-six miles between Steubenville, Ohio and Pittsburgh. For months Cassatt and other officers of the Pennsylvania watched the trials of the air brake. The engineers who ran the trains were suspicious of the new device and reluctant to use it. But the brakers who rode on the roof of each train, ready to jump down and apply the hand brakes, were more than willing to experiment with an appliance which would save so much additional work and, of course, diminish the possibility of injury. In the 1860s, life and labor were cheap while manufacturing new equipment meant an extensive outlay of precious capital.

The decisive demonstration of the efficiency of the air brake occured on the Steubenville train when, on one of the daily runs, a farmer's horse and buggy stalled on the track. The engineer whistled for the brakemen, forgetting for the moment that he had the new air brake available. Just in time he remembered to apply the device and halted the train inches from the rearing horse and its frightened owner. Westinghouse continued to make improvements on his patented air brake, reversing his original design, so that the release of air pressure, rather than the application of pressure, activated the air brake. In November, 1869, Cassatt watched the first passenger train equipped with the air brake pull out of the Altoona station bound for Philadelphia. Within ten years all passenger locomotives of the Pennsylvania were fitted with the perfected Westinghouse air brake, and other railroad lines were forced to follow suit.

Westinghouse acknowledged his great debt to Cassatt for taking a chance on his invention by attempting to persuade the latter to accept a large interest in the company formed to manufacture the appliance. Cassatt declined Westinghouse's generous offer, stating that he was acting for the Pennsylvania Railroad and that encouraging such improvements was only part of his job. Subsequently, he did purchase in the regular market a large block of stock in Westinghouse's company which he held until his death. The men remained friends all their lives. Westinghouse was only one of Cassatt's contacts. He had many other opportunities through the burgeoning oil, steel, and coal industries to amass a private fortune under more favorable circumstances than most. There is no evidence that he took unusual advantage of his situation, but undoubtedly he invested in the nascent industries and augmented his railroad salary. Cassatt always lived comfortably, even luxuriously, but he lacked the acquisitive grasping nature which characterized so many "robber barons" of his day. The exciting speculative games played by many entrepreneurs on the New York Stock Exchange failed to challenge him. He judiciously built up a large income in order to enjoy the sporting and cultural avocations which had always fascinated him. Horses, for example, were expensive, and Alexander Cassatt continued to show a connoisseur's desire to acquire the best. He never emulated Carnegie, Vanderbilt, Gould, or Rockefeller's dedication to the power commanded by a large fortune, and unlike the Standard Oil mogul did not seek to perpetuate his name through lavish contributions to good causes. From the beginning Aleck and Lois Cassatt had tithed their income, selecting the churches and charities which they deemed worthy of support, not publicizing this patronage but accepting such demands as a natural responsibility of their position and good fortune.

Andrew Carnegie, who would challenge Cassatt and the Pennsylvania in a ruthless struggle for industrial power, settled in the Pittsburgh area around 1868. But Cassatt had surely met the steel magnate when Carnegie had been an employee of the railroad and the favored assistant of Thomas A. Scott. As a boy of twelve, Carnegie had arrived in Allegheny City in 1848, the year the Pennsylvania was founded. His parents were immigrants from the depressed cottage weaving industry in Dumfermline, Scotland. He began his career as a $1.20-a-week bobbin boy in a Pittsburgh cloth factory but moved up rapidly to telegrapher and then assistant to Scott, when that fast-moving executive was managing the western lines of the railroad. On Scott's promotion Carnegie, in his turn, had been named superintendent of the western division in 1856, at age twenty-three. His connections with Scott and the railroad established the foundations of his fortune, and unlike Cassatt he took full advantage of them. By 1865 he had resigned from the Pennsylvania, the profits from his bridge company, locomotive works, and iron rail manufacturing giving him an income of $50,000 a year. He bought a country estate, Homewood, for his widowed mother outside of Pittsburgh, but moved his own quarters to New York, although he often returned to the area on family visits. Scott's "white haired Scotch devil" had come a long way from bobbin boy and telegrapher, but his real triumphs, spurred by the introduction of the Bessmer process for smelting steel, lay ahead. Carnegie, only four years older than Cassatt, had moved in and out of the inner circles of the Pennsylvania several years before Cassatt made his mark. In this greatest endeavor he could continue to rely on Scott's favoritism and preferential treatment which would eventually lead him to a confrontation with Cassatt. Carnegie's ally and eventual manager of his steel works, Henry Clay Frick, was just beginning his phenomenal climb when Cassatt became Superintendent of Motive Power and Machinery in Altoona.

Alexander Cassatt spent much time during the first year of his marriage traveling for the railroad between Altoona, Pittsburgh, and Philadelphia. There was much improving to do. In the late 1860s the signals systems remained faulty and spasmodic, the trackage poorly constructed, the rails too light to bear the loads which passed over them, and the roadbeds uncertain: Trains from Pittsburgh to Philadelphia, the pride of the line, required thirteen hours for the trip—and these were considered "lightening expresses." Cassatt set to work to change these conditions, but he never forgot to write to "my dear little wife," who spent as much time in Oxford as she did in the superintendent's house near the railroad tracks in Altoona.

Occasionally, despite her pregnancy, Lois accompanied her husband on his business trips. In Pittsburgh she visited her mother's old haunts, including Trinity Church, and saw former friends of the Fosters. Her mother reproved her for calling on one of the grande dames of the city without first having received a call from that lady: "If they were plain unpretending people, who would be likely to be gratified by a call from you without ceremony, I would not have a word to say, but with persons of their wealth, and so much 'run after', as they are, I think you cannot be too punctilious. I should not have mentioned this, my dear Lodie, but from fear you might be tempted to do something of the same when you come to Philadelphia. . . ." Small wonder with such advice that Lois Cassatt developed a reputation for being somewhat snobbish and "too punctilious." Her mother excused her criticism by concluding, "I know there are cases in which you scarcely know how to act and I thought you might as well know what I think in such matters." Lois' health, conduct, religious observance, clothes, and domestic affairs all received meticulous attention from Mrs. Buchanan.

Lois' constant trips to Oxford, patiently suffered by her husband, at last drew some complaints. He wrote from his Altoona office, "You must not think of staying after next week. My dear child, I cannot spare you a moment longer." He reminded her that he was forced to take his meals at Logan House in her absence. When she was in Altoona, Lois requested a wide variety of services from her family, telegraphing for sugar, asking her mother and sisters to interview a nurse, sending her sister Annie shopping for edging for an underskirt at a dollar and a half a yard, "very expensive," conceded Annie. Aleck, too, was pressed into shopping errands and during her frequent stays in Oxford superintended the renovation of their home. He ordered the stuff for the covering of the parlor chairs, supervised the painting of the back kitchen, interviewed a cook, "because I want everything done before you come home—and I don't want to postpone that happy event."

During the long hot summer while her family vacationed in Cape May, Lois remained in Altoona awaiting the birth of the baby. Edward Buchanan Cassatt was born on August 23, 1869. (As a young man he complained about the choice of his middle name, not regarding his Buchanan connection very highly.) Lois' mother had not been able to travel to Altoona for the birth of her first grandchild being "very weak and miserable." She was also concerned about her youngest son, Willie, then "spitting blood," a warning of the tuberculosis from which he was to die. Except for Lois, the Buchanans were not a healthy brood. Twelve days after the baby's birth, Lois was in Oxford, showing off her son to her parents, convalescing from his birth, and receiving more affectionate letters from her husband, who instructed her "to kiss the dear little boy for me."

Through Aleck the Buchanans met J. Edgar Thomson and his wife and adopted daughter, Lavinia. The president of the Pennsylvania, who shared with his superintendent a talent for engineering and a reserved manner, entertained Lois' sisters in Philadelphia. Henrietta wrote to her sister in Altoona that she enjoyed herself with the Thomsons: "They are all very kind. They talked a great deal about you. I think Mr. T. is very fond of you." He certainly encouraged Alexander of whom he had a high opinion which was translated into rapid promotions. Toward the end of 1869, when, just before the holidays, Edward H. Williams, general superintendent of the Pennsylvania, and Cassatt's immediate superior, resigned to take a position with the Baldwin Locomotive Works, Mr. Thomson named Cassatt to the post. The announcement was received by the Buchanans with mixed emotions. Mrs. Buchanan wrote to her daughter on New Year's Day, 1870, "Of course, my dear Lodie, I cannot but sympathize with you in your delight at Mr. C.'s advancement, though as I said in my former epistle, I could not have desired anything better for you than what you have already."

There was now no question of Aleck's remaining in his Altoona office and running affairs from there. He believed in getting out on the line and was often at the controls of the engines. On one of his frequent tours of inspection of the Pittsburgh division, he started from Altoona in the morning, stopped at every small depot, "and as we came slow and stopped often, it took us all day." Within the next week he had traveled back to Pittsburgh and expected to go on to a superintendent's meeting in Louisville, but these plans might be changed. "I can't tell much about my movements," he wrote to Lois, "as I may have to stay here to meet Mr. Vanderbilt who is coming here on Wednesday to look at our shops etc." The ambitious Commodore did well to inspect the Pennsylvania shops in Altoona, a model of their kind, for his destructive wars with Drew, Fiske, Cooke, and Gould had left the New York Central and the Erie in perilous working condition. More interested in inflating their stock for speculative purposes and securing personal bases of power, few railroad tycoons cared, as Cassatt did, about improving roadbeds or repairing engines on their lines.

Lois, in Oxford while Aleck was in Altoona, had called on the Thomsons and reported to her husband that she had endured a "slight." He tried to soothe her by reminding her that Mr. Thomson had been ill and the household upset. Then he continued with unaccustomed if justifiable severity: "You and I both have reason to feel grateful to Mr. Thomson for many kindnesses and should not be too ready to take offense." Lois' tendency "to take offense" marked many of her relationships through the years, but she learned to control her reactions, temper her attitudes, and profit from her husband's example. Much of her irritability stemmed from a social insecurity fostered by the humorless advice of her parents who cared too much for the proprieties. As Aleck's influence deepened and that of her parents waned, Lois became more tolerant, more relaxed in social affairs.

Mr. Thomson's illness could only have been acerbated by the problems brought on by the New Jersey railroad situation which propelled the Pennsylvania into yet another struggle with Vanderbilt's New York Central. During Thomson's tenure as president he had drawn to Philadelphia first the trade of upstate Pennsylvania and then that of the Great Lakes and the middle west through extending his road to Chicago and St. Louis. The western lines of the railroad to the Mississippi were secure, but there remained the competitive lure of New York, the busiest market place. Because of the fierce struggle for trade among the competing lines, the Pennsylvania had negotiated with the Central, the Erie, and to a lesser extent with the Baltimore & Ohio for equal freight rates, an agreement more observed in the breach than in the practice. But although the problem of the western traffic seemed fairly stable by 1870, this was not true of the city of New York, always Philadelphia's rival as a port, mercantile, and banking center.

New York offered attractive terminals and dockage facilities for the European vessels whose goods were in such demand. If the Pennsylvania would fulfill its pledge to Philadelphia's merchants, additional efforts must be made to make the Quaker City more competitive with New York. This could be done only by extending the Pennsylvania Railroad's lines through New Jersey, by building additional track, gaining rights to the ferries, bridges, and connecting lines north to Manhattan.

Since the Civil War New York had become the nation's chief market place. The city's bankers, merchants, railroad tycoons, steamship owners, traders, and manufacturers did a larger and larger volume of business than their Philadelphia counterparts. Each year Philadelphia fell farther behind its rival and reluctantly conceded that New York had become the number one business center of the nation through determination and what some Philadelphians considered its "ungentlemanly manner" of conducting its affairs. Philadelphia, which in the eighteenth century had been the largest, most sophisticated city in America, had lost out to its brasher northern sister.

Thomson decided to challenge New York's dominance by gaining the vital Camden and South Amboy route to the shores of New York and by leasing the "joint Companies" which supplemented the New Jersey road. His efforts did not go unnoticed, and a stock race began for ownership of the Camden and South Amboy. Aging and ill, Thomson himself could not cope with the ruthless war for New Jersey. The negotiations were entrusted to Alexander Cassatt.

Cassatt came down from Altoona to Philadelphia in the fall of 1870, laid his plans, and announced a few months later that the Pennsylvania had beaten the Central and Erie by buying enough of the Camden and South Amboy stock to give it control. A guarantee of ten percent was given on all the Jersey road stock not secured by Cassatt and his scouts. The Pennsylvania stockholders voted to lease the Joint Companies for ninety-nine years at a cost of $1,948,500 per year. Cassatt's success insured that his road would now travel as far as the Hudson River terminating at the gateway of New York, laying the groundwork for an even more expensive incursion into the heart of the city at the beginning of the twentieth century.

While Aleck had been bargaining for the New Jersey roads, his family had welcomed home his sister Mary, a fugitive from the Franco-Prussian War and the seige of Paris. Naturally the Cassatts expected Lois, Aleck, and young "Tuny," the baby, to spend Christmas with them, the first Mary had spent at home since her brother's marriage. Mrs. Buchanan tried to be forbearing about Lois' absence for the holiday: "It is natural that Mr. Cassatt should wish to be with his family on one of the great days, and of course you ought to be willing to gratify his wish . . . provided that you have a sufficient guarantee that you will be received and treated as his wife should be." Some of Mrs. Buchanan's chagrin over Lois' supposed ill treatment by the senior Cassatts may have arisen from episodes in her own past, when Robert Cassatt and Eliza Foster had been more than friends in Pittsburgh. In a letter on December 13, 1870, she expressed her unhappiness that Lois did not have a more amicable relationship with her in-laws by writing, "I do not think I have ever had a greater disappointment than in the course Mr. C.'s family has pursued toward you, as the fact that he was the son of one whom I had known and been attached to so long ago was greatly in his favor as your suitor." Possibly Katherine Kelso Cassatt's cool demeanor toward her daughter-in-law can be traced to her jealousy of this former "attachment" between her husband and Eliza Foster Buchanan.

Lois' fractious attitude may charitably be attributed to her new pregnancy for she was expecting another baby the following summer. During the Christmas holidays Mary painted a portrait of her new nephew, Edward Cassatt, in a red velvet suit. The painting, not considered by modern critics as one of her best, kept her busy and doubtless pleased Lois. Mary's style, still undefined and unperfected, demanded further study. In March, 1871, Katherine Cassatt refused an invitation from Lois for herself and Mary to visit Altoona, pleading that "Mary must make use of her studio while she has it." She suggested that Lois and the baby visit them in Philadelphia.

Henrietta traveled to Altoona to be with Lois since Aleck was away so much on the New Jersey road business. Mrs. Buchanan sensibly discounted Lois' over-delicate feelings about the presence of her unmarried sister in her home during her approaching confinement. "I think it will have to be borne by both of you," she advised wryly. Henrietta informed the Buchanans that Katherine Kelso Cassatt was born on July 30, 1871. Willie congratulated his sister and mentioned that Aleck had made the Buchanans a "flying visit." Like his late brother James, Willie sensibly evaluated Aleck's character: "If it is not too much flattery for you to bear, I will say that if he has as high a station in the opinion of the rest of the family as he has in mine, he is exalted to a very high pitch." Aleck deserved every kind word the Buchanans could bestow for his attitude toward them had been more than generous under conduct which would have tried a lesser man.

Of equal importance to Alexander Cassatt was the good opinion of J. Edgar Thomson, who was so pleased by his handling of the intricate negotiations to secure the New Jersey railroads through acquisition of the various stock. In the fall of 1871, Thomson informed the directors that a new position, general manager, had been created for Cassatt, "who has during the past year so successfully conducted the business of the Pennsylvania Railroad as Superintendent." The New Jersey lines would now be directly under Alexander's eye from his new headquarters in Philadelphia at the Pennsylania's main offices. In the four years since his appointment as Superintendent of Motive Power and Machinery, Alexander Cassatt had risen into the very front echelons of the railroad and more promotions would follow. He was thirty-two years old.

By mid-December, 1871, the Cassatts had moved from Altoona into a rented house at 2035 Walnut Street in Philadelphia, a dignified, four-story, stone-fronted home on the fashionable north or "right" side of Broad Street. The Buchanans, of course, were delighted to have them so close. But Mrs. Buchanan could not resist offering her daughter some advice about the distractions of the city: "I am much impressed my dear child with the important results which may hang on your removal to the city and pray that you may be led in the right direction and have the strength to withstand the strong current of worldlings to which you may be exposed." Mrs. Buchanan worried constantly about the "extreme" of fashion and the temptations which the "gay" life offered Lois through her position as Mrs. Alexander Cassatt. She warned her against going to balls and parties when Aleck cannot escort her. Under no conditions should she dance the "german" (a stylized Victorian ladies' choice) for fear of being thought fast. In reading over her letter, she must have realized how priggish and presumptuous it would sound to a matron with two children, and even more to her husband. She asked her daughter to burn it.

Fortunately for Lois, the Buchanans' would be away during the next few months. Having finally received his share of the late President's estate, the Reverend Edward decided to take his wife, Harriet, and Henrietta on a tour of Europe. Alice and Annie stayed at home. While they were away, in the summer of 1872, Aleck bought fifty-six acres for $10,000 from Dr. Edmund

Evans in Haverford, some ten miles from Philadelphia on the Main Line of the railroad. Although business forced him to rent a residence in town, he always preferred the countryside where he could enjoy leisurely rides every day. Even when railroad business was most pressing, when struggles between the Pennsylvania and its rivals most intense, when millions of dollars hung in the balance, Alexander Cassatt never abandoned his scheduled rides nor hours with his family. His assistant, William A. Patton, remembered that Cassatt's capacity for work was phenomenal, and in consequence he accomplished so much of the day's work in the early part of the day that he could go home in the early afternoon.

Many railroad executives followed Cassatt to the Main Line, building large homes whose value would be increased by the development of the railroad and the easy commuting to town on the suburban trains. Cassatt's estate, Cheswold, built during the winter and spring of 1872–73 and remodeled several times during the next fifty years, was designed by the firm of Furness and Evans, architects of the future Pennsylvania Station at Broad Street. The cost was $50,000. Late Victorian-Gothic in style, the thirty-room mansion had a vast, walnut-paneled entrance hall lighted by stained glass windows. Marble fireplaces decorated the seven bedrooms which possessed the ultimate luxury of seven accompanying baths. To the right of the entrance hall was Aleck's study, walls and ceiling paneled in mahogany, dominated by a huge globe, a rolltop mahogany desk, and a copper chandelier. Near the window was an armchair where he spent many hours gazing at the gently rolling meadows. Attached to the house was the stable for Cassatt's horses and carriages, a four-in-hand, a brake, brougham pony cart, and Lois' coupe de ville. Two coachmen and two grooms kept the horses and carriages in order, while the indoor staff of a dozen was headed by a butler and a housekeeper. Today, only the gatehouse stands as a reminder of Cheswold's former glories.

One of the attractions of Cheswold for Alexander Cassatt was the space it provided for his horses. For he intended to buy, breed, and race horses. While Cheswold had been built as a summer retreat for the family, they also began to spend occasional weeks during the warm weather at Howland's Hotel in Long Branch, N. J., less for the sea bathing, than to allow Aleck to attend the races. In time, his passion for horses would deeply involve him in New Jersey racing and lead to the purchase of a stock farm ten miles further in the country. In the 1870s, his responsibilities as general manager prevented him from doing little more than acquiring potential thoroughbred winners.

In her diary Lois Cassatt mentions little about the building of Cheswold: "During the year 1872 we bought the property at Haverford Station and built the house in which we have lived ever since. We moved into the house in July, 1873, although it was not really finished until the fall. Bob (Robert) was born there on the 28th of September, 1873." With the birth of Elsie (Eliza) on August 14, 1875, also at Cheswold, the family was complete. They continued to rent town houses in the winter, not buying a Philadelphia residence until the 80s.

Aleck's sister, Mary, who had tragically lost the pictures she had hor d to sell to American art collectors during the Chicago Fire of 1871, sailed for Italy in 1872, where she studied in Parma before briefly staying in Spain. Her parents and Lydia remained at 21st Street in Philadelphia. They did not join Mary permanently until the fall of 1877—the year which brought Alexander Cassatt what his wife later called, "the most trying experience of his life," the Railway Strike in Pittsburgh.

Violence in Pittsburgh, 1877

In the Pennsylvania Railroad's offices at 32nd and Market Streets in West Philadelphia, Alexander Cassatt was the only chief executive at his desk on the hot afternoon of Thursday, July 19, 1877. The president of the road, Colonel Thomas A. Scott, had boarded his special car for a run up to Judge Craig Biddle's estate, Andalusia, on the banks of the Delaware some eighteen miles away. Scott, always eager for convivial occasions, had accepted an invitation to a Farmers' Club dinner at Judge Biddle's. George B. Roberts, first vice president of the line, had fallen ill at his Cape May home. Frank Thomson, whose chief responsibility as general manager was freight traffic, had stopped at Long Branch, N. J. for a rest after a business conference in New York. Cassatt, for the past three years third vice president of the Pennsylvania, had postponed his annual vacation to Long Branch to watch the races. But trouble was brewing beyond the Alleghenies.

Cassatt, distant from the scene, was inclined at first to view the situation as a temporary misunderstanding. True, the country had for the past four years been suffering from a business depression brought on by the manipulations of railroad managers. Cassatt's own chief had played no small part in this chicanery. Scott became president of the railroad at fifty-one, but the presidency of the Pennsylvania was not enough for this ambitious man. His salary and industrial investments, bolstered by his influence with the state legislature, brought him an income well beyond $100,000 a year. Recently, he had met with some obstacles in his efforts to increase his fortune and his power base. He had been deeply involved, along with several other Philadelphians, in the nefarious Credit Mobilier, that dubious organization with the strange French name, formed to finance the building of transcontinental railroads. In 1871–72, when Cassatt had just arrived at the head office from Altoona, Scott had briefly been president of the Union Pacific with the idea of bringing it under the Pennsylvania's control. Nothing came of this plan, but Scott did not readily abandon his efforts to build a railroad empire. He organized the Texas and Pacific, hoping to stretch the Pennsylvania's network to the west coast—despite J. Edgar Thomson's pledge to the contrary in 1869—and challenge Collis Huntington's Central Pacific. Railroads were the biggest business in the country. No matter that too many lines were duplicating routes, that stock was watered, that lines grew unchecked—Scott's ambitions were feverish.

When Congress, prodded by an uneasy public, decided to investigate the Credit Mobilier, Scott rushed off to Europe to find other money for his Texas and Pacific, since government help seemed improbable. Congress in due course discovered that the Credit Mobilier had been charging outrageous prices for construction, lining the pockets of eastern investors at the expense of the public. When the news broke, Jay Cooke & Co., the nation's most prestigious banking firm, heavily into Credit Mobilier financing, closed its doors, bankrupting hundreds of small investors. Railroad stock plummeted, and soon hundreds of other merchants and employers were forced into receivership. Panic swept the country, throwing thousands out of work and earning the railroads a hatred from which they would never entirely recover.

A year later, J. Edgar Thomson, still president of the Pennsylvania, died in Philadelphia while his stockholders were howling for action. Thomson, with Scott's help, had been responsible for the Pennsylvania's phenomenal growth, but the Panic of 1873 finished him. Worried and unable to cope with the economy's impact on his road, he suffered a final heart attack on May 27, 1874.

Scott, still dickering for his Texas and Pacific, more concerned about his power play than with his future with the Pennsylvania, seemed the obvious choice to succeed Thomson. He had never ceased to be first Vice President, and many observers thought he would automatically become the new president despite his other interests. Scott with his mane of white hair, fine features, and incredible energy, looked like a railroad president—and he was bent on being one. He had even considered taking the presidency of the troubled Erie, in a state of collapse after Jay Gould's speculative management. But Scott was a plunger. The depressed economy demanded retrenchment, caution, cutbacks, none of which attracted the colonel. In the inner councils of the Pennsylvania, some of the knowledgeable directors suggested that George B. Roberts and Cassatt, junior officers, were preferable choices. But on June 3, 1874, Scott's partisans prevailed. He was elected president unanimously.

Unfortunately for the Pennsylvania, his talents, which were considerable, were not adapted to the times. He became president during the worst depression the country had endured since its founding. The cheap money of the 60s had led to overexpansion and overbuilding of railroads, particularly east of the Mississippi. The four big eastern trunk lines competed fiercely for the freight traffic which led to huge rebates to favored shippers, cutting into revenue which had already been eroded by falling business. Scott sought other assets for the Pennsylvania. He created the Empire Transportation Company, allegedly a Pennsylvania subsidiary, to haul petroleum, but actually established to challenge Rockefeller in the refinery business. The wily oil baron was not quiescent under Scott's challenge. One of the reasons Scott decided to reduce wages to trainmen in June, 1877 was to release funds for his war with Rockefeller, although he never admitted this.

Meanwhile, Scott had not abandoned his plans for the Texas & Pacific. During the closely fought Presidential election of 1876, he deserted his old friend and railroad lawyer, Samuel J. Tilden, to push the candidacy of Rutherford B. Hayes, who now owed Scott a favor the latter would hasten to collect. Toward the trainmen who kept his "empire" running, Scott showed little interest or concern. Labor was plentiful and cheap. His response to men on strike was to tell them: "If the wages or arrangements of the company did not suit them, to peaceably go away."

On June 1, 1877 Scott had reduced wages ten percent across the board. The men, after sending a delegation in protest to Scott, who gave them no satisfaction, had seemed to accept the necessity. They had objected much more strongly to the recent introduction of more double-headers on the Pittsburgh run. In the past the Pennsylvania had periodically sent out these trains, two engines pulling thirty-four cars instead of the regulation seventeen, with a single crew. The economy move enabled the company to lay off more men and insured jobs for those with seniority. Scott disclaimed all responsibility for the double-headers. He refused to listen to a delegation of trainmen bent on explaining their grievances to the man in the head office. "It is a matter of detail management of the respective divisions that scarcely ever comes to me at all," he explained later. The Pennsylvania paid dearly for the colonel's indifference and intransigence toward his trainmen's complaints. Robert Pitcairn, head of the Pittsburgh division, had unwisely increased the scheduling of double-headers immediately after the announcement of the wage reduction, adding to the men's resentment. All employees on the payroll were promised that their wages would not be lowered below a dollar a day. Many of the senior brakemen were paid up to $2.00 an hour for the actual time on the locomotive. They were now working longer hours in more tiring circumstances for less pay. Cassatt himself had his salary reduced, but he still earned in excess of $30,000 a year. All employees of the road, from the president to the day laborer had suffered two pay cuts since 1873, in response to the depression. Freight rate wars between the competing lines east of Chicago were cutting deeply into the Pennsylvania's revenues as well as into those of its rivals, the New York Central and the Erie, which had also announced pay cuts in the past few weeks. The Pennsylvania's men grumbled, but they accepted the economy moves because they needed their jobs.

On July 11, John W. Garrett, president of the Baltimore & Ohio, who had insisted on paying his stockholders a ten percent dividend that his road could ill afford, announced a pay cut in line with the rival railroads. Garrett, a former provision dealer with no railroad experience, had taken over the B & O before the Civil War and built it into a great trunk line. But not without problems—the B & O's stock capitalization was much too low in comparison with its bonded debt. Garrett tried unsuccessfully to borrow more capital abroad to strengthen his financial base. J. Pierpont Morgan, then beginning his mercurial climb to power, advised him to reduce dividends, but Garrett's answer was to reduce wages. On Tuesday, July 17, a gray morning in the Shenandoah Valley, trainmen of the B & O stopped a cattle car from moving out of Martinsburg, West Virginia. The strike was on. But the trouble seemed local, confined to the B & O.

Yet, two days after the B & O strike, the discontent had spread westward. At two o'clock that afternoon when Cassatt believed that the work of the day had been largely accomplished, his assistant William Patton brought him a dispatch from Altoona. The message was from the general superintendent, G. Clinton Gardner. A fireman and a brakeman in Pittsburgh had refused to take out a double-header that morning. They had been joined by others—the Pennsylvania men were on strike. Information was sketchy because the man in charge of the Pittsburgh office was on vacation. Robert Pitcairn had left the city that morning on the daily express to take his family to Long Branch. David M. Watt, his chief clerk, left in command, panicked at the action of the balky trainmen and called on the civil authorities for protection.

The action of the Trainmen's Union did not appear to be in response to the B & O strike in Martinsburg. Cassatt believed that his trains would run, that the dissatisfaction with the Pennsylvania wage cut and the stepped up use of double-headers was confined to a few malcontents. Despite all evidence to the contrary, he took a sanguine view of the strike: ' 'I telegraphed to Pittsburgh to get extra conductors and engineers, to take the place of those who had gone out, and I thought it would be over soon," he reported later. Having taken appropriate measures he left the office at his usual time, four o'clock, and "went up to the country," to his home in Haverford to enjoy the rest of the day with his family. "I didn't hear anything further until evening," he said.

Cassatt's rural retreat at Cheswold enabled him to put all thoughts of strikers and railroad business aside. Although Haverford and neighboring Bryn Mawr were peaceful summer retreats some of the nationwide labor violence had touched even their protected homes. Cassatt himself had joined "96 gentlemen," a group that met in Bryn Mawr early in July to discuss the threat to safety posed by the hobos who collected at the back doors of estate kitchens for handouts. Most of the tramps were not criminally inclined. They took to the road from desperation, unable to find jobs. But conditions were improving. Vagrants found temporary work on the local farms. Farmers were enjoying a good season, bumper crops, and higher prices. Only the cities were suffering from the industrial malaise.

That Thursday evening Cassat barely had time to greet his wife and family before he was called from his dinner by the station master at Haverford. Conditions at Pittsburgh had not improved. Most of the activity had moved from Union Station in the seething city to 28th Street, where David Watt, still deputizing for his absent chief, Pitcairn, was attempting to move the freight trains. Watt ordered one of the men, Moore, to throw the switch which would allow the cars to pull out on a diversionary track. Moore refused, afraid of the muttering mob of trainmen, mill hands, and roustabouts who had joined the discontented crowd, all spoiling for a fight.

A brakeman named Davis, sensing the mood of the mob, stepped up and addressed them with bravado: "Boys, we might as well die right here." Watt, with more valor than common sense, approached the switch and said, "I will open it." Davis' companion, McColl, supported by the crowd pressing behind him, shoved Watt and then struck him in the face. Watt called to the police for protection. All attempts to throw the switch were abandoned while the strikers tried to prevent the police from arresting McColl, who was finally dragged off to the station. A few stones were thrown, angry words exchanged, and Watt, frustrated and bleeding from a face wound, sent to the mayor's office for more police. Mayor William McCarthy, a man of violent emotions not matched by personal courage, could only enlist a handful of police for duty at 28th Street. The mayor then gave up any attempt to use his authority and left the scene.

Cassatt heard the reports from Pittsburgh when he arrived at 32nd and Market Streets. "On coming to the West Philadelphia office, I then heard no trains had moved up to that time, and I thought my duty ought to be there and I got on a train and went to Pittsburgh," he told the committee which later probed the company-union confrontation. His brief statement does not reveal the real sequence of events. Years later his devoted, austere assistant, William Patton, who brooked no criticism of his chief, remembered the story in more detail in a letter to Mrs. Cassatt. He recalled that Charles E. Pugh, general agent for the railroad, was at dinner in his West Philadelphia home when a messenger arrived from Cassatt requesting his presence at the office immediately. On Pugh's arrival Cassatt told him the situation at Pittsburgh had become critical. The vice president felt he must go west to look into the matter. Cassatt had by this time sent several messages to Scott at Judge Biddle's but had received no reply. He asked

Pugh to get him a car and an engine, to contact Augustus Dowell, a telegraph operator, and also to find a lineman who would accompany them in case the wires should be cut along the route. Since the president's private car, No. 30, had been lent to Governor John F. Hartranft for a tour of the west, the general manager's car was prepared. Cassatt steamed out of the West Philadelphia station at 8:30 Thursday evening. Before leaving, he ordered Pugh to run another special up to Andalusia and get Colonel Scott.

As Cassatt traveled westward across the state, he must have had some hard thoughts about Scott, although he would never reveal them. He admired his chief's drive and expansionary efforts which had benefited the road in the past. Now, Scott's inability to compromise, to temper that drive with sensible restraint might cost the Pennsylvania dearly. At risk were hundreds of locomotives filled with freight, the profit cargo of the railroad. Standing in the yards at Pittsburgh were cars packed with coal, machinery, whiskey, flour, oil, all waiting for dispatch to eastern markets. Stranded refrigerator cars, their ice melting rapidly in the heavy heat, their produce rotting, meant an immediate loss to the company even if the strike could be settled within the next few hours. Fanning out from the 1,300-foot station complex stood repair shops, two roundhouses, blacksmith forges, warehouses, machine shops, hundreds of feet of siding. What was happening to this valuable Pennsylvania Railroad equipment since the civil authorities refused their protection? Where was Scott, and what would he do?

Lois Cassatt, worried about her husband's safety, never forgot his ordeal. Describing that night in 1877 many years later for her children's benefit, she had bitter words for the Colonel and other officers of the road: "When the riots assumed a serious aspect there [Pittsburgh], the President of the Road was away from home, and several of the other officers for reasons best known to themselves, were unable to go to the scene of the action . . . your father, without the slightest hesitation went out to Pittsburgh."

As Cassatt rushed through the night to the striking city, his chief concern was for the railroad property. He had some sympathy for the men, less for Colonel Scott, who had brought the company and its third vice president to this crisis.

While Cassatt was en route, General Agent Pugh ran a car to Andalusia to find Scott. The colonel had left Judge Biddle's home to spend the night with his son-in-law, Howell Bickley, a few miles from the Judge's estate. When Pugh finally tracked down Scott at Bickley's, it was ten o'clock. Bickley at first refused to disturb Scott, who had retired for the night, but the colonel heard the conversation and "in a very peremptory manner" told Bickley to let Pugh come upstairs. Pugh delivered Cassatt's message and waited while Scott dressed. The colonel demanded a horse and buggy for the ride to Biddle's where the special car was waiting at the siding. As the men drove toward Andalusia through a violent thunder storm, Scott never said a word to Pugh about the strike. He kept silent on the way back to West

Philadelphia, only admitting that he had received Cassatt's earlier messages at Judge Biddle's but had thrust them unopened into his pocket. He reached the West Philadelphia station and made preparations for a siege, setting up cots in the office, ignoring the crowd gathering below the windows. He made no attempt to follow Cassatt to Pittsburgh.

On his way Cassatt stopped at Greensburg to see Lieutenant Governor James W. Latta. Governor Hartranft was junketing around the country in Scott's private car, but he had advised his deputy to take charge in case trouble arose. He had been assured on July 16 that all was quiet. Latta told Cassatt that Sheriff R. R. Fife had telegraphed him from Pittsburgh for assistance, but only the Governor had the power to order out the state troops. Scott and Latta were both bombarding the Governor with telegrams. Latta wired Hartranft that on his own he had ordered Major General Alfred L. Pearson, a Pittsburgh lawyer and commander of Pennsylvania's Sixth Division of the National Guard, to the city with four companies. On Friday morning in Cheyenne, Wyoming, Hartranft read the newspaper reports of the disturbances. He wired Latta to proceed to Pittsburgh himself, and from Laramie he proclaimed, "Spare nothing to protect all persons in their rights under the Constitution of the State, in accordance with the policy heretofore adopted. Am on the train to Oregon." He did not intend to return.

Cassatt, unaware of the Governor's proclamation, arrived in Pittsburgh early Friday morning. Two days of pouring rain had left the yards damp and steaming. Late Thursday evening a meeting had been called by the Trainmen's Union at Phoenix Hall on 11th Street. Reporters were barred, but the sense of the meeting was apparent and widely heralded in the Friday morning press. Millworkers and other factory hands in the city were with the trainmen. Pittsburgh was a workingman's town, angry at the railroad for its past efforts to discriminate against the Steel City, and aroused by the recent wage reduction.

Cassatt discovered that Pitcairn had returned from Long Branch and taken charge. He had his locomotives fired and ready to move with crews willing to take out the double-headers when the strikers could be moved from the tracks. Sheriff Fife so far had neither the force of character nor the manpower to disperse the mob. When he tried to reason with them, they shouted him down. "Go to hell, you gray-haired old son of a bitch," one of the angry workers shouted. "Bread or blood," cried another when Fife threatened to use troops.

Cassatt struggled through the excited crowd, which offered him no violence, although he was certainly recognized. At the nearby Union Hotel, where he had planned to stop, the desk clerk refused to give him a room, fearing retribution from the strikers. So he registered at the Monongahela House a few blocks away and returned to the station to confer with Pitcairn and Watt. Cassatt then called in David Stewart, a former railroad agent and local citizen who was sympathetic to the management. He asked Stewart to see Mayor McCarthy. Cassatt wanted the mayor to swear in a posse which could disperse the crowd; he promised to pay the posse's wages with railroad funds. But Stewart's errand was fruitless—the mayor would have nothing to do with it. In the meantime, Pearson, not yet on the scene, had ordered Colonel P. N. Guthrie to take his 18th Regiment and open the road at East Liberty. After a half-hearted try, for the militia were with the strikers in spirit, the soldiers abandoned the effort and most of them remained outside the city at Torrens Station.

When Latta arrived on the Friday noon train, Guthrie had still made no move to clear the tracks. The militia, unable and unwilling, pleaded insufficient troops. In the early afternoon a delegation from the Trainmen's Union appeared at Union Station to give Pitcairn the written demands they had drawn up at the meeting the evening before. Pitcairn and Cassatt went out on the platform to hear them. After reading the terms Pitcairn handed Cassatt the paper. The trainmen wanted their wages restored to pre-June levels, the double-headers cancelled, permission for each engineer to choose his fireman, and, as Cassatt remembered, "a number of other things of the same kind." He handed the paper back to Pitcairn and told him, "Have no further talk with them." Later Cassatt said, "They had demanded such things as we couldn't grant them at all, and it wasn't worthwhile to discuss the matter." He had lost his only opportunity to meet face to face with the dissatisfied men who might have listened to him.

Cassatt may have had no doubts about the propriety of his stand, but the few leading citizens of Pittsburgh who tried to mollify his opinion had many. William Thaw, a railroad director and local steel manufacturer, advised against violence. So did James Park, Jr., another Pittsburgh businessman of substance and influence. Pearson, who had finally arrived, waited at the station with seventy-five of his men. He was not willing to face a confrontation, pleading insufficient force to quell the mob, now numbering in the hundreds and growing. He later said that Cassatt urged him to act: "Mr. Cassatt thought it much better to go out and take possession of the property."

Take possession of the property! That regard for the sanctity of the Pennsylvania's cars, filled with freight, lying untended and unregarded in the yards, forced Cassatt into an action inexcusable in its callous disregard for human life. For the first time in his professional life, he found himself opposed to the men who ran the trains; the men he had worked with, the men who believed in, trusted, and respected him. He had some sympathy for their plight, for the desperate conditions which had forced them to action, but he believed that his duty was to protect the property of the Pennsylvania. In the passion of the moment, he lost most of his usual discipline and objectivity.

By now it was mid-afternoon. After his lack of success with Pearson,

Cassatt visited the roundhouse and persuaded some stand-by crews to take out the double-headers on the understanding that the tracks were clear. The crews seemed willing, and he went back to Pearson.

At this point, Pearson later testified, Cassatt suggested that Philadelphia troops be called. He intimated that the eastern troops would not hesitate to fire over the heads of the mob. Cassatt vehemently denied ever applying to the state authorities for protection and insisted that this step had been taken by Fife before his arrival. But the orders were issued, and Cassatt did nothing to stop them. That evening Latta called out the First Division of the National Guard, commanded by Major General Robert M. Brinton. The National Guard division, known as Philadelphia's First City Troop was distinguished for its social lineage, but also included many Civil War veterans with fine battle records. The Troop left Philadelphia at 2 A.M. on Saturday morning. Cassatt waited uneasily through the night for their arrival. Pearson refused to move the main body of his troops down from East Liberty until the Philadelphia regiment arrived. From the Union Station at 11th Street to the outer depot at 28th Street, the mob continued to grow, blocking the tracks which fanned out from the main station, overlooked on one side by the smoke darkened hills and on the other by a main thoroughfare, Liberty Avenue.

Early Saturday morning the local militia, under a warming sun, stacked their arms and ate breakfast on a hillside by the 28th Street depot. The militia mingled with the townspeople, occasionally trying to move them off the tracks, with good humor on both sides. The militia had no intention of using their arms. Sympathy for the strikers extended to the newspapers, which violently denounced the railroad in their morning editions. *The Leader* contended that the strikers were not violent and displayed "a dignified and manly attitude" towards the soldiers, who "are equally determined to get through this matter without shedding blood." *The Globe* was not so restrained: Scott and Cassatt were martinets. Another editorial protested that railroad employees were no better off than serfs in tsarist Russia. Pittsburgh's blood was up.

Hundreds of people—militiamen, millworkers, railroad employees, their women and children—covered the hillside above the 28th Street station to watch the two battered cars carrying the Philadelphia regiment pull into Union Station that Saturday afternoon. The crowds on the hillside at first cheered the troops, hoping to win their sympathy. But then their mood changed. The cars bore the marks of heavy stoning from the disgruntled strikers at Harrisburg, Johnstown, and Altoona through which they had passed. Rifles protruded from the broken windows; stones and bricks littered the cowcatchers and roofs of the cars. The two shining Gatling guns, which accompanied the troops, were ominously ready for action.

As the troops piled off the train to gulp coffee and rolls at the Union Depot and then form two smart lines across the tracks preparatory to moving up toward 28th Street, the men who had awaited their arrival had widely varying reactions. General Pearson, the militia commander whose men had shown such support for the strikers, eyed them warily. "Meeting an enemy on the field of battle you go there to kill . . . the quicker you do it the better," the general said. "But here you had men with fathers and brothers and relatives mingled in the crowd of rioters. The sympathy of the people, the sympathy of the troops, my own sympathy, was with the strikers. We all felt these men were not receiving enough wages."

Park and Thaw, with heavy investments in Pittsburgh and close ties to the railroad, begged Cassatt, Pearson, and Brinton to wait until Monday before proceeding. By then many of the men in the crowd around the station would have returned to their mills and factories. Cassatt, eager to get his trains moving, aware that every hour's delay meant thousands of dollars lost to the company, took out his watch. "We have now lost an hour and a half's time," he told Park. Thaw put his objections to the troops' movements in writing, but John Scott, the Pennsylvania's attorney, remonstrated with him, and Thaw tore up his note. Thaw then made an unavailing personal appeal to Cassatt. "I had made up my mind not to interfere in any way with the state officials, and I did not. I took the position that we were in their hands, and that it was their problem to work out," Cassatt later explained. But he kept insisting, "We must have our property."

Cassatt overheard Pearson and Brinton plan to deploy the troops. Brinton told Pearson he had given his men orders not to fire on the mob except in self-defense. The First City Troop moved down the tracks in columns of fours, a rear guard pulling the two Gatling guns. At first the crowd gave way with a few hoots and cheers, but as the troops neared the crossing at 28th Street the mob, now over 5,000, pressed nearer, spurred by the watchers on the hillside who yelled their encouragement. Ahead of the troops walked Pitcairn to point out the strike ringleaders for arrest. One of the soldiers remembered later that he looked up and saw Cassatt, in his tall white hat and shirt sleeves, stalking across the top of the freight cars. Inside the 28th Street depot, Watt had the locomotives ready to move, waiting for the clearing of the tracks. There were still crews willing to take out the double-headers provided they were protected.

Brinton's troops formed a hollow square around the 28th Street depot, an impressive professional maneuver, although they were obviously nervous, sweating in their heavy uniforms under the beating sun. Most of them had been dragged from their civilian life in the dead of night, bundled hastily, without food, into those cars for the nightmare ride across the state. These were no enemy which faced them but fellow Pennsylvanians, with a just grievance, stoning and cursing them as they did their duty. They behaved like veterans. The crowd continued to press forward, and the troops fixed their bayonets. A teen-aged boy yelled, "They dasn't shoot." Bricks and coal began to rain on the soldiers. "Shoot," taunted a rioter. A man on a coal car let off a pistol. The rioters began to grapple with the soldiers, trying to grab their rifles.

Cassatt testified later, "I was about one hundred and fifty yards, or perhaps a little less than that away, and I don't suppose the troops could have heard a command, if given, there was so much shouting and yelling. The crowd was very large, and they all seemed to be shouting and hallooing. There was quite a shower of stones before the firing commenced, and when it did commence it was scattering, but then became quite general. It lasted a minute or two minutes, and I could see the officers trying to stop the firing after it commenced."

In frustration, the goaded troops fired impartially from their hollow square. Then they fired over the heads of the mob into the hillside of watchers, who up to that moment had been spectators at what one of them called "the fun." When the firing stopped, twenty were dead and scores wounded, including some small children. The coroner later held inquests on twenty-two bodies. Only one or two were railroad employees, but all were working men. Fifteen of the Philadelphia troops were injured, but none died. Several of the soldiers had fallen from sunstroke. The crowd panicked and ran. Brinton called a cease fire.

Pearson, watching from a window in the telegraph office on the corner of 26th Street and Liberty, agonized over his next move. He asked Cassatt, who had joined him, what to do. Should the troops hold the 28th Street crossing at whatever cost? The tracks were now temporarily open. Would Cassatt send out his double-headers? At his chief's side, Pitcairn, a Union Army veteran of the Wilderness, Cold Harbor, and Petersburg, was appalled at what had happened. Before Cassatt could reply, Pitcairn said for him, "I don't think you have any opinion." Cassatt taking the clue, answered, "I have nothing to do with the movement of the troops. I know nothing about that whatever." Pearson and Brinton ordered the Philadelphians into the roundhouse at the corner of 26th Street and Liberty. Darkness was settling over the hot, seething city while smoke from the gunfire rose lazily toward the littered hillside. The trains remained silent.

"The Most Trying
Experience of
His Life"

What were Cassatt's thoughts as he waited in that beseiged roundhouse? Although he denied all responsibility for the action of the City Troop in firing on the mob, he could not easily forget that he had made no move to stay those shots. His chief concern had not been for men's lives but for inanimate machines, those black monsters waiting on the sidelines, their holds crammed with profitable goods, profits for the Pennsylvania Railroad. In this the "most trying experience of his life," as his wife remembered it, he had not showed to advantage. As the only top officer of the Pennsylvania on the scene, he had abdicated control to weak city officials and an army commander who had not been able to control his men. As a result men were dead, and still Cassatt had not moved his trains.

With Pearson, Brinton, and Cassatt temporarily immobilized, the city smouldered and erupted, frenzied by the slaughter at 28th Street. During the long hours of darkness, while Cassatt and the soldiers waited uneasily in the round house, the aroused crowd went mad. The rioters broke into the freight cars and looted whiskey which further inflamed their passions. They vandalized shops, stole food and guns, lit fires in private homes, terrorizing the more substantial citizens who had hoped to remain aloof. Pearson could not bear the sight. He walked unmolested from the depot to join Brinton and Latta at the Monongahela Hotel. Cassatt and Pitcairn were persuaded to leave the roundhouse, the soldiers fearing their presence would endanger the building and the troops' safety. Some of the crowd had shouted they meant to hang Cassatt from a lamppost.

At one o'clock Sunday morning, Cassatt left the roundhouse, somehow making his way through the rioters to the hotel. Behind him a group of men and boys pushed a burning freight car into the side of the roundhouse. Sporadic fires flared all around the depot. All through the night the fires spread. By dawn the roundhouse sheltering the troops was ablaze, the soldiers shooting from the inferno. At 8 A.M. Brinton ordered his men out of the roundhouse. They retired in perfect order, marching down to Union Station and out toward the Arsenal, across the Allegheny River north of the city to Sharpsburg. By now the fires had spread to the Union Depot and surrounding yards, unchecked by police or firemen. Throughout that awful Saturday night and into Sunday morning, the looting and destruction raged unchecked.

Early on Sunday morning, Cassatt went up to the hillside above 28th Street and watched "the total destruction of the Pennsylvania property in and about the Union Station and the yards." In ruins across the charred and twisted tracks, lay sixty-six passenger cars, 1,367 freight cars, the Union Station and Hotel, car shops, roundhouses, and a large grain elevator. The company estimated the damages at $5,000,000.

Cassatt's mood was bitter. He had not saved the property despite all his exertions; twenty-two people were dead. In no way could he justify his presence in Pittsburgh. For years the Pennsylvania Railroad had treated the residents of Pittsburgh with contempt and indifference. Now the seeds of the railroad's cavalier attitude had borne fruit in a bloody riot whose harvest would never be forgotten. The Pittsburgh Strike of 1877 was the most savage in American industrial history. The Homestead, the Pullman, and the UAW battle at the Ford underpass in Detroit would produce an equal resentment, but never again would so many innocent victims die from army bullets as laboring men fought their managers. The violence in Pittsburgh determined the trainmen to organize for their common rights. They became the first and most powerful of all trade unions, and ultimately, their demands, instigated in the beginning by the railroad's careless and cruel policy in Pittsburgh that torrid summer, would help bring the Pennsylvania to its knees.

Cassatt, in despair, decided he still had a duty to perform to the troops. He crossed the river to Allegheny City that weary Sunday morning to find supplies for the hungry Philadelphia soldiers, who had not eaten since that sketchy breakfast Saturday afternoon at the Union Depot. After a conference with Thaw and other concerned citizens, Cassatt gathered food and wagons and shipped the rations to the troops at Sharpsburg by early Sunday afternoon. The state committee investigating the riots commended his work: "These rations reached the troops through the personal exertions of A. J. Cassatt, who, from the time of the occupation of the roundhouse by the troops, had been unwearied in his endeavors to get provisions for them."

On a gray Monday, as Cassatt prepared to leave for home, fifty United

States regulars arrived from Columbus, Ohio, ordered on duty by President Hayes at the urging of Colonel Scott. Tuesday morning's Pittsburgh newspapers reported that the Trainmen's Union had tried to contact Scott, who would not or could not be reached. On Wednesday, July 25, the freight trains began to move out of Pittsburgh through the still smouldering ruins. Riding with each double-header were soldiers with Gatling guns on flat cars.

In Philadelphia Scott remained at his headquarters throughout the crisis, but he made no attempt to contact Cassatt at the scene, or to follow him to Pittsburgh. Aside from several wires to President Hayes for troops "to protect the nation's transportation line," as he put it, Scott did little. Certainly, he made no concessions to the strikers. Frank Thomson, hurriedly recalled from Long Branch, holed up for two days in the West Philadelphia Station, afraid to face the workers outside who held him accountable for the wage reduction.

Conditions in Philadelphia simmered but never erupted due to the vigilant action of Mayor William S. Stokley, a strong character and a member of the Pennsylvania's board of directors. Stokley, who also rushed back from a Long Branch vacation, had his police well in hand, a loyal force willing to subdue the crowd which threatened to derail an oil train coming into the depot. The mayor wired Washington for auxiliary troops when rioters set fire to a freight train near the Callowhill Street Bridge on Sunday. Stokley arranged 400 police in a hollow square to protect the firemen fighting the blaze. That afternoon General Winfield S. Hancock arrived from fermenting Baltimore and toured the city with Colonel Scott in his carriage. The mayor convened a Committee of Safety and by Tuesday afternoon, when Cassatt arrived at his office, 700 United States regulars and 125 marines were helping the 1,400 police and 2,000 specials to keep the peace. Hancock then sent several companies to other trouble spots, Reading, Scranton, and Johnstown. Angry mobs were threatening as far as Buffalo, Cincinnati, and Chicago.

Up in the country, at Haverford, Lois Cassatt, who had just nursed her children through a bout of typhoid fever, haunted the local station and its telegraph operator for news of her husband. On Monday morning Cassatt left Pittsburgh in a special car which had been ordered to bring him home. The car in which he had traveled to Pittsburgh on Thursday night had been burned in the fire. He wired Lois that he would reach the Haverford station at 9:15 that evening. "This threw us all into a state of agitation," she remembered, "as our friends had collected at our house, fearing that at any moment we might hear of some terrible thing happening . . . and to have him telegraph openly naming a fixed hour at which he would appear in Haverford Station, seemed to us to be almost inviting trouble. He arrived safely and seemed quite surprised that we were all anxious."

Cassatt may have made light of his experiences to his worried wife, but he was exhausted and covered from head to foot with prickly heat from his exposure to the sun during the past few days. Most galling of all, he had to admit that his journey had been fruitless. In after years he never referred to the Strike of 1877. His reactions were too mixed, his ordeal too harrowing. He had been home barely two days when the still brooding trainmen, granted none of their demands and unable to arrange a meeting with Scott, ignited Johnstown. Aleck was again asked to go to the scene of the trouble. Lois was bitter: "He never showed the slightest fear and the company owes him a deep debt of gratitude for his management of the situation and more than all, do the brother officers who thought it best to remain at home. And they let him go back and go back again, and do what they might at least have shared with him."

On his return from this second trip Cassatt's train stopped at Altoona. His fellow travelers suggested it might be prudent if he remained aboard as the crowd of unemployed workers milling about the depot seemed hostile. Cassatt did not heed their advice. He left the car at Altoona and walked into the station restaurant. He ate his lunch and left without incident. In Lois' words: "not a soul raised their voices or gave him one look. It showed the extent of his courage and his confidence that no harm would come to him at the hands of the people amongst whom he had lived for several years."

Cassatt was not unmindful of the trainmen's grievances. Soon after the announcement of the wage cut, he had visited the Altoona shops with General Manager Frank Thomson. He had "remonstrated" with Thomson about the wage reduction at that time, saying, "Why the men cannot buy butter for their bread." "What do they want with butter?" replied Thomson. "Let them make dip." A bitter worker, overhearing this conversation, remarked that they would make dip and fight on "dip." (By "dip" both Thomson and the worker were referring to drippings from cooked meat.) Another disgruntled trainman said, "Mr. Frank Thomson drives his tandem team and draws his big salary, whilst we must do double work at half pay." No wonder Thomson had to hide in his Philadelphia office during those turbulent July days. Cassatt would never have made such a remark, and the Altoona workers knew it.

His attitude, nonetheless, is not easily excused or explained. He made no attempt to justify lowering wages to the investigating committee. The strikers' other demands he found unwarranted: "We looked upon this objection of the men to the running of double-headers as an interference with our business. . . . We might as well give up the management into their hands." Cassatt's implacable drive to protect property at the expense of men's lives shocks today's observer. Cassatt was not insensitive. His acts of private philanthropy prove that he had understanding and sympathy for those less fortunate. Typical of his age, he responded to the social and economic inequities which engaged his attention with paternalism. But in this crisis, he allowed his respect for property and his duty to the stockholders to overcome his humanitarianism. Honestly appalled at the deaths and destruction which resulted from the strike, he never actually faced his own responsibility in calling in the City Troop. His personal courage cannot be doubted, but his actions, especially his acceptance of Pitcairn's rebuke before Pearson, reveal that he allowed his concern for the railroad's machines and freight to overcome his sense of justice and decency. In the frenzy of the moment, he acted with stubborn arrogance rather than with the cool judgment and compassion which governed most of his life, both personal and professional. He never answered his critics. Whatever his guilt or justification, he bore the brand in silence.

Scott, on the other hand, had no doubts about the wisdom or humanity of his own actions. At jeopardy was his financial empire, his Texas & Pacific, his petroleum war with Rockefeller. He testified to the committee that ninety percent of his employees were loyal, stirred to rebellion by a lawless ten percent. James P. Barr, editor of *The Pittsburgh Post,* pointed out that the general populace of the city shared the strikers' hatred of the railroad, which imposed heavy, discriminatory rates on local traffic and kept competing lines out of Pittsburgh. Barr himself had wired to Scott to come to the scene and "make some proposition to convince our people your company has rights and grievances." Scott refused. He replied that the strike had begun without any employee complaint. Scott had conveniently forgotten the delegation from the Trainmen's Union—or he lied.

As a result of the Strike of 1877, Scott lost all chance of raising capital for his Texas & Pacific. He was forced to cancel the Pennsylvania's October and November dividends to stockholders, for the first time in the line's history. Worse, President Hayes, who owed his election in part to Scott's efforts on his behalf, began to consider government regulation of the railroads. Scott's reasoning, that since railroads were public transport they must be protected, was a two-edged sword. Hayes natural conclusion was that if the railroads demanded government protection, they also had to accept some government regulation. Another prophetic result of the strike, was its effect on the workers. Their demands had not been met but the brotherhoods of trainmen, hitherto little more than fraternal organizations, realized that they must widen their scope and form effective trade unions to bargain from a base of power with the employer.

The Pennsylvania State Investigating Committee, created by the legislature in early 1878 to inquire into the reasons for the strike, came to few conclusions. The members were still intimidated by Scott who made a brief appearance before them as did Cassatt, Pearson, Thaw, Park, and many workers, minor officials, and militiamen. After 1,000 pages of interviews, the committee decided that the Pennsylvania Railroad was not the real culprit: "True the capitalist himself has not been blameless. He should meet the workers half-way. The Pennsylvania was responsible only in so far as the order to send out the double-headers and the reduction of wages had brought on the violence." Once the rioting began, it had to be suppressed. The committee severely criticized Mayor McCarthy, of Pittsburgh, for his failure to go to the scene and enforce order. Sheriff Fife also should have used the full force of his civil authority to put down the strike. Finally, "when a great line of public travel and traffic like the Pennsylvania Railroad is blockaded by a mob, the public interests suffer more than the railroads, and every day it is allowed to continue damages the community to thousands of dollars." The troops were not accused of inciting the rioters, but commended for their steadfastness under provocation. Indeed, the First City Troop had conducted itself well.

Scott received no admonishment from the committee. Since many of them were officials both impressed with the railroad's almighty influence and recipients of the railroad's largesse, this is not surprising. But Scott's power was broken. Not only were millions of dollars of railroad property destroyed during those hot July days in Pittsburgh, but so also were Scott's authority and ability to manipulate the state and federal governments, and the nations's bankers and money men.

Writing after Cassatt's death, Gustavus Myers, in his tirade against robber barons, accused Cassatt of the utmost depravity and ruthlessness. He insisted that Cassatt had ordered loyal employees to fire the engines and commit arson to justify his brutal treatment of the strikers. To compound the crime, Myers believed that Cassatt, with the cooperation of corrupt political bosses, had pushed through the state legislature a Riot Endemnity Bill which gave the Pennsylvania Railroad $4,000,000, in compensation for property destroyed during the strike. Some legislators rebelled, and an investigation did reveal bribes, although there was no evidence that Cassatt had exerted his influence. It was Scott not Cassatt who controlled the Pennsylvania legislature. Myers pilloried Cassatt to no avail. The railroad did not receive $4,000,000 recompense for the destroyed property, but $1,600,000, much less than half the amount lost in the strike.

The roundhouses and shops at Pittsburgh were rebuilt. The strikers did not have their wages increased. The double-headers continued to run. Scott advised his stockholders at the annual meeting: "It is hoped that the present depression will soon end, and that with improved results a higher rate of compensation can be paid to employees." For the trainmen it continued to be "dip" not butter, but as the fortunes of the railroad rose, so eventually did those of its workers.

Scott did not tell the stockholders that he had not needed to cut wages at all—freight business was rising. Cassatt informed the investigating committee ruefully: "That very day (of the outbreak) I had a message from the Vice President of the western lines, stating that there was a brisk demand for cars. If only they had waited a couple of weeks, they could all have had enough to do." But they had not waited, nor had Scott. He failed to mention this in his annual report, just as he omitted any mention of the role of his lieutenant in rushing courageously to the scene of the strike.

Cassatt's own testimony to the committee had been laconic in the extreme. He did not attempt to justify or excuse his actions. From the strike he had learned several valuable lessons—about himself, about the management of the railroad, and about the men who worked for the line. He never made such mistakes again. For the first time he doubted his future. And not the least result was that he was forced to reassess Scott. In the months ahead his chief would suffer the most agonizing defeat in a lifetime marked with unusual success. In his battle with Rockefeller, Colonel Scott would not find Cassatt again ranged enthusiastically and uncritically at his side.

Rockefeller
Wins a Round

Cleveland in mid-August 1877 was hot. The slight breeze off Lake Erie failed to penetrate the austere offices of the Standard Oil Company in the Sexton Building on Euclid Avenue, the city's chief thoroughfare. Here John D. Rockefeller and his associate Henry M. Flagler had consented to meet with the Pennsylvania Railroad's emissary to work out peace terms on the oil refinery war which had significantly reduced the railroad's revenues. That emissary should have been Thomas A. Scott, but the Pennsylvania's president, in failing health and wearied by his struggles with Rockefeller and the striking trainmen, could not face the meeting. Instead he sent Alexander Cassatt.

Present at that first meeting were Rockefeller, Flagler, and William Warden, a Philadelphia banker with large interests in the Standard Oil Company. But there was no doubt in Cassatt's mind that Rockefeller was the controlling figure. Rockefeller had a quiet friendly manner which belied his reputation as a fierce competitor who allowed no quarter to his adversaries. Cassatt was not deceived by that mild appearance. He agreed thoroughly with William Vanderbilt's assessment of the Standard Oil organizer and his associates: "These men are smarter than I am by a great deal. They are very enterprising . . . I never came into contact with any class of men so smart and able as they are in business." In the yards beyond Rockefeller's Euclid Street office in Cleveland, the Standard was refining 10,000 barrels of oil a day, outstripping all rivals. And sixty-five percent of that oil was shipped over the Pennsylvania lines. In return, Cassatt later testified, the railroad paid its biggest shipper, more than $10,000,000 in rebates during an eighteen-month period. Naturally, Scott loathed parting with that kind of money. The obvious solution was to thrust his railroad into the oil refinery business. Cassatt was in Cleveland to do Scott's bidding.

Cassatt later reviewed for a congressional committee how his railroad came to be involved in this struggle with Rockefeller: "The Empire Transportation Company had a contract with us by which they provided the cars, the soliciting agents, and did all the business connected with the transportation of oil, except the mere hauling of the cars, from every district except Pittsburgh . . . there they did not go; there we carried our own cars as a local business." Certainly, one of Pittsburgh's reasons for supporting the strikers had been this monopolistic practice of the Pennsylvania Railroad in relation to the trade of that city. Pittsburgh merchants and laborers alike believed, with every justification, that the Pennsylvania kept other roads from entering the city on a competitive basis.

Cassatt explained the role of the Pennsylvania's subsidiary, the Empire: "For the work they did in soliciting, collecting freights, and managing the business generally we paid them a percentage of our net receipts from the business after paying the rebates, etc." So there would be no misunderstanding, he added, "Those rates were made by the Pennsylvania Railroad Company always." He made it quite clear that the Empire was a creature of the Pennsylvania, although it had not been put in quite that way to the stockholders in the annual report. The New York Central's fast freight lines prevented the Pennsylvania line from acquiring "that class of business, without interfering with the ordinary tonnage of the road."

Cassatt did not tell the committee, if indeed he knew, of Scott's special arrangements with Joseph R. Potts, president of the Empire. Potts, like Scott a former colonel in the Union Army, had organized the Empire Transportation Company after Appomatox. An astute manager, shrewd and reserved, the stocky Potts had expanded his fast freight oil feeder for the Pennsylvania Railroad into a lucrative company paying ten percent dividends yearly on an annual gross of $11,000,000. At the beginning of 1877, when the battle with Rockefeller began, Cassatt described the assets of the Empire: "They had a thousand in round numbers, tank cars—iron tank cars —for carrying crude oil, and they had 400 cars known as rack cars for carrying refined oil; that was the extent of their car equipment. The Empire Transportation Company also owned or controlled the Union Pipe Line Company which had pipe lines from the region reaching nearly every source of supply and carrying oil to the railroad connections in the region; those were the facilities."

The Empire, in the twelve years since its organization, had become the single most effective fast freight feeder of oil into the eastern markets. Naturally, the other three trunk lines, the Central, Erie, and B & O, were alarmed at the Pennsylvania's subsidiary. They would not support the road in its struggle with Rockefeller.

In January, 1877, Potts and Scott sealed their agreement in Philadelphia. They had decided to go into the refinery business, ostensibly at the request of the independent producers of oil in western Pennsylvania, who were being squeezed to death by Rockefeller. The Empire immediately began building refineries in New York and Philadelphia. Cassatt believed that the capacity of the Philadelphia refinery was 6,000 barrels of crude oil a day. As he put it later to the committee, "This was entirely new to Philadelphia." But it set a pattern which continues today.

In 1874 Potts had been chiefly responsible for pushing through an agreement between the trunk lines on freight rebates, a pooling agreement which guaranteed each of the lines a certain percentage of the shippers' output. In return for this guaranteed carriage, the railroads rebated twenty-two and one-half cents on each barrel shipped to Standard. Potts felt, as the largest transporter, that he was in a prime position to act as regulator of national railroad traffic, and he had been urged by the independent oil producers to assume such a role. He believed Rockefeller's growing monopoly threatened the rail business itself: "There were three great divisions in the petroleum business—the production, the carriage of it, and the preparation for market. If any one party controlled absolutely any one of these divisions, they practically would have a very fair show of controlling the others." The Pennsylvania Railroad's official historians, Burgess and Kennedy, in most cases apologists for the line, regarded the Potts-Scott merger with only qualified enthusiasm: "Foolishly or not, it decided that one way to protect its transportation business was to have refineries of its own, so that in the event of practical monopolization of the remaining business by Standard, it would still have an outlet for oil."

Potts really feared that Rockefeller's control of oil would allow him to ship over whatever line he pleased, the Erie, the Central, the Pennsylvania, or entirely through the pipe lines he was building to the seaboard. Such a situation could only intensify the already ruinous rate wars among the trunk lines. If Potts did not trust Rockefeller, the oil baron returned the compliment. He considered the Empire president, "a shrewd, oily man, as smooth as oil." He knew that the presidents of the other trunk lines would never allow Potts to become an arbiter of their business.

Scott's motives for entering into the refinery contract with Potts owed little to the independent producers' pleas for help, to distrust of the Standard, or to any thought of becoming a spokesman for his industry. He hoped to fight Rockefeller at least to a draw, neutralize the other's monopoly, and then secure a major share of the oil profits after the war had ended. He underestimated the Standard. Potts' motives were more respectable, but experience should have warned him to trust his ally as little as he trusted Rockefeller. He considered Scott completely unprincipaled. Soon after the outbreak of the Civil War, Potts had seen Scott and congratulated him on his appointment as Assistant Secretary of War. "Yes," Scott reputedly replied to Potts, "this place is worth $100,000 a year to me." The oil refinery profits could provide an even more attractive windfall.

Scott believed that the Empire would quickly develop a considerable refinery business before Rockefeller knew what had happened. And Rockefeller had a reputation for negotiating which could further delay matters. But neither Potts nor Scott had reckoned on Flagler, Rockefeller's associate, who had his ear close to the track, railroads being his special province within the Standard Oil Company. Henry M. Flagler, whose fame today rests chiefly on his development of Florida as the nation's playground, had rented office space from Rockefeller soon after the Civil War. The son of a western New York Presbyterian minister, he had worked in several Ohio towns, chiefly as a grain seller, and had won and lost a fortune. A distinguished looking man in his late thirties with dark hair and mustache, and a sharp eye for the main chance, Flagler also possessed a bold imaginative mind which Rockefeller admired. The oil baron appreciated Flagler's qualities, so different from his own rather thoughtful, cautious manner, and he asked him to become his partner in 1867. Thus began a relationship between Rockefeller and Flagler which was unique. The former never felt quite as much regard for any other business associate. Potts had rather unwisely revealed his grandiose plans in a phamphlet published during the Centennial Exhibition of 1876 in Philadelphia. Undoubtedly, Rockefeller and Flagler read of Potts' designs and made their own plans to thwart his attack on their company.

Since Cassatt was in charge of all the freight that was carried over the Pennsylvania, these intricate machinations of Scott, Potts, Rockefeller, and Flagler were of paramount concern to him, although there is no evidence that he was a party to the decision of his railroad to enter the refinery competition. Soon after Scott had signed the contract with Potts, the latter was surprised by an approach from Rockefeller. Cassatt was present at that meeting. Rockefeller told the railroad executives that unless the Pennsylvania abandoned its plans to challenge the Standard in the refinery business, he would cancel his agreement to ship sixty-five percent of his oil over the Pennsylvania lines. Faced with this ultimatum and despite Cassatt's urging to give up the idea, Scott refused to abandon his plans. Even the protests of fellow railroad presidents, Hugh J. Jewett of the Erie and William Vanderbilt of the Central, failed to move him.

Rockefeller's biographer, Allan Nevins, insists that Cassatt was not so confident: "For a time Cassatt wavered. He even talked to Potts about leasing the Empire refineries to the Standard or selling them to third parties. But Potts indignantly refused . . . He exhorted both Cassatt and Scott to stand by him." Nevins concludes succinctly, "There is no evidence that Scott ever wavered." Scott believed in the power of the Pennsylvania, which had rarely been frustrated, in his appraisal of the Standard as a loosely knit corporation which had yet to endure a real fight, and ignored the pleas of

Jewett and Vanderbilt who were constantly at each other's throats with little energy for outside fights. The battle between the Pennsylvania and the Standard was joined, with Cassatt a loyal if reluctant commander in the field.

Almost ten years later Cassatt could easily remember the details of the war: "About March or April of 1877, it [Standard] ceased to ship any oil by the Pennsylvania Railroad Company's lines." He explained to the committee investigating the oil trust why the Standard took this move and unwittingly revealed much of his own distaste for the battle: "The Standard Company complained to the officers of the Pennsylvania Railroad Company that they did not get fair treatment from the Empire Transportation Company in the matter of distribution of cars when cars were scarce; that they did not believe they got as good rates . . . and that the Empire favored their own refineries against The Standard; they would not transport their oil by an organization which was also a rival of The Standard in the refinery business. *We endeavored to try to get those difficulties harmonized.*" The endeavoring was mostly on his part. Scott and Potts showed no interest in compromise in the beginning. Cassatt continued to suggest remedies: "We talked of getting the Empire to lease its refineries to the Standard or put them into other hands but we did not succeed in doing that . . . it resulted in a complete breach."

Although the independent producers had pleaded with Potts to enter the refinery business, they did nothing to support him once he began his fight with Standard. Cassatt and the Pennsylvania were caught in the middle: ". . . All the other refineries not connected with Standard Oil, we induced to come on our line and ship, but we did it at a very great loss to the company. We paid very large rebates; in fact, we took anything we could get for transporting their oil, in some cases we paid out more than the whole freight. I recollect one instance where we carried oil to New York . . . at 8 cents less than nothing." His distaste for the struggle is evident. The experience hardened his opposition to the whole rebate system.

Six months after signing his contract with Potts, in June, 1877, Scott, eager for more capital to continue his contest with Standard, cut wages on his railroad. The Pittsburgh strike resulted, and the Pennsylvania, already over-taxed, could not continue to challenge Rockefeller. So Cassatt, not Scott, went to Cleveland, as he had gone to Pittsburgh in a time of crisis, hating every minute of the negotiations he was forced to undertake, to reverse a policy he had never endorsed.

Cassatt went twice to Cleveland to work out the terms of the Pennsylvania's surrender. Scott had been forced to abandon his Empire Transportation Company and to let the independent oil producers shift for themselves in a struggle with Rockefeller. The conversations between the Standard and Cassatt were not acrimonious. That was neither Rockefeller's style, nor Cassatt's. But the iron entered Cassatt's soul at those meetings. He worked out the terms by which the Standard would again allow his railroad a lucrative share of the oil traffic, but he never forgot the humiliation he suffered as Scott's emissary.

During mid-August Lois Cassatt visited her friends, the Gardners, in Altoona. There she learned first hand about the bitterness of the railroad employees, pawns in Scott's game with Rockefeller. Her young son, Edward, at home in Haverford, only eight years old and caring more about his pony than railroad affairs, was influenced enough by his father's troubles to write to his mother on August 15, "My dear Mama, the children are all well. Papa took them out riding in the gig and I rode on Louy and Wasp. How is Mrs. Gardner and all the children? Mama is the strike all over?"

"Papa" at least had some relief from his worries in riding with his children, enjoying their company, a relaxation he always found soothing. On Lois' return from Altoona, the whole family left for the Howland Hotel in Long Branch, then as famous for its race track and gambling halls as for its sea bathing.

While Aleck and his family vacationed at Long Branch, Scott was digesting the bitter surrender terms Rockefeller demanded. He had no choice but to accede, although Potts brought heavy pressure against him to stand firm. By September the battle was all but over. Rockefeller and Flagler came to Philadelphia and met with Scott and Cassatt in the St. George Hotel. In answer to a congressman's question later about the subject of that meeting, Cassatt recalled, ". . . to see whether we could not make some contract or agreement with the Standard Oil Company by which this contest would cease, which was costing our company a great deal of money and loss of revenue, and the object to be obtained was that of making some arrangement with them, which was done."

He continued: "We made up our minds that it was a mistake for the Empire Transportation Company, as a transporter, to be in the refinery business. The New York Central, and the Erie Railroads, and the Baltimore and Ohio Railroad, looked upon it with jealousy and the Standard Oil Company also, and we endeavored to get the Empire Line to dispose of its refining interest, which they declined to do." Cassatt expressed the company line. Potts was still determined to fight, although his ally had deserted him. But Scott was adamant. The refineries would have to go. The failure to pay the August dividend had shaken him as well as his stockholders. As Cassatt remembered it, Potts finally agreed that rather than get out of the refinery business he would prefer that the Pennsylvania buy him out, "and close our contract with you."

Potts had little recourse. If the Pennsylvania abandoned him, he would be forced to bow to the demands of Standard since the independent producers, once so eager for him to take on the Rockefeller giant, now seemed unwilling or unable to support him. When Cassatt presented Scott with Rockefeller's terms, which were simply "between us we shall buy it (the

Empire) out," Scott, too, had little choice. At the meeting in the St. George Hotel in Philadelphia that September, Rockefeller and Flagler proposed to Scott and Cassatt that the Standard take Potts' refineries and that the Pennsylvania buy the cars and pipe lines. Scott and Cassatt, determined to surrender on the best terms possible, objected. If they were not allowed by Standard to be in the refinery business why did they need pipe lines? Rockefeller then agreed to take the refineries, pipe lines, oil terminals, some tank cars, harbor tugboats, and barges, leaving the Pennsylvania the rolling stock.

Rockefeller himself has described the scene at the St. George Hotel. All the officials of the Standard and the Pennsylvania had gathered in the room for the signing of the agreements. Scott was late. When he arrived he showed none of his discomfort. Rockefeller wrote, "I can see him now, with his big soft hat, marching into the room in that little hotel to meet us; not to sweep us away as he had always done, but coming in with a smile, walking right up to the cannon's mouth." Scott then sat down and signed the contract with a flourish. On September 17, the Pennsylvania directors formally approved the purchase. The cost to the Standard was $3,400,00, to the Pennsylvania, $3,000,000.

Scott explained the sale to his directors as gliby as he had explained the original subsidizing of the Empire. The Pennsylvania, he stated, had established the Empire because it felt that it was not receiving its share of the oil freight, that the Central, Erie, and B & O had more than a fair share. This is hardly borne out by Cassatt's later testimony that sixty-five percent of Standard's oil was shipped over the Pennsylvania. Scott reported to his directors: "The net results of the operation of the Empire Company's lines have been very favorable so far as the transportation of oil is concerned, and reasonably profitable in the transportation of merchandise." Not a word was said about Joseph Potts and the contract signed between them. Potts met his stockholders on October 17 and announced the sale from which he personally profited well. He told his stockholders that he would have continued to hold out, "but for Tom Scott's desertion." That evening Scott, Cassatt, Flagler, and Rockefeller met in Potts' office on Girard Street in Philadelphia and signed the final papers incorporating the agreements made in September. Potts himself shook hands with all the executives calmly, bowed them out of the office, and then returned to his desk, buried his head in his hands, and sobbed. Potts was later to revise his attitude toward the Standard and join Rockefeller in a pipe line project, but he never forgave Tom Scott.

Cassatt was embittered, as much as a man of his equable temperment could be, by the experience with Standard. Later, he testified to the congressional committee investigating the oil monopoly about Standard's actions: "they [the Standard] manipulated the market. They did it to our detriment all they could; no doubt about that; they endeavored to injure us and our shippers *all they could* during the fight." Even more galling to Cassatt was the arrangement concluded with Rockefeller at that same October 17 contract signing for considerable rebates to Standard on all the oil shipped by the Pennsylvania. Most sordid of all, was the Pennsylvania's promise to allow to the Standard rebates on the oil shipped by the independent refineries, the Standard's competitors. Since no independent producer, or combination of producers, could guarantee the Pennsylvania the percentage of oil freight of the Standard, Rockefeller insisted that if the trunk line wanted his business, Scott and Cassatt must assure him that he would get the rebates on his competitors' carriage. Of course, this arrangement would drive the independent producers out of business. They protested to the Pennsylvania, and Cassatt later reported that Scott's reply to them was "that unless they would guarantee us the same quantity of oil that the Standard had agreed to ship, we could not make them the same rates." Cassatt explained, "They said they would never agree to any arrangement by which they did not get the same rates as the Standard, and from that time forward they commenced to arrange in some way to get some other route to the seabord."

For the Standard Oil Company and John D. Rockefeller the triumph over the Pennsylvania was complete. Two big organizations, the Empire and the Pennsylvania Railroad, had been neutralized as competitors. By acquiring the Empire's pipe lines, the Standard now controlled the means by which the oil would go to the railroads. Also signed at that October 17 meeting, was a new trunk line agreement, providing quotas for the roads. The division would allow forty-seven percent of all shipments to the Pennsylvania, twenty-one percent each to the Erie and the Central, and eleven percent to the B & O, which had tried to service the independent producers and earned the Standard's wrath. This contract guaranteed the Pennsylvania not less than 2,000,000 barrels of oil a year. For this guarantee the Standard would receive a commission of ten percent on all its own shipments and also on "whatever other freights it might produce," successfully barring the few independent producers left from posing a future threat to the Rockefeller interests. Rockefeller wrote to Scott: "we feel the location of our refineries, all of which can be reached by your lines should naturally create a close alliance between your company and ours." It was an unholy alliance which would greatly strengthen both corporations to the public detriment.

All of this business was conducted with Cassatt's cooperation and consent, if not with his approval. Basically, he was opposed to secret rebates and did not hesitate to say that the Pennsylvania had had the action forced upon it through lack of any other method of securing equal and open rates.

Loyalty—to his family, his friends, his company—was always one of Cassatt's dominant characteristics. He knew that both the Standard and the Pennsylvania had acted less than honorably and had engaged in nefarious business practices in pursuit of profit and power. He protested in private, but publicly he supported Scott, lending credence to those critics who accused him of robber baron tactics. Again, as in the strike, he made no attempt to defend himself. To a man of Cassatt's reserve, such an indignity was abhorrent. Unlike his chief, Cassatt had a standard of personal ethics which governed his conduct in the business arena. He refused to explain or justify his decisions, whether through shyness or arrogance is difficult to discover. But the day would come when Cassatt would show how deeply the Rockefeller negotiations had affected him.

Years later, when Congress investigated the Standard, Cassatt came forward to urge action: "If all the roads in the United States were compelled by law to publish their tariff, and if it were made a misdemeanor upon the part of any officer, punishable by law, to make such secret concessions from them, and such a law could be enforced, there would be little difficulty in maintaining rates." In other words, since the railroads were unable to regulate themselves and compete in an open market, it was up to the government, the newly formed Interstate Commerce Commission, to enforce fair practices.

As 1877 ended, the Pennsylvania's revenues were rising, the directors pacified, but the other three trunk lines were riled at the terms their rival had obtained, secretly, from Rockefeller. Scott still felt vigorous enough to repell some of his liberal board members when they suggested it might be well to outlaw free passes and abolish all secret rebates. The motions, made at every annual meeting for some years, were tabled. Ahead lay further conflicts for Scott, battles with his rival roads over those secret rebates. His health failing, his spirit quenched, he felt unequal to the contests. Again he sent his deputy, Cassatt, to negotiate terms at Saratoga Springs in mid-July of 1878.

At the "Hall of Springs," thirty-five miles north of Albany, at the gateway to New York's Adirondack Mountains, the nation's social elite had been gathering since before the Civil War to take the waters. A regimen of twenty-one baths offered at the recuperative springs was advertised to ease sufferers of jaundice, dyspepsia, gout, dropsy, "depraved appetite or bilious affections generally." Although the therapeutic waters attracted the first visitors, Saratoga's race track and gambling casinos had an equal following. Unlike its newer and more staid sister resorts, Saratoga, welcomed all comers: Presidents Chester A. Arthur and Ulysses S. Grant rubbed shoulders at the long mahogony bar of the Grand Union and United States Hotel with such disparate types as "Bet a Million" Gates, John Jacob Astor, "Diamond" Jim Brady, actor Otis Skinner, and composer Victor Herbert. August was the most popular month at Saratoga when the yearling sales brought Vanderbilts, Whitneys, Paynes, and the Southern stable owners to inspect and buy the thoroughbreds. Both Derby winners Man o War and Foolish Pleasure were sold at the Saratoga ring.

In the 70s and 80s Saratoga pleasure seekers came on the railroad which unloaded its passengers right on the main street, Broadway. In July of 1878 the railroad also brought Cassatt, who would have little time to visit the races or inspect the horses he might buy for his growing stables. He registered at the United States Hotel, that impressive hostelry, long since demolished, with its towering three floor facade, ornamented grill work, and wide pillared veranda flanked by spreading elms. Not for Cassatt was the leisurely round of race meetings, drinking the waters, and taking the air on the hotel promenade. Behind a barred door in the hotel, he met with the representatives of the Erie, the Central, and the B & O to talk about oil freight.

The executives finally agreed to reduce rates on refined oil shipped by their roads to eighty cents a barrel, forced by the Standard into further reducing their profits. Independent producers would have to pay $1.44½ a barrel. When asked later by the Congressional Committee why the Pennsylvania and the other lines had agreed to this reduction at Saratoga, Cassatt replied carefully, "I do not know what moved them to do it, unless the trade required that it be done. That is to say, the trade would not bear a higher rate." Such pooling agreements were not unknown. Four years earlier the railroad executives had met at Saratoga to initiate a similar freight rate, but secret rebates had nullified this arrangement. Cassatt had been forced into this new contract by the other roads who had discovered that they were making higher rebates to the Standard than was the Pennsylvania. They were determined to equalize the situation, and they had the power to compel the Pennsylvania to accept their demands. If the New York and Erie had refused to pay the higher rebates, if the B & O had kept its character as a competing route, if the Pennsylvania had not discriminated against the independent oil producers, if the politicians had not been intimidated and corrupted by the Standard's power, then Rockefeller's monopoly could have been broken. A contemporary railroad historian, James F. Hudson, writing about railroad power in 1906, believed that the trunk lines, and particularly the Pennsylvania, had practiced "the greatest commercial crime of the last decade," by knuckling under to Rockefeller.

Cassatt never recovered from the Standard experience and the perfidious role the Pennsylvania had played. The canker rankled so deeply that he discussed it with his wife following the visit to Saratoga. Lois in turn, confided in her mother, who discussed Cassatt's concern in a letter to her daughter on August 1: "Your father repudiates the idea that Mr. Cassatt is responsible for the deficencies of the road in any degree, and thinks it would be well not to countenance such an idea." It would take more than these comforting words or Lois' reassurance, to erase the remembrance of the Standard pressure. In an effort to lift the gloom, the Cassatts took their 1878 holiday in Newport, then just beginning its lavish "cottage" colonizing, the gathering place of such established New Yorkers as the

Belmonts, the Livingstons, the Stuyvesants, and the Van Rensselaers. Newport had been a resort since 1844 when a Virginia merchant had built the first $100,000 "cottage," a princely sum for a house in those days. Until the decline of the clipper ship, the small Rhode Island town had been an active trading port. What later generations have come to call the "social" Newport, began about mid-nineteenth century when Southerners, dissatisfied with the casualness of Saratoga, discovered Newport's more rarefied atmosphere. At first they stayed in boarding houses, then in the modest hotels which sprang up before the Civil War. By the 70s most of these hotels had disappeared as the lavish "cottages" appeared along Bellevue Avenue, and the fabled Bailey's Beach was established for those who could afford to belong to its exclusive precincts.

Lois, who always had social aspirations, adored Newport, writing to her mother in early September of "all the wonderful things" that greeted her upon arrival. Unfortunately, she could not enjoy the lavish dinners, the coaching parade along Bellevue Avenue, and the sea bathing, for upon her arrival she became ill. While Lois was unable to attend the noted Newport functions, Aleck undoubtedly had leisure for the Reading Room, the resort's men's club, patronized also by such patrons of the turf as Pierre Lorillard, the tobacco tycoon, and A. H. P. Belmont, the New York socialite, both of whom shared his interest in racing. In time, Alexander Cassatt would join these two millionaires in an ambitious rack track venture in northern New Jersey. But, however much the Cassatts enjoyed the "regal" month in Newport, neither the congenial company nor the sea and sun dispelled Aleck's gloom about the railroad and his position as an officer of the Pennsylvania.

On his return from Newport, Aleck wrote to his parents abroad where they had established a home with his sister Mary, who was struggling for a foothold in the Parisian art world. For the first time he mentions resigning from the railroad and coming to join his family in France. His mother, discouraging the idea, replied, "What you say of resigning makes me hope to see you soon, but I am afraid you will find it hard to get out of it. As to coming over here to live, think well of it before deciding. However, you are still young enough to make friends in a strange land, and you might like it. I am too old for that now and naturally see things differently."

Mrs. Cassatt found living abroad difficult and only justified her sacrifice by acknowledging that Mary's work was receiving the recognition in France that the artist had failed to find in her native land. Mr. Cassatt, anxious to see his son and grandchildren, reported that he had heard that Tom Scott had not recovered from his contest with Rockefeller and found this news disturbing for Aleck's plans. From a lady who had traveled on the Nile with the Scotts, Mr. Cassatt learned that although the President of the Pennsylvania now seemed in good spirits, "he would never again be able to attend to business. How is this going to affect you? Will you be able to carry out your plan of getting over here for six months?" Aleck had decided to take his family to Europe for an extended stay as a prelude to residence. But before he could carry out his plans for a leave of absence from the railroad, further demands were made upon him as a result of the Standard situation.

Early in 1879, the Pennsylvania courts began to hear suits initiated by the independent oil producers against the Standard Oil Company. By March important testimony had been publicized from the Harrisburg hearings. Ida Tarbell, who had few kind words for industrialists at this stage of her journalistic career, commended Cassatt for his testimony before the Pennsylvania courts: "The most important witness who appeared was A. J. Cassatt. Mr. Cassatt's testimony was startling in its candor and its completeness, and substantiated in every particular what the oil men had been claiming: that the Pennsylvania Railroad had become the creature of the Standard Oil Company; that it was not only giving that company rates much lower than to any other organization but it was using its facilities with a direct view of preventing any outside refiner or dealer in oil from carrying on an independent business."

In the spring of 1879, the New York legislature under the direction of Alonzo B. Hepburn began an investigation into railroad rates and rebate discrimination. The Hepburn committee originally confined its probing to the New York Central and the Erie, primarily New York lines, but it was evident that the scope of the committee would broaden to include the Pennsylvania, which again in this critical stage of its affairs would call on Cassatt to be its spokesman. The Hepburn committee soon discovered that although there were many practitioners of long-haul, short-haul discrimination (for example, flour went from Milwaukee to New York for twenty cents a barrel while the charge from Rochester to New York, half the distance, was thirty cents) the chief benificiary of the railroads' abuses in rate practices was the Standard Oil Company.

Many critics of the oil monopoly insisted that not only did the Standard receive rebates from all the trunk lines ranging from forty cents to $3.07 on each barrel shipped, but that the trunk lines were selling their tankers to Standard and agreeing to build no more. The committee determined that the Standard controlled the four trunk lines' terminal facilities for handling oil, that it had prevented independent producers from refining oil, that the officers declined under oath to give testimony about these practices, and that when and if they were forced to testify they lied. This was no news to Cassatt who spoke openly to the Hepburn committee about the Pennsylvania's dilemma: "We made our first contract with Standard Oil Company for the reason that we found that they were getting very strong, that they had the backing of the other roads, and, that if we wanted to retain our full share of the business and get fair rates on it, it would be necessary to protect ourselves." He made no excuses for the arrangements, which he had not endorsed, but he explained candidly to the committee what had forced the Pennsylvania into such dubious actions.

William Vanderbilt, standing in for his dying father, the old Commodore, was not so forthright. So distraught was Vanderbilt by the Hepburn committee's revelation of the condition of his road, its watered stock, its rebate schemes, that he negotiated with J. P. Morgan to buy 250,000 shares of Central stock. This assured Morgan of a seat on the Central's board of directors, which would in years to come have a decisive affect on the Pennsylvania. The Hepburn committee may have revealed much, but it was powerless to initiate reforms, and the Pennsylvania courts were no more effective. The suits against the Standard were abandoned.

While New York and Pennsylvania continued their investigations and suits, Ohio, too, began a court case indicting Rockefeller and Flagler on eight counts of criminal conspiracy. Cassatt had set an example, and others were called. But few answered willingly, and many refused to honor the subpoenaes, so powerful was the Rockefeller influence. At the very opportunity to shake the yoke of Rockefeller from their shoulders, the railroads turned aside, restricting their own freedom by mutual agreement. If the government would not intervene, the financial community had no such scruples, no such fear of Rockefeller, where millions of dollars were invested. The real railroad owners, the stockholders, sought the advice of J. P. Morgan, who after 1880 became a major force in the direction of railroads.

All these developments worried and concerned Cassatt, who saw much earlier than many of his colleagues the necessity for government regulation of the railroads, either with or without the cooperation of the lines' officers. His experiences of 1877–1880 intensified his hatred of rebates and manipulation of rates to favored shippers. When the hour arrived, Cassatt would see that Rockefeller and his fellow robber barons paid dearly for their arrogant dictation to the Pennsylvania Railroad. Cassatt's treatment at the hands of the Standard, the investigating committees, and his own chief, Thomas A. Scott, would bear bitter fruit for these public maurauders.

While Aleck had been traveling from New York to Philadelphia to Harrisburg on railroad affairs, he had not forgotten his family in France. With his usual foresight he had drawn up a trust for his mother, to ensure that she should never be in need. Living in Europe was less expensive than America, and Robert Cassatt had gathered a comfortable income during his own business days, but he was far from wealthy. He had, moreover, been forced to spend some of his assets to rescue his younger son, Gardner, from financial embarrassment. Gardner, scorning the railroad business to Aleck's dismay, had become a banker and made some injudicious investments in "Denvers," railroad stock. Then, too, Gardner, a bachelor, lived handsomely. Unlike Aleck, Gardner caused his parents much concern, for he wrote to them infrequently and told his father little of his affairs. Mrs. Cassatt wrote to her elder son: "I suppose you don't see much of Gard. What a strange life he leads! He doesn't tell us much about himself or anyone else. Says he never sees or hears anything. Is his business getting on well do you know?" Some of the gossip about Gard's lively bachelor life penetrated the apartment at 13 Avenue Trudaine where the Cassatts were spending the winter. His father also confided his uneasiness about the younger brother to Aleck: "I could not help continuing to feel uneasy and shall, I suppose always do so (knowing G.'s domestic habits and how much alone he must feel himself) until I hear of his marriage to some suitable person."

Aleck's generosity was welcome for it would enable the senior Cassatt's to live more comfortably. Robert Cassatt acknowledged his son's gift on May 26, 1879: "Your Mother, my dear Son, is very much touched with your kind intentions with regard to the Trust which she accepts in the same frank and loving spirit in which it is offered. She bids me to say that she really is not in need of anything except a carriage which her growing infirmities make her long for sometimes."

Mrs. Cassatt had her carriage, but the senior Cassatts, although popularly believed by French acquaintances to be rich, lived modestly. In the winter they rented various apartments in Paris; in the summer they usually moved to Marly-le -Roi, beyond the city, where their household was staffed with four servants including the new coachman. Mary spent much of her time, when not painting, at household chores as her mother and sister Lydia were often ill. Mr. Cassatt appreciated his daughter's talent but indicated to Aleck that Mary herself was bored with her growing fame. "Too much pudding!" she called it.

About his son's financial affairs, he gave paternal advice: "I am glad to hear your financial success has been so good. The thing now will be to keep it from wasting. Most anyone can make money, only the wise know how to keep it." The senior Cassatt had a strangely ambivalent attitude toward worldly success. He did not seek it for himself, but he enjoyed his elder son's meteoric rise in the executive ranks of the Pennsylvania Railroad and deplored Gardner's inability to do likewise as a banker. In October, 1882, Gardner would somewhat allay his father's apprehensions by marrying Jennie Carter, of Virginia, who unlike Lois Buchanan, managed with Southern charm, to get along well with her in-laws.

Aleck certainly knew how to make money, keep it, and use it, to increase his already impressive income. But wealth was not his chief concern, then or ever. He wanted leisure to enjoy the benefits of that wealth, to spend more time with his family. The railroad, once such an adventure, began to impose chains. Unlike many of his contemporaries in the business world, Cassatt did not share the desire for more and more power and luxury. In this he followed his father. At forty, with success assured, he found the pace of the competitive arena uncongenial. A complex man, Cassatt on the one hand wanted achievement, and on the other spurned the demands which success imposed. He was young to consider abandoning the struggle. His health was good and his energies in full spate, but he hesitated. The exigencies of his executive responsibilities had pushed him into a position which he disliked. Only his father understood. Robert Cassatt wrote to his son: "If what I wrote proves true about Scott's never being able to resume business again a change must be made in the next election when I suppose Roberts will succeed. How will that suit you? With the fearful competition in railroading now going on I should think the business anything but agreeable?"

Anything but agreeable! Aleck agreed, and George P. Roberts, the proper staid Philadelphian, did not suit him as a chief. But how to retire gracefully from the scene? He pondered the problem and prepared for the future by drawing up a new will which protected his children's interests. In this he observed the elder Cassatt's strictures to tie up his daughters' money, so that their eventual husbands could not gain control of it. For his day, the senior Cassatt was liberal in his views about women's rights, and life with Mary, a strong-minded woman, amazingly independent for her day, had intensified those views.

Aleck's mother urged him to come abroad to see them before his sister Lydia, suffering from an incurable disease, should die. Mary and her mother traveled on an extended tour of Switzerland, Italy, and southern France during the summer of 1879, and consequently the artist had few paintings ready for the Paris exhibition of 1880, in which her friend Degas' work was acclaimed. By the turn of the new year, 1880, Aleck had decided to take his family to Europe that spring. Thomas A. Scott, although only fifty-six, found his health so deteriorated from the struggles of 1877, that he announced his retirement for June, 1880. The railroad's official biographers wrote, "his years in authority must have been a great disappointment to his expansive nature"—surely an understatement of Scott's frustrations. He was succeeded, as Robert Cassatt had expected, by George B. Roberts, who had risen rapidly in the company to become first vice president and comptroller. Cassatt also was promoted, to first vice-president. Scott died in his home less than a year later, a disillusioned and defeated man who had failed in his dream of a Pennsylvania and Scott-controlled transcontinental railroad.

By June 22, the Cassatts and their four children were sailing for France. This first visit to Europe since he had left Germany as a boy of seventeen, promised Cassatt not only a reunion with his family, but a time of decision. He had come to the crossroads of his life. His fortune and reputation were made, but what of his private hopes and needs for the future? The railroad strike, the humiliation at Rockefeller's hands, the succession of the uncongenial Roberts shadowed his achievements. Did he want to continue? His father had turned to Europe in a similar crisis. Would this be the answer to his own doubts, the life of an expatriate abroad? His boyhood had been peripatetic, imposed by his father's restlessness. It had had the advantages of travel and exposure to a sophisticated culture, but had also robbed him of roots and a settled home. Would his own children benefit from such an upbringing? The railroad and his established position in Philadelphia's business and social world meant security. He had worked single-mindedly to achieve that status. Now at forty he must assess the years which had brought him from comfortable obscurity almost to a place on the pinnacle of power in his country's rugged dynamic industrial world.

The $14,999,999 Check

The senior Cassatts with Mary and Lydia, met the visitors at the Gare du Nord and accompanied them to the Hotel Meurice where they would stay temporarily. Aleck had not seen his family in three years, and it had been twenty eight-years since he had been a schoolboy in Paris. Now, he was a distinguished, successful man of almost forty, with an upright stance, well-buttoned into a dark conservative suit, his hair and mustache with a reddish tinge. That air of reserve hid not only a painful shyness which prevented him from speaking to large groups, but also a passionate nature, well disciplined and under tight control. Mary, not at ease with male sitters, would paint him on this trip, again not one of her best efforts. Her brother appeared wooden, disdainful, exuding pride, with the warmth and kindliness his family had come to depend upon, concealed. The oil portrait, a three-quarter view of Aleck sitting in a chintz-covered chair with his right leg crossed over his left, was the first of several paintings of her brother Mary attempted. None was a success.

Robert Cassatt, reluctant to let his grandchildren out of his sight, spent the night at the Hotel Meurice, and then escorted the party to Marly-le-roi, a few miles from Paris, which would be their headquarters for the summer. In the Cassatt's French rural retreat, the four children from America would be indulged by their grandparents and aunts, treated like kings and queens,' while Aleck and Lois were free to travel. Lois Cassatt's reaction to her in-laws was tempered but she admitted to her sister Henrietta that "I took them just as I found them." Lydia offered to escort Lois to the dressmakers. At first Lois was inclined to refuse, but she accepted when she saw that her sister-in-law "really wanted to do it." Both Mary and Lydia dressed elegantly, buying their frocks from Redfern, Doucet, and La Ferrière. Mary's most recent biographer, Nancy Hale, believes that "Mary's grasp of chic was in fact what made her able to render Lois the only service that lady ever appreciated from her," introducing Lois to the couturiers. Aleck, who intended to buy his clothes in London, spent his leisure driving a rented carriage to Longchamps to see the races. He was delighted to revisit the scenes of his youth, but Lois found much of the sightseeing tiring. Aleck escorted her to the Louvre and then accompanied her to the dressmakers, but "would not stand more than ten minutes of that so he left Lizzie (Lydia) and me to buy." And buy she did, not forgetting her Buchanan sisters who had given her fashion commissions.

Lois worried about Cheswold and had "several bad dreams about the house." In her letters home she constantly inquired about the rennovations before discussing her shopping expeditions. "I got several pretty white dresses, or rather ordered them, not that they are cheap, but because the trimmings are new and very pretty. Underclothes at the best places are very high," she complained to her mother. Aleck, generous and indulgent, encouraged her purchases. He wanted to spend as much time as possible with his parents and sisters and missed his children who remained at Marly. It took an hour and forty minutes to travel from Paris to the country. Lois confided to her parents: "It is a pity on his account that they are not in town for they are so anxious to have him there and it really takes up too much time to come and go."

In mid-July Aleck and Lois went to England where they intended to stay ten days before going up the Rhine to spend two weeks in Germany and Switzerland. The children remained at Marly.

Lois made the tourist rounds in London: Madame Tussaud's, the Changing of the Guard, the Tower. For Aleck, London's main attraction was horses. He rented a four-in-hand and after some instruction from a famous whip, drove Lois to Richmond for dinner at the Star and Garter. They also rode frequently in Rotten Row to see and be seen by the "swells." Lois, still preoccupied with shopping, was pleased that carpets for Cheswold were so inexpensive. She enjoyed visits from Philadelphian friends, the Fairman Rodgers and the Hutchinsons, but didn't care much for Londoners—"in fact it is nothing but blasted Englishmen everywhere," she wrote home. (What did she expect in London?) At the opera they shared a box with the Rodgers and caught a glimpse of the Wales', Prince Edward and Princess Alexandra. But Queen Victoria was in seclusion, to Lois' disappointment. Aleck missed his children, and Lois confided to her mother that they might have to change their plans about a tour of Germany and Switzerland.

The chief reason for the trip to London had been Aleck's desire to buy some horses, which Lois did not entirely approve: "He went there expecting to find everything he wanted, I won't say needed, for he needs none, but the horses, good ones, are scarce and very high." He bought some clothes, expensive outfits, and had trouble being properly fitted. These experiences with the tailor and the horses dampened his enthusiasm for Europe. Lois, pleased, wrote her mother: "He finally came to the conclusion to waste no more time on clothes as he thinks his tailor at home an *excellent* one. On the whole, do you know, I think even Aleck is going back to America very well satisfied with his own country. As for me, although I am entirely enjoying the experience, I know ours is the only country to live in. But isn't it lovely to have Aleck go back so pleased with home?" For years Aleck had been cherishing his memories of Europe. How disillusioning it was for him to have to admit that he would never be able to settle there permanently.

However much Aleck wanted to escape from the Pennsylvania Railroad, he continued to follow the events at home closely, informed by his faithful assistant, William Patton. One of his concerns was a tragic accident on the New Jersey Lines for which he felt much responsibility. During the 70s and 80s, railroad accidents were frighteningly frequent. In 1876 a fast Pacific express on Vanderbilt's line crashed through a bridge at Ashtabula, Ohio, and more than twenty passengers were burned to death. Massachusetts reported over 200 deaths a year from train crashes in the 80s. The Pennsylvania, better managed than most roads, its officers more eager to try the newly-invented safety devices, had a safer record but was not immune from railroad holocausts. Cassatt read a brief mention of the New Jersey wreck in the English newspapers and promptly cabled Patton for particulars.

In Patton's words: "It was a very unfortunate affair and much regretted by everyone. Eighteen persons have died from the results of their injuries and the wounded number some 40 or 50 more . . . An investigation is now in progress. The responsibility of the accident is placed upon the engineer of the second train. I think there is but little if any truth in his statement that the air brake failed to work when he applied it. In fact, in his testimony yesterday before the coroner's investigation, he admitted the new automatic brake had been applied to his engine the day before and that he had not been instructed as to its its workings and did not know how to apply it." George Westinghouse's safety device was scarcely ten years old and not yet perfected or understood when it was used at all.

Patton also described the business climate and the Pennsylvania's progress: "Mr. Roberts keeps well and sticks pretty close to the office. Everything moving very quietly. . . ." The oil shipments had fallen off, but the grain traffic had grown steadily, and the road's revenues showed an increase of $500,000 over the same month last year. Cassatt, still troubled by the Standard Oil situation and his fellow officers' reaction to Rockefeller, learned that there was no change in attitude between Roberts and the Standard. As Patton put it there seemed to be "no further show of open hostility between the two companies."

Aleck and Lois visited Switzerland and southern France before a final reunion with the Cassatts in Paris. Lois still fretted about Cheswold. She wrote to her mother from the Hotel Meurice on August 5: "It is a strange but sad fact that since we landed we have heard nothing of the new house. Neither Gard nor Mr. Evans (the architect) have written a line. Alice tells me of the cook but not of the house." She had had quite enough of her in-laws and hastened to complain to Harriet: "Everything is still lovely between me and the C's, that is to say as far as I know, but the truth is I cannot abide Mary and never will. I cannot tell why but there is something utterly obnoxious about that girl. I have never heard her criticize any human being in any but the most disagreeable way. She is too self-important and I can't put up with it. The only being she seems to think of is her Father. She tries to be polite to me, so we get on well enough. The children all seem to prefer her to the others, strange to say, enough of this."

Lois never altered her opinion of Mary Cassatt. Certainly, there were faults on both sides—Mary found Lois stuffy, too interested in her position in Philadelphia society, and as "self-important" as Lois found her. Mary's deep family feeling, which encompassed her ailing sister, Lydia, her parents, and her brothers, never extended to Lois. Their relationship steadily deteriorated, although the artist was genuinely fond of the Cassatt's four young children. Throughout their lives, when allowed, they returned her love.

However much the young Cassatts were enjoying their indulgent grandparents and aunts and life at Marly-le-Roi, they were as anxious to return to Haverford as their mother. Lois wrote again to Harriet: "We are all full of our various experiences but everybody says how nice it will be to get home. Aleck is fully convinced that America is on the whole a better country to live in. How long this will last after we get there I can't tell." Aleck's familiarity with Europe, his appreciation of its older culture, his enjoyment of his parents and sisters obviously rankled.

Lois prepared to sail with trunks full of presents and furniture for Cheswold: "This room and the anti-chamber look like a large shop with all the boxes from the Louvre and other shops standing about." There were watches and music boxes from Switzerland, silks from Paris, carpets from London, winter coats and towels,—and the paintings Mary had encouraged Aleck to buy. He did not get the Degas she wanted for him because the artist refused to finish it. But there was a Pissaro and a Monet, bought by Mary for 800 francs a piece (about $150). Aleck, together with Mary's friend Minnie Hagenmeyer, was the first collector in America to own French Impressionists. Mary herself had painted the four Cassatt children with their grandmother as well as the portrait of Aleck. Her family remained her favorite models—if not always her most successful.

By September the Cassatts were back in Haverford after what Lois described as a "very painful voyage," to a Cheswold still not fully remodeled. Mr. Cassatt informed his son that although American lines were no doubt "safe and staunch," they cared little for the comfort of their passengers, and in the future he would be wiser to sail Star or Cunard. The senior

Cassatt was already looking forward to his son's next visit. He missed his grandchildren, felt his age, and was disturbed by the rumors of another French war with Germany.

Aleck's intention of resigning, expressed so often to his parents, had not diminished over his two-month holiday. But his plan would have to be deferred for a time. A confrontation with the B & O in New Jersey loomed which Cassatt was to handle. Whatever his opinion of Roberts, he could not abandon the Pennsylvania at this juncture. Repeatedly, newspaper articles referred to Cassatt's distaste for Roberts and his reluctance to work with the new president. Although later denied by Cassatt's assistant, these rumors persisted. Observers believed that Cassatt's resignation was prompted by pique at Robert's election rather than his own. Certainly, he had been among the most favored candidates. But there is little evidence that Robert's election to the presidency was decisive for Cassatt's wish to resign. Other factors were more important—his family life for one. With his usual reserve, he declined to comment on any suppositions in the press or from friends. His mother wrote one sentence in a letter to him after his return to America which throws some light on her son's real attitude: ". . . How do you manage with Roberts as chief? I think you didn't like the idea of serving under him."

Whatever he told his mother, Cassatt never commented publicly. His ideas on how the Pennsylvania should be run differed fundamentally from Robert's cautious approach. An open clash of personalities never occurred, but a distance widened between Roberts and his first vice president. Cassatt and Roberts had many common bonds: They came from similar backgrounds; were both well-to-do Main Line Philadelphians; had both graduated from Rensselaer; and had risen through hard work and ability, under the aegis of Thomson, to top executive rank in the Pennsylvania.

In an era when it seemed vital that the president of the Pennsylvania Railroad be a "gentleman," George Brooke Roberts, like Cassatt, fulfilled that criterion in every way. Born on the family estate, Pencoyd, in Montgomery County, a few miles from Philadelphia, Roberts, was descended from a Welsh settler who had come to Pennsylvania in 1683 to join those Quakers who formed a colony on William Penn's famous Welsh tract. By the mid-nineteenth century, the Roberts family had shifted from malting to ironmaking, from the Quaker allegiance to proper Episcopalianism. After his education at a local academy and Rennselaer, George Roberts had joined the Pennsylvania Railroad as a rodman, and like Cassatt, quickly gained his superiors' attention for his engineering skill. While Cassatt was working in Georgia and on the Frankfort Junction, Roberts joined the corps which was locating the line over the Alleghenies. In 1862 Thomson named him his special assistant, a post created for Roberts, "in whose judgment and experience as an engineer I have the fullest confidence," Thomson reported to his board of directors.

Roberts rapid rise through the executive ranks of the railroad to first vice president under Thomas A. Scott in 1874 has been attributed by the road's historians to "sheer hardworking ability." His background and natural temperment inclined him to modesty and gentleness: "None of his contemporaries accuse him of undue aggressiveness." Sober, quiet, tight-lipped, Roberts devoted much of his leisure to good works, a family tradition. He encouraged the Young Men's Christian Association, served on the board of the Free Library, and was vice president of the Fairmont Park Association. Near his home in Bala Cynwyd, on the Roberts' tract, he built the Church of St. Asaph, decorated with murals by the family artist, his sister Elizabeth Roberts. Elizabeth was an artist inferior in every way to Mary Cassatt as her brother was a pale copy of Alexander Cassatt. Aggressiveness, even ruthlessness, would be necessary to promote the Pennslyvania's interests in the 80s, a period of bitter rate wars and intense competition among the great trunk lines. In these qualities Roberts was deficient. It would be up to Cassatt, as gentle and modest in his family circle as Roberts, but much more capable of confronting a Vanderbilt or a Garrett. He could counter every move of his rivals with a driving, hardheaded flair for negotiations which Roberts would never have contemplated. The most spectacular performance of the Roberts regime, the acquisition of the Philadelphia, Wilmington, and Baltimore road from under the very eyes of the B & O, was the canny work of Cassatt, not Roberts, who would have stood by, in his gentlemanly way, and watched his rivals challenge the Pennsylvania's access to the New York markets.

The Baltimore and Ohio and its testy president, John W. Garrett, realized that if the B & O did not have a direct approach to New York, the line would have little voice in setting rates in the freight wars so prevalent in the 80s. Its competitive position as a great trunk line would be weakened. The B & O must get into New York, and arrive there before the Pennsylvania.

Six months before his retirement, Scott warned Roberts about Garrett and his intentions: "You want to keep your eye on Mr. Garrett, however, very closely, and take all his protestations with a large grain of allowance. His ambition and his necessities are such, that I do not think you can trust him at all." Scott also realized that Cassatt understood as well as Garrett that his line's prestige, power, and profit lay in New York. Cassatt, not Roberts, must handle the challenge from the B & O. In that same letter to Roberts, written from Florence, Scott wrote: "Mr. Cassatt, I think, understands the question very thoroughly and will quickly see the necessity of meeting the enemy on all points." To Scott any competitive thrust against the Pennsylvania meant war.

The instrument of Garrett's challenge to the Pennsylvania was the main line of the Philadelphia, Wilmington, and Baltimore road which formed the middle third of the through route between Washington and New York. Both the B & O and the Pennsylvania ran their cars over this vital line under an agreement with the P. W. and B. The upper third to the north was the

line of the United New Jersey Railroad and the lower third was either the
B & O's Washington branch or the Pennsylvania's Baltimore & Potomac.
For years the B & O had run its trains across the United Jersey line in a
competitive position with the Pennsylvania, but now Garrett wanted to
upset this precarious balance. He began secretly to build a new route east
from Philadelphia over the Reading line and then north to the Central
Railroad of New Jersey where it reached the west bank of the Hudson
River. On December 1, 1880, Garrett suddenly announced that the B & O
would withdraw its passenger trains from the Pennsylvania's New Jersey
lines immediately and its freight trains in the first month of the new year.

The New Jersey lines had been acquired for the Pennsylvania on a long
lease by Cassatt during those delicate negotiations in 1870 which had led to
his promotion to general superintendent. He took a proprietary interest in
them and refused to see them slip from the Pennsylvania's grasp. But the
New Jersey lines had always maintained an annoying independence of
action, leasing right of way to the B & O and to whomever else they saw
fit. The Pennsylvania could not rely on the Jersey lines cooperation in any
war with the B & O.

Even more distrubing than Garrett's secret maneuverings, was the announcement on February 1, 1881 that Jay Gould, that dubious financial
despoiler of the Erie, had been elected president of the Central Railroad
Company of New Jersey. Jay Gould was suspect, capable of any maneuver
which would line his pockets at the expense of the stockholders and the
public. An alliance between Gould and Garrett promised only trouble.
Obviously, the Pennsylvania would have to try and buy the Philadelphia,
Wilmington, and Baltimore or see its hegemony in New Jersey and its trade
with New York endangered.

Most of the stock in the P. W. and B. was held by a group of Boston
financiers whom Garrett hastened to approach, hoping to steal a march on
his rivals. He had gathered a group of interested backers—Gould, Russell
Sage, August Belmont, and John Jacob Astor—for the B & O could not
effect such an expensive deal without outside resources. He began his dealings with the Boston stockholders in mid-February, and by mid-March,
they agreed to sell him 120,000 shares, a controlling interest in the road. On
February 19, Cassatt was invited to meet with the members of Garrett's
syndicate and offered a third interest in the Philadelphia, Wilmington, and
Baltimore for the Pennsylvania. He refused.

Garrett, secure in the knowledge that he had the Boston men in his
pocket, lost no time in crowing over his competition. He bustled into
Roberts' Philadelphia office to boast of his coup on a crisp wintery day in
early March. "Mr. Roberts," he said jovially, "we have secured the control
of the Philadelphia, Wilmington, and Baltimore railroad. We are not disposed, however, to disturb your relations with the property and you need
not give yourself any uneasiness on that score."

Roberts and Cassatt knew better, but they listened unmoved to Garrett's insincere protestations. Roberts only replied quietly, "Well, I did not know that you had progressed so far in your negotiations." Garrett left that meeting chuckling at his rivals impassivity before certain defeat. Unknown to the aggressive, bristling head of the B & O, however, were Cassatt's arrangements for just this contingency. Behind Garrett's back, the Boston stockholders of the P. W. and B. road had determined that Garrett's offer of $70 a share for the controlling 120,000 block of stock was not enough. They hoped that the Pennsylvania might give more. Tentative feelers had been made by the Bostonians long before Garrett appeared in the Pennsylvania's executive suite. Garrett, highly pleased with his injudicious visit to Cassatt and Roberts, returned to Baltimore on the night of March 6, unaware that his competitors were slamming the door on his road's entry into New York.

Once Garrett had left the office, Cassatt told his president that he was sure that all the stock had not been secured by the B & O. That very hour Cassatt left for New York where he contacted the Boston men and offered them $78 for a block of 91,000 shares of stock Garrett had overlooked. He promised them the same price for the remaining controlling stock if they would deliver by April 1. The Bostonians, eager for such a profitable sale above the market price, agreed to abandon Garrett for cash in hand. Cassatt sat down and wrote a check for $14,999,999, the largest single transaction in the history of American business to that date. The Pennsylvania did not have $14,999,999 in cash in its running account, but the next day, March 8, 1881, was the annual meeting of the Pennsylvania's board of directors, who would be asked to vote the money.

Roberts reported to the board that the purchase of the Philadelphia, Wilmington, and Baltimore road, so recently and opportunely consummated, had been financed through the sale of $10,000,000 in trust certificates, bearing interest of four percent. The stockholders gave their approval and authorized an issue of an additional 400,000 shares of Pennsylvania stock, which would give the company $20,000,000 more. The total cost of the new acquisition was $17,032,879.25. Roberts explained the need for the purchase: "From the further examination made of the condition of this property since its acquisition, your Board are more than ever convinced of the wisdom of its purchase, although the price paid thereof was at the time thought to be fully equal to if not in excess of its value. It not only gives your company the ownership of a continuous line between Washington and New York, and makes directly tributary to your system the valuable traffic originating in the productive section traversed by its auxiliary lines, but also secures extensive additional terminal facilities at Philadelphia and Baltimore, of such a character as could not now be acquired at any reasonable cost, if at all."

No mention was made of the crucial role played by Cassatt in these maneuvers. The purchase of the new lines brought the total of Pennsylvania mileage on the Main Line, branches, and leased roads to over 6,500 miles. The road employed 95,000 people, carried 75,000,000 passengers and hauled 160,000,000 tons of freight yearly. It had become the largest industrial employer in the nation. Cassatt saw no reason to stop there. On the executive wall, framed discreetly, hung the $14,999,999 cancelled check for the Philadelphia, Wilmington, and Baltimore road, a reminder of the Pennsylvania's imaginative and pioneer financing. The check would move, along with the other office paraphanelia to the new station on Broad street, a monument to the company's preeminent position in the railroad world.

Garrett, balked of access to the New York market, began bargaining to build a parallel road, linked to the Reading's tracks east of the Schuykill River. *The Philadelphia Record* felt that all these moves on Garrett's part were unneccesary: "The B & O has been offered terminal facilities in this city several times that would give it direct connection with the Reading Railroad and a line across the city, but it has always refused the offers and stated that it would wait and see how the Pennsylvania Railroad Company treated it before placing a plant between Baltimore and Philadelphia. . . ." The *Record* and Garrett soon found out how the Pennsylvania treated it. In 1884 the Pennsylvania refused to transport B & O cars over its road. But Garrett had completed his parallel road the year before, just in time. Garrett was beseiged on all sides, by the Pennsylvania, by the rate wars, and by Vanderbilt. In the end, the aging tycoon was forced to retire from the leadership of the road. Roberts wrote to Cassatt, who was in Europe, that Garrett had managed the B & O "into the most complete financial and administrative wreck we have had for some time."

His triumph over Garrett did not alter Cassatt's intention to retire. Railroad conditions were competitive and bitter. Vanderbilt plagued the Pennsylvania, forcing it repeatedly to lower freight rates. The public was now aroused. The state legislatures of Pennsylvania, Nevada, and Indiana sent general resolutions to the House of Representatives requesting federal intervention in the railroad wars. The National Grange, formed by irate farmers who felt victimized by the railroads, circulated a petition for "such laws as will alleviate the oppressions imposed upon us by the transportation monopolies. . . ." Cassatt fully agreed with the public and the farmers. He told the House committee investigating the Standard Oil Company that government intervention was the only remedy. Albert Fink, vice president of the Louisville and Nashville Railroad, had tried, after the Strike of 1877, to initiate an informal division of freight traffic and a pool structure, but the trunk lines refused to take his suggestions seriously. The secret rebates to favored shippers continued. The same month that Cassatt directed the purchase of the P. W. and B., saw Vanderbilt's Central, under pressure from New York merchants, cut its rates to the lowest percentage in history. Fink's efforts to make the railroad men see where their tactics were leading failed.

About rate wars and government intervention, Cassatt and Roberts were poles apart. In the words of the the Pennsylvania's historians, Roberts looked upon the subject of government control as "an absolute absurdity" and did not believe that any man—no matter what laws were passed to aid him—"could successfully manage the entire transportation system of the United States." Roberts claimed that men selected for "partisan and political reasons" could only contribute to the injury of the public welfare. Ironically, he held faithfully to the free pass, also used for "partisan and political" purposes, a view that Cassatt did not share.

Since government intervention was manifestly impossible at this stage, Cassatt realized that the only way to shake off the oppression of the secret rebate system was to build the Pennsylvania into such a powerful position that it could defy its rivals and force them to be more reasonable to the independent shippers and the public. Cassatt had urged that Roberts buy the P. W. and B. years before when its cost would have been considerably less. He wanted the Pennsylvania to buy the Reading, a hostile force in his company's backyard. President Roberts, in the words of a popular journalist of the day, "was too weak and too cautious to support this intrepid policy."

With his advice unheeded in the board room, Cassatt turned his attention to one last effort for the Pennsylvania before he left the executive offices. The new Broad Street Station would signify to the Pennsylvania's competitors how impressive was his road's position. The acquisition of the new line proved an added impetus to the station which had been planned under Scott, but was not completed until well into Roberts' presidency. Furness, Evans and Co., the architects of Cassatt's country home in Haverford, were hired to build the new station opposite Philadelphia's City Hall. The Moorish-Gothic ten-story building, with its great arched train shed, would house the general offices of the company, until then inconveniently located in West Philadelphia at 30th and Market Streets. To move the trains from the main tracks into the center of town, a great stone causeway was built, cutting across the city between the main avenue, Market Street, and a parallel artery, Arch Street. This giant causeway, forcing the bisecting streets to pass underneath through damp dripping tunnels, was called the "Chinese Wall" by Philadelphians who admitted its ugly necessity and in time grew quite attached to the railroad's arrogant gesture. The Broad Street Station, towering over the "Chinese Wall," was opened on December 5, 1881, although not fully completed.

Nathaniel Burt, sardonic observer of the Quaker City, thought that the Broad Street Station represented Roberts, inbred, parochial, and convinced that Philadelphia was the center of the universe. Cassatt, on the other hand, never shared this illusion. The primary purpose of his road was to channel the riches of the west to the port of Philadelphia. New York, not Philadelphia, was garnering the chief rewards of the hinterland. By acquiring the

Alexander J. Cassatt. Statue by Alexander Weiner which stood at the foot of the Grand Staircase, Pennsylvania Station, New York. *Courtesy of the late Mrs. John B. Thayer, Jr.*

A.J. Cassatt in 1866, aged 25. *Courtesy of the late Mrs. John B. Thayer, Jr.*

Harriet Buchanan, *c.* 1865, first fiancee of A.J. Cassatt and niece of President James Buchanan. *Courtesy of the late Mrs. John B. Thayer, Jr.*

Maria Lois Buchanan at her marriage to A.J. Cassatt, November 25, 1868, Trinity Church, Oxford, Pennsylvania. *Courtesy of the late Mrs. John B. Thayer, Jr.*

Mr. and Mrs. A.J. Cassatt and children drive from Haverford estate, *c.* 1880. *Courtesy of the late Mrs. John B. Thayer, Jr.*

Cassatt family on the terrace of Cheswold, *c.* 1882. L. to r. Elsie, Edward, Mrs. Cassatt, Robert, A.J. Cassatt, Nancy and Cornelia Ewing, Mrs. Maskell Ewing. *Courtesy of the late Mrs. John B. Thayer, Jr.*

Four Acres, Bar Harbor, Maine. Built by A.J. Cassatt
1902-1903. *Courtesy of the late Mrs. John B. Thayer, Jr.*

Chesterbrook Farm, Chester County,
Pennsylvania in the early 1900s. Bought
by A.J. Cassatt in 1881. *Courtesy
of the late Mrs. John B. Thayer, Jr.*

Cheswold, Haverford, Pennsylvania, built 1872-
1873. *Courtesy of the late Mrs. John B. Thayer, Jr.*

Cassatt town house, 202 Rittenhouse Square, Philadelphia. Bought from architect Fairman Rogers in 1888. *Courtesy of the late Mrs. John B. Thayer, Jr.*

Edward Buchanan Cas-
satt in his Saint Cyr uniform, *c.* 1887-1889. *Courtesy of the late Mrs.
John B. Thayer, Jr.*

Edward, Katherine, Elsie, and Robert in the 1880s.
Courtesy of the late Mrs. John B. Thayer, Jr.

A.J. Cassatt with his granddaughter Lois, 1900. *Photograph by T.H. Voight, Bad Homburg, Germany.*

.J. Cassatt, 1887. Pastel by Mary Cassatt, ainted in France. *Collection of Alexander assatt, Charleston, S.C.*

Lois Buchanan Cassatt, 1883. Pastel by Mary Cassatt, painted in France. *Private collection.*

Lois Buchanan Cassatt, 1900. *Photograph by T.H. Voight, Bad Homburg, Germany.*

Mr. and Mrs. A.J. Cassatt aboard the *Enterprise, c.* 1896. *Courtesy of the late Mrs. John B. Thayer, Jr.*

WILL HE SLAY THE DRAGON?

Interstate Commerce Commission investigation brings A.J. Cassatt home from Europe. *Philadelphia Public Ledger,* May 27, 1906.

President of the Pennsylvania Railroad presides at a board of directors meeting in Broad Street, Philadelphia office, July 1905. *Courtesy of the late Mrs. John B. Thayer, Jr.*

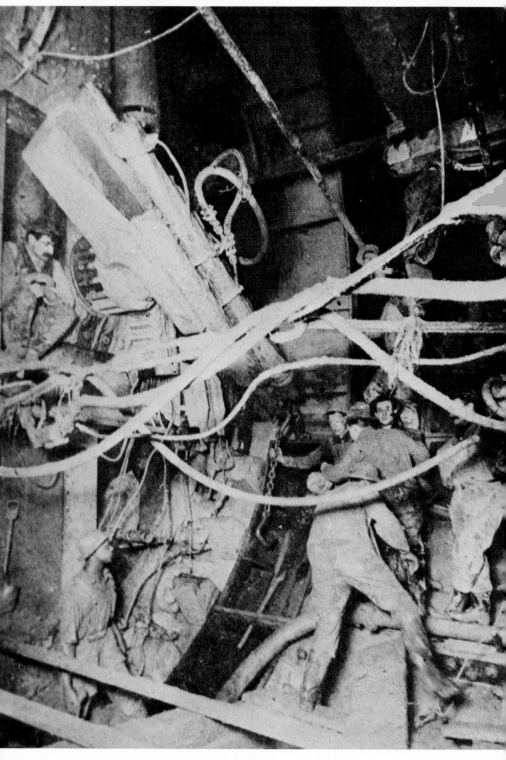

Sandhogs constructing tunnels under the Hudson River,
1902-1903. *Courtesy of the Free Library of Philadelphia.*

Concourse, Pennsylvania
Station, New York, 1911.

From the street level to track platforms, Pennsylvania Station,
New York, 1902. *Courtesy of the Free Library of Philadelphia.*

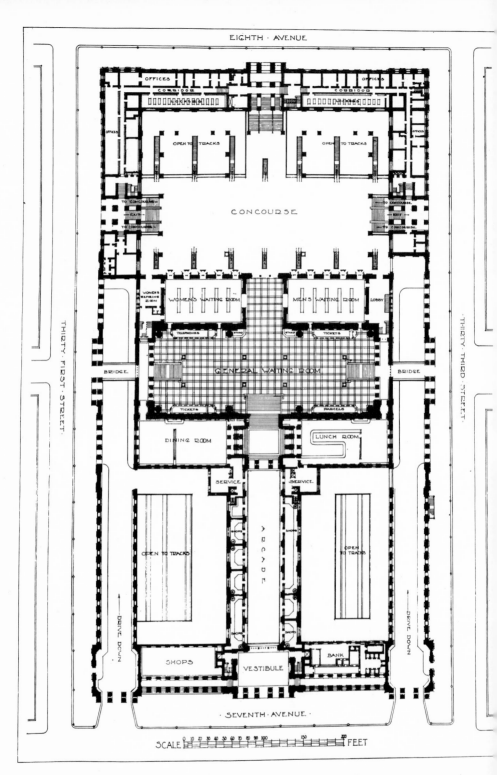

Block Plan, Pennsylvania Station, New York, 1911. *Mckim, Meade, and White.*

Front Facade of Pennsylvania Station, New York,
1911. *Courtesy of the Free Library of Philadelphia.*

Pennsylvania Railroad Station, New York. Seventh Avenue
Entrance, 1911. *Courtesy of the Free Library of Philadelphia.*

nnsylvania Station, the arcade looking from the
venth Avenue entrance toward the main waiting
om. *Courtesy of the Free Library of Philadelphia.*

Pennsylvania Station, detail of main
entrance on Seventh Avenue. *Courtesy
of the Free Library of Philadelphia.*

Main waiting room, Pennsylvania Station, New York, 1911.

P. W. and B., Cassatt had moved his road up to the very gates of the great market place. But he watched his trains stop dead at the Hudson, while Vanderbilt's lines traveled right into the center of Manhattan—an intolerable situation. But for more than two decades, no executive of the Pennsylvania saw any need to acknowledge the New York Central's ascendency. After all, over a million passengers a day passed through the Broad Street Station. Why be concerned about Cassatt's pipe dream of pushing the Pennsylvania into New York City?

By Christmas of 1881, Aleck had still not set the date for his retirement. The Cassatts were spending the winter in Haverford, so that Aleck could superintend the improvements at Chesterbrook, his 600-acre farm near Valley Forge. He seemed reluctant to abandon the Pennsylvania which sorely needed his expertise, although his advice to expand the road fell on deaf ears. His mother understood his dilemma: "I am afraid you are having a very worrying time of it this winter. I see continually in the papers that there is no end of the railroad wars and I know what that means. I am afraid you will be fretted to death and hope sincerely that before long you will be done with it."

Lydia continued to fail. She could not enjoy the oysters, ducks, and apples that the Haverford Cassatts sent their relatives in the Christmas box that year. Mrs. Cassatt took her elder daughter to the south of France in the New Year, hoping that would improve her health. Her condition had finally been diagnosed as Bright's Disease. Preoccupied with Lydia's health, Mrs. Cassatt worried too about Aleck's welfare: "You ought to watch yourself and when you find that business troubles keep you awake or make you nervous it is time to quit. I feel anxious knowing yours is a nervous temperament."

Aleck certainly showed no signs of a nervous temperament, and nothing in his youth indicated such a condition. He did suffer from headaches and his mother may have remembered some childish symptoms, perhaps his obsessive shyness, which she thought revealed such a problem. His warmest feelings were expressed within the family circle. Neither his business associates nor his social circle ever glimpsed a nervous temperament behind his stern facade.

In March, 1881, at the annual meeting, he was re-elected first vice president. He may have entertained thoughts of the presidency. His father wrote: "I see by the paper that you have been re-elected first vice president from which I conclude that you have given up the idea of getting the road for some time to come," a clue to his son's desire to run the railroad. Robert Cassatt knew that Aleck disapproved of Roberts' executive policies. While the senior Cassatt wanted his son to retire if he could not carry out his plans for the railroad, he was concerned that Gard, who could ill afford it, might follow Aleck's lead: "Gard writes in very good spirits about his business which it seems is even better than he expected." Robert Cassatt believed

Gard's success was due in no small part to Aleck's friendship with the father-in-law of Gard's partner. The family owed much to Aleck's influence, but Gard had not achieved his brother's position. His father worried: "The foolish fellow talks of retiring in a couple of years."

Mrs. Cassatt continued to press Aleck: "I hope you may stick to your present intentions of resigning for I am persuaded that 21 years of the kind of life you have led is quite enough for a person of your nervous temperament." In truth, she wanted him and her grandchildren in France, and used every opportunity to coerce him. She reminded him that his children, now so proficient in French, would do well in foreign schools. Aleck at last had made up his mind to leave. His final weeks of business were spent as a consultant to the New York and New Haven Railroad on the purchase of sleeping cars for that line. The New Haven urged him to take some compensation for they would want to call upon him again, and "we certainly are debarred from it in case he will take no fee for his services. He is too able a man to be left out of the field altogether."

The New Haven's vice president was only expressing what every knowledgeable railroad man in the country felt. Cassatt was too able to leave the railroad, but leave it he would. On July 3, Mr. Cassatt learned from the newspapers that his son had definitely fixed the date of his retirement from the Pennsylvania Railroad Company. "May God in his kind providence grant us a happy and safe meeting," he wrote Alec when he read the news.

The Resignation

Cassatt's decision to retire as first vice president of the Pennsylvania came as no surprise to railroad and financial circles in Philadelphia. As early as June, 1882, rumors abounded. *The Record* of June 13 headlined: "Mr. Cassatt's Future. A Report That He Is To Be President of Vanderbilt's Southwestern System." Such a suspicion shook Third Street, the city's business center, for Vanderbilt and his New York Central were the sworn rivals of the Pennsylvania. Would Cassatt go over to the enemy? The article described Vanderbilt's intention to consolidate all the lines controlled by him in Pennsylvania and south of New York under one management. It would be called the Southwestern System, and its new president would be Alexander J. Cassatt. The disturbing report concluded: "It was stated by many that the position was not regarded as one of any more importance than that now held by Mr. Cassatt, but would be more lucrative."

But more money was not Cassatt's chief concern. Whatever the rumors on Third Street he never considered lending his talents to the enemy. Despite many attractive offers, his allegiance remained with the Pennsylvania. While a Gould or a Scott could move with impunity from road to road in search of more power or money, such an action would never occur to Cassatt. Surprising as it seemed to these hard-headed, Victorian businessmen, here was a man at the pinnacle of his career, who wanted to sacrifice position and prestige to the doubtful pleasures of life as a country squire. It was unbelievable—there had to be more to it than that, and the rumors continued.

Since he had definitely decided to retire in the fall, Cassatt spent the summer on the job. His father, "now very full of your coming," wished that his younger son was as diligent as the elder: "Gard is a good for nothing scamp. I have been writing him positive orders about money matters and he answers my letters and never even alludes to their contents nor obeys the orders. If he treats his customers generally this way he will never become the founder of a great banking house that is certain." One of those customers was George B. Roberts, who entrusted all his stock and bond buying to Gard's firm, a bonus for the younger Cassatt, secured, no doubt, through the good offices of his brother.

On September 2, 1882, President Roberts received the following letter from his first vice president: "I beg to tender my resignation of the office of First Vice-President, to take effect as soon as it may be convenient to you." Cassatt, not unaware of the rumors on Third Street about his dislike and jealousy of Roberts, attempted to quiet the gossip in another paragraph: "My only object in taking this step is to have more time at my disposal than any one occupying so responsible a position in railroad management can command. If I were to remain in active railroad life I could not desire a position more agreeable to me than the one I now occupy, nor would I be willing to connect myself with any other company than the one in whose service more than twenty-one years of my life have been passed." So much for Vanderbilt—*The Record* was answered.

Such a clear statement might, nonetheless, not be enough to settle the suspicions once and for all. To underline his attitude, he continued: "During the whole of this time I have been treated with the kindest consideration by the Board of Directors, by my superior officers, and by my associates, and all of my labors have met with an appreciation far beyond their merits." He assured the company that he would not seek preferment elsewhere. "For this I shall always be grateful, and although about to sever my official connection with the company, my best wishes will, at all times be for its continued prosperity, and for the welfare and happiness of all connected with its service." Aware that his resignation letter would receive wide publication, Cassatt was not content with a simple statement. In the end, as throughout his career, he remained loyal and modest.

When President Roberts read the letter to the assembled Board, he stressed again that Cassatt's resignation was entirely based on his wish to enjoy some leisure. Roberts expressed his own deep regret at the loss and promised his directors that Cassatt had assured him that, if he thought about returning to the railroad world in the future, "he would make the Pennsylvania his first consideration." The Board then drew up a resolution commending Cassatt for his service and the pleasure it felt "that in the future as in the past, everything tending to promote the welfare and prosperity of this company will receive from him earnest and cordial support." Those rumors had evidently disturbed the tranquillity of the board room to no small degree.

Elected to succeed Cassatt as first vice president was Edmund Smith, a

Philadelphian who had also begun his career with the railroad as a rodman and then served an apprenticeship on the construction of the Main Line west and in the company's repair shops. At his election Smith was acting as treasurer of the Pennsylvania. He would remain as first vice president for only six years. A company historian, William Bender Wilson, reported that Smith had moved ahead by "working hard, keeping his habits correct, and by being suave of manner," hardly a glowing endorsement. He was a safe, if not inspired, replacement for Cassatt who was in fact irreplaceable.

Cassatt's letter had done nothing to quiet the speculation in the press, which hastened to review the late vice president's accomplishments and qualities. *The Philadelphia Evening Telegraph* speculated that "in the fullness of time" Cassatt could have expected the presidency, but that title could "hardly have given him honors greater than he has already won." *The Record* reminded its readers that Cassatt was not only surrendering his Pennsylvania executive office, but also the vice-presidency of the Northern Central, the Baltimore and Potomac, and the Philadelphia, Wilmington, and Baltimore, all Pennsylvania subsidiaries. *The Record's* glowing assessment of Cassatt's contribution to the growth of the Pennsylvania suggested that his tact and comprehension had been vital assets. Mindful of the conjectures that his resignation had been inspired by the company's present policy of stopping all expenditure on improvements, *The Record* concluded: "Mr. Cassatt pointed out the danger of a violent retrenchment policy. He urged, too, . . . that an increased business during the present fall would demand increased facilities which retrenchment would render impossible. Events have justified the wisdom of his position. In matters such as these his judgment has rarely been at fault."

Since the days in Altoona when he had demanded and received more repair shops and engines, Cassatt had always advocated creative expansion. In this policy he was at odds with Roberts. Professionally, the men could never agree. The railroad would suffer from Roberts' tight-fisted, conservative policies for more than fifteen years. Poor Mr. Smith must have needed all his suavity to cope with press opinion that no replacement existed for a man of Cassatt's wisdom, leadership, and practical experience.

The Pittsburgh Dispatch stressed Cassatt's achievements, introduction of the Westinghouse air brake, revolutionizing the road's motive power system, insisting on uniformitty in engines and cars, permanent track improvements, the reorganization of the New Jersey lines, the change in employee morale, and "thousands of details." Even his exertions during the strike of 1877 received a commendation from the Pittsburgh editorial writer who concluded that Cassatt's most outstanding characteristic was that "he never neglected an opportunity." Considering Pittsburgh's traditional hostility toward the Pennsylvania Railroad, these were complimentary words indeed.

For a man of Cassatt's temperament, such public recognition was unwelcome. He would have preferred to slip away to Europe with little fanfare, but the board of directors determined to give him a testimonial dinner. The nine course banquet at the Bellevue Hotel included oysters, terrapin, saddle of mutton, duck, and bombe glacé, washed down by Chateau d'Yquem and six other wines. Unable to face a public speech, the acknowledgement of these honors tried his nerves and his modesty. Roberts led the banquet guests, testifying to the amicable personal relations between the two men.

As the time grew near for Cassatt's sailing, Roberts belatedly reconsidered how the Pennsylvania would survive the loss of his talented lieutenant. Whatever their differences, Roberts knew well what Cassatt's departure would mean. He did not intend to sever business relations completely, nor allow Cassatt to cease advising the company. On October 2, 1882, he wrote to Cassatt offering him a desk in his office: "I forgot entirely on Saturday that that would be the last day for you at the office or probably I would have come in." Mindful that Cassatt's sailing date was still a month distant he suggested that his former vice president might occupy his private side room: "In this I am probably a little selfish, as I feel that we would then have an opportunity to avail ourselves of your council and good judgment on various matters that will arise until our new officers get accustomed to their duties." Roberts did not want Cassatt challenging him in the board room, pressing him to expand the road, but he was not averse to picking his brains behind the scenes. He planned to keep in close touch, profiting from Cassatt's advice without having to give an accounting.

While Aleck wound up his business affairs and settled conditions at his farm in preparation for a long absence, his parents waited eagerly for his arrival. Every letter brought disturbing news of Lydia's condition. Her feebleness and pain were increasing, and now even morphine failed to ease her suffering. By late September it had become apparent that Aleck must hurry, or he would not see his sister again. But eager as he was to reach Lydia's bedside, another, much happier family event, took precedence. Aleck and Lois delayed their sailing to attend his brother Gardner's wedding to Eugenia (Jennie) Carter of Virginia in St. Mark's Church in Philadelphia on October 18. The senior Cassatts, who feared that Gard, now thirty-three, might be a perennial bachelor, felt that a wife might settle him down and curb his tendency to extravagance.

On November 7, 1882, as Lois, Aleck, and their four children prepared to leave Cheswold for New York to board ship, they received a cable from Robert Cassatt informing them that Lydia had died peacefully in her sleep in the Paris apartment. Although not unexpected, Lydia's death affected Aleck strongly. He clung to his family as he grew older and regretted not seeing his sister one last time. Lois, who recorded their European trip sparsely in a diary, wrote: "We all left Cheswold in sad spirits the morning of the 8th of November." They traveled to New York in President Roberts' private car 60, accompanied by relatives and William Patton, Aleck's devoted assistant. After a sumptuous lunch at Delmonico's, the Cassatts boarded the *Servia*, "the worst old roller on the sea," at 1:30 on the afternoon of November 8th.

The trip was a nightmare, stormy, foggy, with high winds buffeting the ship. Even Lois, normally unaffected by wild seas, was ill, and Aleck himself "was uncomfortable the whole way." They arrived in Liverpool on the 17th to be met by a representative of the American Line, who took the Cassatts off on a tug at once. No waiting at the customs shed for such a distinguished American railroad executive. A special car, filled with flowers and fruit, courtesy of the British Railways, whisked them to London where they arrived at the Bath Hotel in Piccadilly at 9:30 that evening.

Aleck, Lois, and the children spent nine days shopping and sightseeing in London. On the day after their arrival, they watched the "Egyptian soldiers," commanded by Sir Garnet Wolseley, parade in a grand review from Green Park to St. James. "The finest display I have ever seen," Lois commented.

Lois ordered her mourning clothes at Redfern's; took the children to Westminster Abbey; attended a concert in Albert Hall. Aleck spent his time riding in Hyde Park with Rob and Eddie, shopping at Poole's, and buying a carriage. Horses as always were Aleck's chief interest in England, and a few days after their arrival, taking Lois and his sons with him, he "went down to the country to see a Fox Hunt." Aleck hunted frequently with a local pack, the Radnor Hunt, near his Chesterbrook farm and was eager to see an English hunt in action.

After a week-end in London the family embarked for Paris, enduring the rigors of a choppy Channel crossing "in a recumbant position," thus escaping active illness. That evening they arrived in Paris to be met by the Cassatts and escorted to the Hotel Chatham in the Rue Damon. Again, they had a large suite of rooms with a parlor, dining room, playroom, and four bedrooms. The Cassatts traveled in luxurious style, Lois insisting on spacious accomodations.

The children were enrolled immediately in Parisian schools. Lois rode daily with Aleck in the Bois and enjoyed her shopping expeditions with Mary, the one activity which they could share without acrimony. Again, Mary made a great effort to be friendly to Lois during this visit. The senior Cassatts and their artist daughter were then living in an apartment on 13 Avenue Troudaine where Degas was a frequent visitor. Lois wrote her mother that she met Degas but said nothing of her impressions of Mary's colleague. On Aleck's forty-third birthday they rode in the Bois and bought a new Victoria, an early Christmas gift to Lois from her indulgent husband.

Mary began a new portrait of Aleck. Lois may have resented the hours Aleck spent closeted with his sister in her studio, but during this visit at least, she felt that her relationship with her sister-in-law had improved. Lois wrote her mother: "Mary seems most anxious to be friendly and proposes something for us to do everyday. She is very lonesome . . . and says she feels now that perhaps she would have been better off to have married when she thinks of being left alone in the world. She has not had the heart to touch her painting for six months and she will scarcely now be persuaded to begin. . . ."

With Lydia gone Mary relied on her nieces and nephews as models. Children would always be her favorite subjects. Critics have suggested that she did not do men well, and Aleck in particular failed to develop on canvas. The half-length view of him, wearing a blue jacket, his brown hair and reddish mustache highlighted against a turquoise background, did not capture his warmth, kindly manner, or restrained energy. Nancy Hale, Mary's latest biographer, suggests that Aleck appears wooden in this portrait because in fact, he was, an assessment not sustained by a closer study of his temperament. Reserved he might be, wooden, never. But this was a difficult time for the Cassatts. Lydia's death made for a somber family reunion. Lois returned one afternoon from a shopping expedition and found "Mrs. C. and Mary talking in a most solemn manner to Aleck," discussing Lydia's death no doubt. Katherine Johnston Cassatt had borne seven children and only three remained to her.

Lois did not accompany Aleck and his father when they traveled to Marly on January 6, 1883 to see Lydia placed in the special vault there. Mr. Cassatt had delayed burying Lydia until Aleck's arrival. Lois recorded on that sad occasion, "Agnes and I spent the afternoon in doing errands and arranging for our going to London." With the children settled in school (the girls attended classes in the Faubourg St. Honoré), and their grandparents keeping an eye on them, Aleck and Lois felt that they could return to London. He wanted to buy a four-in-hand coach and return to the hunting at Wansford.

By January 10, they were back at the Haycock in Wansford where they would remain for ten days. Neither rainy weather nor exhaustion dampened Aleck's enthusiasm for the sport. In London at the Bristol Hotel, Aleck met an old schoolmate from Heidelberg. Albert Schiff, a German industrialist with a flaming red beard, had read of the Cassatts arrival in the newspapers and called at the Bristol. The Cassatts dined with the Schiffs in their London house which Lois thought was "very fine." She liked Mr. Schiff, "but the Madame was rather common," she decided. In a terse and typical addition to the diary, Lois also noted: "They are evidently very rich. They are Jews."

By the end of January, 1884 Lois and Aleck were back in Paris, eager to see their children. But after a short reunion, they continued their continental tour. In Rome, Aleck left cards with John Jacob Astor, a fellow tourist. As Episcopalians, the Cassatts did not expect an audience with the Pope, but they left beads to be blessed by his Holiness. They visited the Forum and Colosseum. "I am amazed at the whole place . . . The amount of things to be done here makes me feel tired before I begin," Lois wrote to her mother. The baths of Caracalla impressed Aleck, who would remember their architectural wonder and insist on their recreation later in his life. Lois disliked the catacombs, but predictably, with her religious background, thought "the most beautiful and grand thing I have seen was St. Paul's." Her descriptions were neither literary nor perceptive. She became much more lyrical when describing the set of glass she ordered in Venice ($135), or the gold chain necklace three yards long Aleck bought for her. In Florence she shopped for Leghorn hats and mosaic pins. After visits to Turin and Naples, they returned to Paris on March 3. "We both suffered all the trip for homesickness for the children," and to their dismay, they discovered that the boys had contracted measles.

Among the many letters waiting for them in Paris, was a long report to Aleck from Roberts, who began: "The railroad world has been making some great revolutions especially in our own State since you went abroad." Vanderbilt had invaded the Pennsylvania territory in the bituminous coal country to the northwest. After an alliance with the Reading, he intended to build a line from the coal fields up through New Jersey and into New York. Construction of the Southern Pennsylvania, the line which rumor had indicated Cassatt might head, would give Vanderbilt's Central an independent outlet to the seacoast, gravely affecting the Pennsylvania's revenues. Roberts did not seem to know how to cope with this incursion into his territory by his rival. Most of the letter is a fulmination against Vanderbilt with little evidence that Roberts had decided upon a plan to thwart the Central. Roberts wrote about Vanderbilt: "I think he has been prompted into seemingly aggressive movements against us largely through jealousy, being goaded by a class of people by whom he is surrounded. Their characters you know as well as I do." Cassatt not only knew their characters, but he also knew how to repel the Central threat. This was exactly the challenge he had feared from Vanderbilt. Cassatt would have stepped in dramatically and stopped the Central, but that role was now to be J. Pierpont Morgan's. Dissatisfied European investors, who saw their dividends endangered by a ruinous railroad war, asked Morgan to intercede. In the summer of 1885 he summoned Roberts and Chauncey Depew, president of the Central, to a secret conclave aboard his yacht *Corsair* and insisted they settle their problems. If Roberts had followed Cassatt's policy of bold expansion, the Corsair surrender might have been avoided.

Always much more concerned with coal than with other aspects of the Pennsylvania, Roberts cheerfully turned to one of Cassatt's pet projects: a line from Chestnut Hill, the suburb across the river from the Main Line. Roberts urged Cassatt to come home and "lend a hand with this." He ended his report, "everybody desires to be remembered to you," as well they might. Several Pennsylvania officers realized that Cassatt was needed to direct the fight against Vanderbilt with the doggedness, ingenuity, and qualities of leadership for which he was known and for which Roberts was not.

Lois and Aleck spent March, 1883 in Paris while he finished his sittings with Mary for his portrait. Lois, too, wanted her portrait painted, but obviously Mary was not the artist to do it. She painted only one portrait of her sister-in-law, sometime during the winter of 1883, although Lois herself does not refer to it. Mary's most recent biographer describes the three-quarter view of Lois in a blue evening dress as showing "a tight-lipped lady. The sitter looks rigid; doubtless was." A family member, years later, looked at the picture which hangs in the dining room of Lois' granddaughter, Mrs. John B. Thayer, and said caustically, "It shows all of Lois' bad qualities." In the definitive catalogue of Mary's works, Adelyn Breeskin, notes briefly below the description of the painting, "They were not fond of one another." Lois would have to look elsewhere for a suitable portrait. Aleck asked Mary's advice, and she suggested Whistler or Renoir. On April 1, the Cassatts, once again leaving their children in his parents' care, traveled to London to seek out the famous artist.

Whistler had a reputation for being unreliable and sarcastic, but a furious worker. On her visit to his Chelsea studio, Lois found the artist "most polite and most curious looking." Lois tried on five gowns and was most disappointed when Whistler chose to paint her in her traditional black riding habit. By April 11, eight days after the first sitting, Lois wrote in her diary that the picture was so well advanced that she would not have to go often. She found posing tiring, but was grateful to the artist for introducing Aleck to the Beefsteak Club where he could meet "some nice men here this time." While Lois posed for Whistler, Aleck spent his time "trying horses" as Lois put it. Although she felt the painting was coming along well, the artist would prove agonizingly slow, accepting payment in full, but procrastinating about finishing it. His excuse, later, was that Lois had not allowed him enough sittings, but Mary could not accept that. She thought it an inferior portrait, "by no means a striking likeness." She wrote later to Aleck: "It is a work of Art, and as young Sargent said to Mother this afternoon, 'It is a good thing to have a portrait by Whistler in the family.' " (It was a good thing to have a Sargent in the family, too, but that artist waited many years to paint a Cassatt.) The Whistler portrait continued to give trouble. Mary concluded that Lois should have been painted by Renior after all, as she had first suggested, but neither Aleck nor Lois liked his work. After the Cassatts had returned to America, Whistler came to Paris and called on Mary. Her nephew Eddie wrote to his parents that the artist arrived with a cane about three and a half feet high and a glass in his eye. Mary met Whistler again at Degas' studio where his fellow guest was Oscar Wilde: "Oscar Wilde and he together are just as crazy a pair of men as can be found on the face of the earth."

Lois had hoped to be presented at Court before she sailed for home at the end of April, but Queen Victoria postponed the Drawing Room much to her disappointment. Mary brought Robbie, Katherine, and Elsie to London, visited Whistler, and said goodbye to her brother. Eddie would stay in Paris, much against the advice of the Buchanans, who wanted their grandson in Philadelphia. Mary had different ideas. After his initial difficulties Eddie did well at the École Monge, stood third in his class, and his aunt saw to it that he did his homework. Mary wrote a few months later to her brother: "I cannot understand you and his mother putting him in Haverford amongst those Quakers . . . their grammar alone is enough." Eddie remained at school until late July, writing home to his parents about his grades, his outings with Aunt Mary, his euchre games with his grandmother, and his cricket matches. Back in America, Aleck plunged into his farm where he was raising Shropshire sheep, Berkshire pigs, Guernsey cattle, and, he hoped, a winning stud. Although he had employed a resident manager, he felt the farm demanded his personal supervision. In fact, to all questions about his retirement, he replied, "Had to do it. The farm needed me." Chesterbook was always a solace and a pleasure.

The Pennsylvania Railroad, however, could not endure Cassatt's absence from the executive suite. And there is every evidence that much as Aleck welcomed his leisure and his hours with his horses and farm that he, too, wanted to keep in close touch with railroad affairs. On September 12, 1883, he was elected to the railroad's board of directors and made chairman of the road committee which considered the operations and additions to railroad equipment. William Patton echoed the prevailing opinion in a congratulatory letter: "Upon the reestablishment of your relations with your old associates. I have no hesitation in saying that the company is *more* to be congratulated upon securing the valuable aid which from your knowledge and experience will be able to render to its Directors and Officers." By this action Cassatt quieted the fears of many in his former company that he would desert them for a rival.

Racing took up most of Aleck's winter in 1883–84, but he told his father that if his horses did well, if he had a few winners, he might retire from the track. Just before his resignation in 1882, he had been elected a supervisor of Lower Merion Township, running on the Democratic ticket in this still heavily Republican Philadelphia suburb. Good roads were always a passion with Cassatt. Driving his four-in-hand out Montgomery Avenue to his Chesterbrook farm, he found the coarse gravel track exasperating, dusty, rutted, and hard on both horses and passengers. Soon after his election he began to macadamize Montgomery Avenue and then widened his scope to include all the main thoroughfares of Lower Merion Township. Within a few years, the township, under Cassatt's guidance had the finest system of macadamized roads in the nation. Roads were the first step, for in the 80s Cassatt's borough had few suburban amenities, no street lighting, no police force, no civic ordinances of any kind. Believing that the best materials were an economy in the long run, he insisted on granite curbstones and sturdy iron street signs, saving the Lower Merion taxpayers a tidy sum, for those curbstones and street signs are still in use.

Each year he won re-election as Supervisor with only token opposition until 1898.

Paralleling Montgomery Avenue was the main artery from Lancaster and the west, historic Lancaster Pike. The pike, too, was in deplorable condition. After the Civil War when Cassatt had first moved to Haverford, he assumed the burden of its repair and maintenance. He persuaded some of his wealthy neighbors to join him in buying the road, at a cost of $8,000, and formed the Lancaster Avenue Improvement Company. Tolls were collected at strategic stopping places along the 62-mile pike to help defray the expenses of maintaining the road. Lancaster Pike was operated as a private road until World War I, years after Cassatt's death, when the motorists he despised forced the state to assume the burden of operating the road.

While Cassatt was the guiding genius in their improvement, the actual details of the Lower Merion road supervision were entrusted to a young man, John Dunne, who remained on the job until 1922. Before one of his numerous trips abroad, Cassatt tried to persuade a neighbor to oversee the roads in his absence. The neighbor refused, pleading lack of time. Cassatt replied, "Why, Joe, there's nothing to it at all, but *damn Dunne.*" Behind his joking explanation lay a fundamental belief: Delegate authority, give your employees your trust, but if they fail to achieve results, see to it that they are reprimanded or removed. Cassatt had no patience with excuses. He made none for his own mistakes.

After Christmas of 1883 Aleck felt that Cassatt restlessness which could only be assuaged with travel. The Pennsylvania Railroad offered him a private car, No. 180, which he had used as first vice president, for a tour of the west. In late February he set off with Lois and Robbie for New Orleans. With them went Mrs. Sidney Hutchinson, her daughter, Cintra, and the Thomas McKeans and their son, Harry. The girls, Katherine and Elsie, were left at home with a German fraulien and Aunt Annie Buchanan. Eddie, at fourteen, had entered Haverford College. In New Orleans the party attended the Mardi Gras where Lois met the Jefferson Davises, and then they steamed on to Galveston, Texas, a rough voyage of forty-eight hours in a coastal ship. Car 180 met them in Mexico City, and they continued through Mexico, not knowing that the president of the country had attached a car to their train which was packed with $60,000 in silver, which reached its destination, as did the passengers, without incident. They intended to go home from El Paso but instead, at the last minute, extended their trip to California. Lois wanted to see her brother, Edward, his wife and two daughters who were living in San Francisco.

Edward Buchanan caused his family considerable anxiety. He could not hold a job because he drank more than was good for him to the agony of his wife, parents, and Lois. Aleck found him another job that year, in Colorado, but he did not prosper there and within a few months he resigned and returned to California. Edward Buchanan never conquered his alcoholism, and eventually his two daughters became the responsibility of their maiden aunts, Henrietta, Harriet, and Annie. In their letters to Lois about Edward's problem, the sisters were amazingly frank in discussing their brother's devotion to demon rum, unusual in Victorian days when such family disgraces commonly were covered with the decent hypocrisy of illness.

Grandfather Cassatt's letters followed Aleck to California. His wife's health had deteriorated, and by summer, Mary was suffering from bronchitis. He intended to send them to the south of France for the beneficial air. He missed his grandchildren a good deal and worried, too, about their health. Still believing in the beneficial qualities of sea bathing he gave his approval to Aleck's plans to take his family to Long Branch again that summer. At the racing resort Aleck's horses had a losing season, but he planned to send his horse, Brookwood, to England for the Derby that fall. To his father's delight, he wrote of coming to Europe soon himself. Whistler had still not completed Lois' portrait, and Aleck hoped to chivvy the artist personally. He was forced to delay his trip on Robert Cassatt's news that a cholera scare had swept Paris. But in late November he decided to go with Robbie, leaving Lois and the other children at home.

Except for this brief trip abroad and even shorter business trips, Aleck rarely traveled without Lois and his children. By temperament monagamous and genuinely devoted to his wife and family, he did not enjoy being away from home alone. He certainly could have created opportunities for the back street dalliance so prevalent among some industrial tycoons of the 90s, whose public propriety masked private lives reeking with scandal. He could have gone to Europe in the fall of 1884 alone, but he took Robbie. Alexander Cassatt possessed an austerity of character and a gentlemanly reticence about his private life which prevented any but his most intimate circle from penetrating his natural dignity. His family provided all the warmth and affection he needed.

After a brief family reunion in Paris, he left Robbie with his parents and traveled to London to discover why Whistler was delaying Lois' portrait. After checking into the Bath Hotel and ordering "a lot of clothes . . . two dress suits, riding suit, and a heavy warm top coat, boots from Lobb and stockings and gloves," he went to look at a stallion near Cambridge. A day later he appeared at Whistler's Chelsea studio, unannounced. The painter at the sight of his disgruntled client, gasped out in a frightened whisper. Aleck "heaped coals of fire on his head," whereupon Whistler took him into the studio, took down Lois' portrait, sponged it all over to bring it out, and "promised most faithfully to have it finished by my return here in two or three weeks."

Aleck did not like being alone in London and was not inclined to look up his friends. He watched the horses at Tattersall's, went to the theater, and caught a cold. By January 19 he was back in Paris at the Westminster Hotel and promised Lois to engage a cordon bleu cook, buy her a fan, and see to it that his sister, Mary, attended to all her commissions at the dressmaker, Armonds. Then, after still another abortive visit to Whistler, Aleck and his son sailed from Liverpool on the *Germanic* on January 29, 1885. They had been gone about six weeks.

By March, Aleck, who had been so anxious to retire from the railroad, was deeply immersed in a most ambitious scheme. He wrote to a fellow horseman, a Mr. Patterson in Toronto, about the horses he had bought in London but admitted, "I have been so busy with our Norfolk Railroad matters that I have had no time for anything else." The Norfolk Railroad matters evolved into the "Cassatt Line South," which absorbed his whole attention in the next few years.

The Cassatt
Line South

Norfolk, gateway to the rural heartland of Virginia, the Carolinas, and
Georgia lies over one hundred and forty-five miles to the south of Philadelphia. In the 1880s sophisticated Yankees hungered for the fresh delicacies
from Dixie—crabs, oysters, shrimps, berries, and peaches. Separating the
eager consumers from this gourmet fare was Chesapeake Bay, thirty-six
miles of choppy, treacherous water which prevented rapid shipment. Every
pound of produce had to be unloaded at Norfolk, shipped across the Bay
by steamer, and then reloaded onto boxcars or wagons for the North, an
interminable process, which raised the prices to unprofitable heights. Even
then, there were problems for no through rail line to Philadelphia existed.

Cassatt had never lost his interest in the agricultural and marketing
possibilities of the South since those long ago days when he had contemplated managing a Georgia vineyard. He realized that Southern produce
offered attractive profits, if only the trains could move the goods quickly and
economically across Chespeake Bay. He was not the only railroad executive
to understand the marketing future from Norfolk, even then a chief rail
terminus. But he was the first to expedite a plan which would move that
produce north at a speed rapid enough to put berries on the breakfast tables
of Philadelphians and the luncheon tables of Bostonians at the peak of their
freshness.

In 1881, while still vice president of the Pennsylvania, Cassatt was approached by William Lawrence Scott, a coal magnate with railroad interests
in the west, who had early seen the opportunities in an express line from
Norfolk. Scott, no relation to the late Pennsylvania president, had tried to

promote a line for some years but had found no backers. Like Cassatt, Scott bred race horses and cattle on his farms in Erie County, Pennsylvania, and Virginia. He was also deeply involved in politics, a legacy from his days as a page in the House of Representatives. He had served a term as mayor of Erie and would be a Democratic Congressman for two terms and his party's delegate to three presidential conventions. Upon his marriage to an Erie heiress, whose family had been pioneer railroad investors, he added to an already respectable income from Pennsylvania coal mines. Scott was a railroad man himself, but no engineer. He knew he must find an expert ally who could solve the problem of the Chesapeake if the Norfolk line were to become a reality. That expert was Alexander Cassatt.

Cassatt immediately warmed to the idea, his imagination stirred by the thought of linking the South to the Pennsylvania's expanding trackage. In 1881 his road purchased the charter to build a line down the Delmarva Peninsula from the Pennsylvania state line through Delaware and Maryland to Cape Charles, Virginia, and the right to operate a steamship from that port to Norfolk. Surveys began that same year, but Roberts refused to carry the project any further. He believed the line to be impractical. Cassatt did not agree. Before he thought of investing a penny of his own money, or even persuading the Pennsylvania to devote its assets to such an experiment, he decided to investigate the terrain. In the summer of 1882, he rode down the eastern shore of Maryland on horseback, a sixty-five-mile tour through forest and farmland which had drowsed since the Revolution, unaffected by the technology which was altering the face of the industrial northeast. That timber struck a responsive chord. Cassatt saw that not only farm produce, but also the untapped timber of the Southern forests would be eagerly welcomed by the Northern states whose own woods were fast being denuded by rapacious lumberman.

All along his route residents from the small Maryland towns pressed their demands for the line to run through their hamlets. Wherever the railroad traveled, wealth and progress followed, and Marylanders were not averse to sharing the fruits of railroad expansion. Cassatt, always the practical engineer, even when planning an unlikely venture, refused their requests. With his ruler he drew a straight line down the map of the peninsula. This would be the route of the railroad. Let the townspeople bring their business to his line, for it would not come to them.

He notified Scott that although the Pennsylvania was dubious about the scheme, he had decided to invest his own money in building the New York, Philadelphia, and Norfolk. Scott was willing to commit his own resources, but he worried about that thirty-six miles of water barring access to Norfolk. "How will you transfer your freight across the Chesapeake Bay expeditiously?" he asked Cassatt. "We will build powerful and fast transfer tugs that will transport loaded trains across the Bay . . . We can equip them with engines of sufficient power to make the run in three hours," was the reply.

Here was a revolutionary idea. Every railroad man who had thought of building a through route north from Norfolk had been stopped by the Chesapeake Bay and the reloading problems. Scott, too, believed the waterway to be too turbulent. At times it was rougher than the English Channel. But Cassatt never doubted that he could design tugs which would navigate the water barrier. He set to work to draw blueprints for steel barges which could carry eighteen railroad freight cars. When the design proved practical on paper, Cassatt once again offered Roberts the opportunity to let the Pennsylvania build the route, and again Roberts refused. Undaunted, Cassatt and Scott invested their own money and persuaded friends who had faith in the Cassatt magic to buy bonds in the proposed road.

In April, 1884, construction began on the New York, Philadelphia, and Norfolk, which would be known for many decades as "The Cassatt Line South." An existing branch line, nine miles long from Kings Creek, Maryland, to Pocomoke City, was the starting point. Tracks were laid from either end of this short line, north to the Pennsylvania border and south to Cape Charles. Mishaps occured at every juncture. The annual report of 1884 suggests some of the difficulties: All the switches had to be renewed to fit the Pennsylvania's standard, as did the sidings. Rosaris Garcia, an Italian laborer, had his arm crushed by a construction train running into some cars standing on the main track south of Accomac, Virginia. He was just one of the many victims of the construction. Two conductors were injured jumping from an engine. A brakemaster hurt his hand while trying to couple two flatcars. Accidents on the line continued. The Virginia legislature insisted on the road installing standard cattle guards to comply with the state law. The road beds proved so rough that oyster shell ballast was introduced to even the grade.

Progress, nonetheless, was rapid. By November 1, barely seven months after work had begun, the final foot of track was laid into Cape Charles at the tip of the Delmarva Peninsula. Ahead lay the Bay yet to be navigated. As a temporary measure, until his barges could be completed, Cassatt leased a steamer, the *Jane Moseley,* to take passengers from Norfolk to the Cape Charles station along with freight goods. In 1884, 53,874 tons of freight were carried and the net profit, after construction expenses, was $50,236.34.

Cassatt went to Washington that fall to urge the federal government to dredge a 1,000 by 600-foot channel in the Bay which would afford his heavy steel barges the proper draught. When the Departments of War and the Interior both refused, Cassatt paid for the dredging himself. By April, 1885, the barges were operating. Repair shops had been built at Cape Charles to service the flat cars and engines. In February Cassatt was elected president of the new line whose net earnings had fallen that year, 1885, to a meager $18,499.81. Twenty years later "The Cassatt Line South" showed a net return of more than $500,000. The barges had proved immensely successful. Railroad men the world over were influenced by Cassatt's feat. In Russia, the Trans-Siberian Railroad used his barge plan for transferring its trains across Lake Baikal, and later the Great Lakes introduced the same system.

Cannily, Cassatt had insisted that his independently owned road, which consistently paid a twelve percent dividend to its stockholders no matter what the profit and loss sheet listed, should give first option on future purchase to his previous employer the Pennsylvania. Cassatt held no grudges. His loyalty to the Pennsylvania overrode his disagreement with Roberts' shortsighted executive policies. While his former colleagues and the public believed that Cassatt had retired to breed his horses and holiday in Europe, he was devoting much of his time and energy to the Norfolk road. From 1885 until 1899 Cassatt remained head of the line, never accepting a salary for his services.

By the end of 1885, the harbor dredging was finished and "the high standard of excellence of our floating equipment was fully established by the performance of steamer and engines during the exceptionally severe winter which had prevailed," according to the annual report of that year. "The Cassatt Line South" encountered some rough financial periods, but the president contributed from his own resources to tide it over. Soon these emergency infusions of capital were unnecessary. Two years after Cassatt's death the Pennsylvania assumed ownership of the New York, Philadelphia, and Norfolk as he had intended. The great road offered $3.00 in bonds for every $1.00 in stock held by the investors and paid $7,478,000 for "the Cassatt Line South." The Pennsylvania, if it had heeded Cassatt's original advice, need not have paid a cent.

The opening of the new road caused considerable anxiety in the offices of shipping lines and rival railroads. If "The Cassatt Line South" were to prosper, its president had to overcome the animosity of the Southern railroads in order to cultivate advantageous interchanges with these lines. Eight roads entered Norfolk, and by 1898 the traffic had become clogged and competitive. Unwilling to endure these conditions, which endangered his line, Cassatt decided that a beltway around Norfolk should be constructed to ease the problem of interchanges. He secured a charter and directed a corps of engineers to make a survey for a ring line around the city. When the estimates were in, Cassatt sailed to Norfolk and anchored in the harbor. Then he called a meeting of the representatives of the eight competing railroad companies to discuss his plans and his estimates.

"Now, gentleman, if you feel that you would like to take an interest in this project, I am willing to turn it over at actual cost and give each line an equal share of the stock and equal representation in the management." Since the generous offer involved very little capital outlay on the part of each railroad, the offer was gratefully accepted and the beltway was completed by the end of 1898. Cassatt was far from altruistic, but he never pushed for an unreasonable profit, realizing that in the long run a sensible accommodation with his rivals was more to his benefit than a vindictive urge to triumph. He was not a greedy man.

By the summer of 1885, with his railroad off to a promising start, Aleck was able to take his family to Long Branch for the racing and the sea bathing so enthusiastically endorsed by his father. While he followed the fortunes of his horses on the track at Monmouth Park, his former chief, George P. Roberts, had entered deep waters, indeed. Vanderbilt's efforts to challenge the Pennsylvania in the coal lands had reached a climax. With the cooperation of Carnegie and Pittsburgh business interests, William Vanderbilt, aging but still indomitable, began constructing the South Pennsylvania Railroad, which would parallel the Pennsylvania's line east, connect with the Reading, and free Pittsburgh from the "thralldom" of the Pennsylvania. Already too many lines crisscrossed the heavily populated northeast, duplicating services and forcing ruinous rate wars which pushed many under-capitalized roads into bankruptcy. While the late nineteenth century was the great era of railroad building, it also ruined many roads. In the twentieth century there would be too many highways; in the late Victorian Age there were too many railroads.

Vanderbilt entered the competitive struggle with zest. He told his board of directors in October, 1884: "Our old road will not be behind any of its rivals, whether they are young or old . . . The fact is there has got to be further liquidation. Some companies among the trunk lines have confessed that they were not making much money . . . I feel the depreciation." Liquidation and depreciation would not be entertained by Vandebilt for a minute. He was convinced that the Pennsylvania, which had already weakened the Baltimore and Ohio's hegemony south of Philadelphia, would use similar tactics on his Central. The Pennsylvania planned to enter New York state.

Vanderbilt based his fears on concrete evidence. A year before he began his South Pennsylvania, yet another trunk was about to cross New York. The West Shore Line, surveyed to run along the Hudson, began operation, its stock held by the Pennsylvania, Vanderbilt discovered. In 1884 five trunk lines ran between Chicago and New York when three would have been ample. Now the West Shore accelerated the competition. Vanderbilt refused to allow this incursion into his territory without a fight. He countered with a raid on the Pennsylvania's heartland. First he enlisted the aid of Carnegie, always a foe of the Pennsylvania's freight monopoly in Pittsburg. Carnegie promised to put up $5,000,000 for the South Penn if Vanderbilt would match it with an equal sum. The New York Central head agreed, and work began immediately, proceeding at a furious pace.

While Cassatt, who had warned Roberts of this very contingency, pushed his independent New York, Philadelphia, and Norfolk toward completion, Vanderbilt's crews blasted through mountains, built bridges and laid track across Pennsylvania. The railroad rivalry raised frantic alarm among the industrialists and money men of Wall Street. The insuing rate war might benefit shippers for a time, but in the end losses would be heavy to both adversaries, and wages would be cut, markets decline, and business generally would suffer. In no way could the railroad war benefit the general public. Building two railroad lines over identical routes meant an enormous waste of capital which both the Pennsylvania and the Central would have to replace by raising passenger and freight charges.

It must be stopped. In New York, J. P. Morgan, who cared little for the general welfare—"I owe the public nothing"—refused to permit the railroad securities on which so much of his own personal wealth rested to be endangered by the egotism of warring railroad barons. Already, New York Central stock had declined in European markets between eight and four percent. Morgan made up his mind to "bring more harmony between the trunk lines." Some years earlier, in response to investors' pleas, Morgan had forced Vanderbilt to surrender to his dictates, and he now held a commanding position on the Central's Board. Vanderbilt must listen to his arguments for restraint.

Acquisitive by nature, Morgan collected first editions, paintings, cameos, tapestries, stained glass, but his deepest avarice was for power. Since the most powerful industrial force in America during the 80s was the railroad, Morgan collected trunk lines too. A complex man Morgan, whose chief ambition was to control the financial destiny of America. He had begun with the New York Central.

In July, 1885, Morgan summoned Chauncey Depew, Vanderbilt's surrogate and president of the Central, to a meeting with the Pennsylvania's Roberts aboard the Morgan yacht, the *Corsair*. While the opulent boat steamed idly in the Hudson River, safe from prying eyes and ears, Morgan pushed Roberts and Depew to an accomodation. While the two railroad presidents argued, Morgan sprawled in a chair, smoking his eternal black cigar, his large cold hazel eyes staring arrogantly from his craggy face, occasionally interrupting the protagonists with a sharp, brusque comment. He suggested that Depew sell the South Penn line to Roberts, and in return the Pennsylvania would turn over the "blackmailing" West Shore road, now on the verge of bankruptcy, to Vanderbilt's Central. Roberts refused. "I am not anxious to buy a hole in the ground," he argued contemptuously. Morgan continued to press him, reminding Roberts that the Central would pay fairly for the West Shore. The powerful financier ignored the Pennsylvania state law which expressly forbade any state railroad to purchase a competing line. Morgan was prepared to evade the law by acting as nominal buyer himself. The wily banker never allowed legality to obstruct profits, although he was always careful to observe the letter, if not the spirit, of a statute. Roberts at first seemed implacable, unwilling to yield to Depew or Morgan. On and on steamed the *Corsair* while the gentlemen argued, but Roberts was no match for the brooding Morgan, who allowed the two railroad heads to talk themselves to a standstill while saying little himself. Roberts refusal to compromise rested on his belief that he would be rescuing the Central, his chief rival, from sure financial debacle. Why should he do that? Finally, Morgan broke the deadlock. The Central would pay, and pay dearly, to the Pennsylvania for acquiring the West Shore.

Roberts capitulated. Morgan agreed to reorganize the West Shore and South Penn. Outside investors lost heavily but Morgan earned a profit of between one and three million dollars. The South Penn was abandoned, never to carry an engine along its tracks. The West Shore had its bonded indebtedness cut in half and became yet another Morgan asset. The chief gainer in these complicated transactions was Morgan, who now wielded a power in railroad affairs equal to the head of any road.

Neither Depew nor Roberts had been able to resist Morgan in a crisis. How would Cassatt have fared? In his less flamboyant fashion, Cassatt was as ruthless in the market place as Morgan. Astute enough not to place himself in Robert's humilating position, he dealt with Morgan subtly, allying with the financier, but never becoming his creature. If Cassatt had been the president of the Pennsylvania in the summer of 1885, it is doubtful if he would ever have found himself confined with his competitors aboard the *Corsair* at the mercy of Morgan.

Cassatt shared with Morgan an ability to take the long view, to reorganize and recapitalize, to commit his energies and talent to a profit-making venture whatever the odds or the obstacles. Both men realized that the stability of the country's economy rested on the railroads. They were willing to work together to assure the healthy condition of this vital industrial force, even if it meant government supervision. Morgan respected Cassatt and that respect was returned. Surely, a meeting aboard the *Corsair*, if it had come to that, would have had a different outcome if Cassatt's hand and not Roberts' had been directing the Pennsylvania that July day.

But while the *Corsair* was steaming in the Hudson River, Cassatt was watching the races at Monmouth. Railroad executives around the country shuddered at the Morgan coup and its implications, but Cassatt remained impervious to the machinations of the financiers and trunk line presidents. He had an opportunity to enter the war in a position of equal power to Vanderbilt and Roberts. The newspapers were constantly discussing the chances of Cassatt again entering the arena, heading a rival road, but the gentleman himself continued to express disinterest. Through his independent New York, Philadelphia, and Norfolk, however, he kept in close touch with railroad affairs. He did not yearn for greater power, and his directorship in the Pennsylvania insured his continuing loyalty to the road which had brought him prominence.

But the railroads were in trouble. Farmer and labor unrest throughout the nation during the late 1880s accelerated the demands from all sections of the public for government intervention. In 1886 the American Federation of Labor was organized to combat the Knights of Labor's effort to destroy the craft unions. The Haymarket violence in Chicago shook the complacency of all employers and serious disturbances in the steel industry were building toward a bloody crisis, the Homestead riot. All the great trunk lines, in a frantic effort to secure more business, increased rebates to favored shippers and cut rates at the expense of their employers and the public. Even the Pennsylvania, so conservatively managed by Roberts, was under fire.

In the 80s stockholders' demands for higher dividends became increasingly vociferous. Cassatt had an answer to these critics: "The existence of 'free railway laws' in nearly every state makes it possible for any group of men to parallel any existing road. The existing roads are therefore always subject to such attacks, and to maintain their financial position through bad and good years must pursue a policy that will hold their capitalization within bounds. The immense extent and complexity in this country makes a reasonable control of competition and the maintenance of remunerative rates a very difficult task. The tendency of rates is constantly downward, and all efforts that railway managers have made to maintain them have been practically fruitless. . . ." Tonnage had increased, and shippers, with larger profits, could afford to pay advanced rates, but the competitive situation and the lack of any effective regulatory agency kept the railroads in a state of flux. Naturally investors complained. Publicly, Cassatt defended Roberts' conservative financing and his insistence that profits be plowed back into improvements, but privately, he believed that recapitalization of the Pennsylvania was a more imaginative way to satisfy investors. Cassatt always showed an adventurous spirit, daring the impossible, which scared Roberts. In sum, investors were chafing and the public was angry.

In 1886 Congress investigated the Standard Oil Company and its dubious relations with the railroads. Cassatt, alone among railroad executives, had testified about the Rockefeller combine's blackmailing efforts to force the railroads into compliance. The situation was a disgrace, and now the public demanded government intervention in railroad management. If the trunk lines could not manage their affairs honestly and effectively, then they must be regulated. In April, 1887, Congress responded to the outcries by establishing the Interstate Commerce Commission.

This law answered many of the popular criticisms. Discrimination, rebates, and pooling of traffic were prohibited. No carrier would be allowed to charge more for a short than for a long haul, that detested practice which had earned the Standard such hatred. The Commissioners, five men appointed by the President for six years, were empowered to investigate all carriers and use appropriate measures to obtain any needed information. These measures were not spelled out, and, indeed, the language of the law was so vague that it would prove simple to circumvent. The ICC, on paper, answered many of the critics' protests, but, in fact the law did not appreciably alter the arrogant attitude of shippers or railroad executives.

Almost alone among railroad men, Cassatt applauded the Commission. He had urged the passage of such a bill as early as 1874, when the Pennsylvania had been forced into humiliating compliance with Rockefeller's demands. He hoped that the act would be vigorously enforced, but he was to be disappointed. The commissioners became figureheads, suspected of connivance with the railroads, rather than disinterested public servants. Astute lawyers, hired by the trunk lines, quickly learned how to evade the law. Not until the arrival of trust-busting Theodore Roosevelt in the White House would the Interstate Commerce Commission effectively control the rampaging railroads and the profit-swollen shippers. Ironically, one of the ICC's first victims would then be Cassatt.

In June, 1887, the Cassatts sailed again for Europe, this time remaining abroad for fifteen months, during which time Edward, was admitted to the Ecole Militaire at St. Cyr, through the good offices of the U.S. Secretary of War, W. C. Endicott. By mid-June, 1889, he had passed his entrance examinations and been admitted to West Point.

The senior Cassatts hailed their arrival, for Mr. Cassatt felt, at his advanced age, there could not be many more reunions. Lois wrote home that although he "was a very old man," he insisted on walking up the six flights to his Rue de Marignan apartment, ignoring the automatic lift. He also rode daily in the Bois but remarked that his horse bucked badly.

The following year, Lois and Aleck, after years of renting a winter residence in Philadelphia bought 202 Rittenhouse Square from architect Fairman Rogers for $100,000 and agreed to take it furnished for an additional $100,000. The Buchanan sisters, in Lois' continued absence abroad, hurried to inspect it. Harriet wrote: "I don't think the furnishing in the best of taste but we must remember it was done at the time when it was very hard to get pretty things in this country. . . ." Eventually, Lois auctioned off most of the offending decor for almost $2,000 and replaced the furniture with pieces she bought in Europe.

Lois' shopping trips in Paris and London were legendary. An account at London's Thomas Goode & Co. alone totaled over $1,500 and included two dozens each of hock glasses, sherry glasses, finger basins, and "ice" plates all monogrammed. The Cassatts now owned the Chesterbrook farm, the Haverford estate, and the Rittenhouse Square mansion. Still to come was another house and a yacht. All this in an era when mortgages were rarely offered and most real estate was paid for in cash. Where did the money come from for such lavish expenditure? The newspapers implied that Cassatt made most of his fortune during his retirement from coal, steel, and railroad stock. He held large blocks of stock in Westmoreland Coal Co., Pennsylvania Steel Co., and the Northern Central Railroad. Then, there were his Westinghouse investments and The Cassatt Line South. Certainly, by the end of the 80s he was worth several million dollars, and, of course, paid no income tax. Just twenty years before, he had regarded a $3,000 a year salary as princely.

Yet the expenses of a busy social life made inroads even into Cassatt's wealth. Eddie wrote in response to unsettling news from his mother, "Your letter about selling Cheswold was a great blow to me but if it is a question of financial necessity selling one of the places I am sorry to say that Cheswold seems pointed out to be the one to go. It would be very hard to ask Papa to give up Chesterbrook, especially as he would have nothing to do afterwards . . . Though I always opposed the house in town I recognize it as almost a necessity for Sister and Elsie when they go out into society . . . Of course it would break my heart to have to give up Cheswold and I could never consider anyplace else my home but I have only to submit with patience to what you and Papa decide is best to do."

Edward's letter is in dramatic contrast to contemporary reports of Cassatt's financial condition, and the only indication that the tremendous expenditures he made on houses, travel, and horses during his retirement caused any worry. This must have been a temporary situation for no further mention was made of selling Cheswold. George Roberts wrote to Cassatt that winter about the possibility of Aleck buying the Reading Railroad which was in dire straits. The Morgan *Corsair* pact had further eroded the position of several trunk lines, and the Reading was the chief loser in that agreement. He suggested that Cassatt take title to the Reading, after which the Pennsylvania might buy it from him. Possibly, the contemplated purchase of the Reading required Cassatt to realize all his assets and hence Cheswold. Nothing came of the plan, but all the roads were in difficulties. Mrs. Cassatt, who rarely commented on business affairs, wrote to Aleck from Paris that winter about "the trouble at the Penna. Railroad office."

By 1889 there had been a shift in the ownership of stock in the Pennsylvania, and 46.7 percent was held by foreign, mostly British, investors. The overseas stockholders pressed Roberts to revise his conservative policies, and a confrontation loomed. Roberts continued to insist on investing the major share of the company's profits in improvements and extensions which assured that its securities were safe and well regarded, but did not soothe the foreign owners, who began to sell their stock. From 1880 to 1896, the years of the Roberts' presidency, earnings failed to increase appreciably, due in part to the rate wars and the proliferation of lines over existing routes.

In the spring of 1889, the Pennsylvania Railroad sustained a disaster to its track and rolling stock more damaging than any since the strike of 1877. On May 30th a steady rainfall began in the middle of the state continuing throughout the night. By the next morning the waters at the South Fork below Johnstown were so swollen that the dam containing a reservoir of 15,000,000 tons of water was threatened. At mid-day the dam gave way, flooding the area, the rolling water sweeping all before its path—bridges, trains, cars, stations, and finally inundating Johnstown itself. More than 1,600 houses were destroyed, and 2,500 people lost their lives in the Johnstown flood. Roberts told his stockholders that the destruction to the Main Line of the Pennsylvania totaled over $3,000,000, and this amount did not include losses from the disruption of service. It was two weeks before the first passenger train could use the Main Line to Pittsburgh, all trains having been detoured by the North Central Line from Harrisburg and then the Erie to Pittsburgh. It was the greatest disaster the railroad ever faced , and Cassatt was not there to help.

Horses and Holidays

All his life Cassatt had been enamored of horses, even of the smells and noises of the stable and race track. His career as a racing owner had begun long before he left the railroad. The purchase of Chesterbrook enabled him to take up racing and breeding seriously. The Cheswold home, although a country residence, did not offer enough scope or land, barely forty acres for grazing. In April, 1881, he finally found the stock farm which satisfied his demands, twenty miles from Philadelphia, near a small hamlet called Howellsville. Piece by piece he added to the farm through the years until eventually Chesterbrook included over 600 acres. He remodeled the Revolutionary farmhouse into a suitable residence with two sunporches, five bedrooms, four baths, and servants quarters, a comfortable gentleman's dwelling of fieldstone set amid the green pastures, well hidden from curiosity seekers. Half a dozen wooden barns were added for the horses he now began to buy from all over the country and abroad. He installed a manager to oversee the farm, but whenever possible supervised the horses' exercise and breeding himself.

Because of his position in the railroad he initially entered his horses under the name, Mr. Kelso, but after 1882 he abandoned this soubriquet for his own name. His first winner was Rica, named for his friend August Belmont's daughter. In 1878 Cassatt formed a syndicate to purchase the Monmouth track in New Jersey. Joining him in the venture were Belmont, Pierre Lorillard, the Virginia tobacco titan, newspaperman James Gordon Bennett, and D. D. Withers, a New York merchant with South American business interests.

Monmouth had opened in 1870 to provide the patrons of nearby Long

Branch with sophisticated racing. Under the aegis of its distinguished association, Monmouth offered the largest stakes and the best facilities for racing in the East, rivaling Saratoga, Coney Island, and Jerome Park, the latter founded by Winston Churchill's father-in-law, Leonard Jerome. Included in Monmouth's 600 acres were two huge tracks, an enormous grandstand 210-feet deep and 700-feet long, a broad balcony dining room which shaded seventy-five feet of lawn, and box stalls for ninety-six thoroughbreds. The Monmouth Clubhouse, which attracted every prominent racing figure in the country, measured 1,100 feet, dwarfing race courses of today. Lorillard, president of the association which had developed Monmouth, was eventually succeeded by Cassatt, about to enter the apex of his career as a breeder and racer of champions.

Racing, with its betting, the sport of New York's high livers, appalled the Buchanans, strengthening their belief that marriage to Cassatt had introduced Lois to the path of frivolity if not of outright sin. Aleck's parents, his sister Mary and Lydia, shared his feeling for horses and followed his progress on the turf with passionate interest. His mother wrote him from Paris: "We were glad to hear the racing was so much better than usual this year *because* you know you said if you once made a good hit you would quit . . . it seems to me to be pretty nearly as hard work as any kind of business a man could go into." Expensive, demanding, frustrating, the life of a race horse owner, however, offered all of the excitement and challenge Cassatt wanted. He persisted in his efforts to find the perfect horse and in the end, he succeeded.

In May, 1884 Aleck bought The Bard, a bright bay yearling with black points, for $1,800 at a Tennessee auction. Turf critics insisted that the pride of the Chesterbrook stables was not a "pretty" horse, but acknowledged his immense stamina and "great dimensions."

Cassatt entered The Bard in his first race on June 25, 1885 at Coney Island, where the two-year-old came in second in the Great Post Stakes, a rewarding beginning. A month later he won his first race at Monmouth; and several other victories followed that summer. The Bard, whose considerable success on the track was to be interrupted by injuries, suffered his first mishap that autumn at Coney Island when he was crowded into the rail and badly scraped. Cassatt worried over the injury but was convinced The Bard would recover and become the constant winner he had always sought. The next year The Bard placed second in The English Derby, a great satisfaction to his owner.

The Bard's season as a three-year-old was phenomenal, justifying all Aleck's hopes. He beat his stable partner, Eurus, in the Preakness and went on to win five more races on the eastern tracks. In August and September, 1886, The Bard triumphed over every competitor at Monmouth, Jerome Park, Baltimore, Coney Island, and Washington. The crowds at Monmouth adored The Bard, and by the time he was a four-year-old, racing fans hailed

him as one of the most brilliant horses in the sport's history. His stable
mates proved less exciting during the 1885–1886 season. Mrs. Cassatt wrote
to her granddaughter Katherine: "You speak of the disappointments in the
racing at Long Branch. I was disappointed too and it seems to me that I
should prefer a breeding farm and let the racing alone"—a view her son
would also eventually take.

But in 1886 Cassatt had no intentions of leaving racing. Then, at the top
of his form, The Bard suffered a sudden and seemingly fatal illness, drown-
ing all Cassatt's visions of another winning record. Veterinarians diagnosed
The Bard's trouble as stoppage of the bowels and gave the horse injections
which further injured the delicate tissues. For weeks the gallant horse
hovered on the verge of death at Chesterbrook, but incredibly he rallied and
at last recovered fully. Back on the track, however, his old form seemed
gone, and he lost several races during 1887. Cassatt, discouraged, sent The
Bard to Saratoga where the bracing air revived the thoroughbred.

On August 4, 1887 The Bard returned to his home track to race in the
Freehold Stakes against Troubadour, the champion of Pittsburgh millionaire, Captain Sam Brown. The odds that day were three to five against The
Bard and habitués of the track thought that the great horse seemed stiff and
tired as he began the mile and a half contest. But as the two rivals entered
the home stretch, he pulled even and then passed Troubadour to the frantic
excitement of the crowd which chanted "The Bard, The Bard," when he
crossed the tape, the winner. Cassatt, in France with his family that summer, missed the triumphant win at Monmouth.

As a five-year-old in 1888, The Bard continued to win races, but the tragic
finale to his career came in August. At Monmouth before his ardent cham-
ions and with his owner again in Europe, The Bard pulled up lame in the
Freehold Stakes. The "turf idol of his time" was finished, retired to Chesterbrook and put to stud. The Bard had proven equal to all Cassatt had asked
of him, and his triumph was shared by another Chesterbrook champion,
whose success capped Cassatt's final year of racing.

On August 15, 1889, from his owners box, Cassatt prepared to watch his
champion, Eurus, compete in the Monmouth Handicap, a mile and a half
contest with a purse of $3,000. A night's rain had slowed the course, which
in racing terms, "was pasty and holding, very trying for a horse to run
over." The odds against Firenzi, the 1888 winner of the cup and a favorite
to repeat his victory, were 6 to 5. Cassatt's magnificent six-year-old had
many previous laurels in his crown, but the thousands of excited fans did
not expect him to beat Firenzi. A large and distinguished crowd thronged
the grandstand and the newly planted green lawns before the course to
watch this running of the Monmouth Handicap, the fifth race of the afternoon.

Eurus, under the guiding hand of jockey Hayward, started slowly but
moved up confidently during the final half mile, beating off the challenge

of Firenzi early and wearing down Senorita in the stretch. Eurus neared the tape, a length and a half ahead, then suddenly he faltered. As the stunned crowd watched, his foreleg buckled, but Hayward, whipping him on, brought him in a clear winner. The victory of the 1889 Monmouth Cup proved to be a costly one for Cassatt. The injury to Eurus' foreleg was permanent. He would never carry Cassatt's colors again. The champion's final race had been the last of many triumphs, for the Texas bred horse had won the Suburban Handicap at Sheepshead Bay in 1887 and at odds of 20 to 1 had captured the Brooklyn Handicap that same year, as well as several purses at Jerome Park and Coney Island. August 15 was not only his last appearance, but the last of any Cassatt thoroughbred on a New Jersey race course.

New Jersey racing had long been clouded by venality. Outlaw tracks sprang up around the state, as the popularity of racing and the gambling which attended it attracted a growing coterie of fans. Cassatt and his syndicate had insisted that Monmouth Park become the most luxurious in the country. Just the year before, the association had vastly increased the acreage at Monmouth, enlarged the betting ring and the stables, and paved the muddy ground before the repainted grandstand. Only the best thoroughbreds were invited to race at Monmouth. Answering the challenge of the outlaw tracks which thrived at Brighten and Harlem, the Jockey Club insisted that horses which were entered in these unsupervised races would be barred from Monmouth. The outlaw tracks had dangerously enlarged the field in order to increase betting profits. Naturally, owners of the maverick tracks were not willing to surrender their profits because of the probity of Cassatt and his associates. New Jersey law did nothing to protect the upright patrons of the turf, and conditions deteriorated rapidly as racing authorities in the state succumbed to bribes and inducements from the outlaw track owners. Cassatt and his association had decided to close Monmouth after the August 15 racing day.

His horses' injuries and the maneuverings of the outlaw track owners had greatly diminished Cassatt's enthusiasm for racing, but on this final day, worse was in store. The outlaws had finally secured the cooperation of the state racing authorities. As Eurus was led from the winner's circle by Cassatt, two constables approached him. While he was still receiving the congratulations of his friends, Cassatt was arrested by the New Jersey state authorities. The charge on the summons accused him, under an old state blue law, of "running a disorderly house" at the Monmouth race track. This shocking charge, especially repugnant to a man of Cassatt's dignity and reserve, implied only one thing: In the parlance of the times, a disorderly house was a brothel. What could be more abhorrent to a man like Cassatt!

Although the constables made no attempt to detain him or his fellow defendant, D. D. Withers, treasurer of the association, the publication of the arrest created the effect for which the pool sellers had hoped. A *New*

York Times reporter, who interviewed Cassatt that day at his Long Branch vacation home, believed that the arrest was "an act of retaliation" done solely "to annoy the gentlemen." Cassatt himself made little attempt to answer the charges. A spokesman for the association, J. N. Galway, insisted that the arrest had been in revenge for its refusal to allow the poolroom off-track betting shops to run a telegraph wire into Monmouth. Galway said the pool halls were "kept by disreputable people . . . their effect was demoralizing." The pool hall owners on the other hand charged that Monmouth had denied permission for the wire because it would keep fans from attending the races. Galway dismissed this complaint disdainfully: "Pool room customers are not the sort of people who go to race tracks. They could not afford it."

Cassatt, never eager to be interviewed either in trouble or in triumph, told the *Times* reporter that he "was satisfied that the Association was conducting a proper and lawful business under the New Jersey statutes." He did not know whether the matter would be pushed by the pool room people. He implied that he did not care, that the matter was beneath his notice. The arrests were a technicality. But the purpose of the pool hall owners had been achieved. Monmouth Park closed on August 15, 1889 and removed its stakes to Jerome Park and Coney Island. The Park reopened briefly in 1890 and 1893, but repressive legislation again forced its closing, and thoroughbreds did not race again at the best track in New Jersey until 1946.

Of more importance to racing in the 1890s, the arrest publicity forced Cassatt into a decision he had contemplated for some time—to retire from the competition. He had assured his mother that if he ever trained a big winner he would do just that, and he kept his promise. Two champions had carried his colors, Eurus and The Bard. He had satisfied his dream, but the scandals surrounding those final days at Monmouth left an indelible impression. The whole affair was distasteful, making Cassatt a figure of notoriety in the public eye, endangering his reputation for upright sportsmanship. In 1891 when his fellow defendant, D. D. Withers, formed a Board of Control to combat corrupt racing tactics in New Jersey, Cassatt consented to be a member, and when the board's function was taken over by the Jockey Club, he was among the founders. Cassatt took an active role in the Monmouth Park Association for another three years, but he never raced again.

Not mentioning the scandals, Cassatt wrote to his racing companion, William Pattison, in the fall of 1889: "I have come to the very sudden determination to retire from racing, temporarily at least, and sell all yearlings at the New York Horse Exchange on the 29th of this month." Cassatt's thirty-four yearlings and twelve race horses from the Chesterbrook stud brought the disappointing price of $46,515. The auctioneer on announcing the sale attributed it to Mr. Cassatt's temporary retirement from the turf. No other explanation was offered, even to Pattison. A knowledgeable racing reporter for *Harper's Weekly* wrote: "Cassatt's judgment, integrity and liberality made him for a time one of the most successful as well as the most prominent figures of the American turf."

Both The Bard and Eurus enjoyed an honorable old age at Chesterbrook, not sold at the auction which signaled Cassatt's retirement from racing. He had accomplished what he had wanted: the proud distinction of capturing both the great spring handicaps, the Suburban with Eurus, the Brooklyn with The Bard. *Harper's Weekly* reminded its readers: "This is a feat no other turfite has yet accomplished. It is earnestly hoped that Mr. Cassatt will at an early date reconsider his determination not to race."

But Cassatt resisted all such blandishments. Diamond Jim Brady, that orotund and flashy New York bon vivant, adopted the Cassatt racing colors, blue, red, and white, and they were not seen again under the Cassatt name until Aleck's elder son, Colonel Edward Buchanan Cassatt, took up breeding and racing after World War I. With his usual singlemindedness Cassatt turned instead to hackneys, cross breeding the English horse with the American trotter. The April 9, 1892 *Harper's Weekly* published an article by Cassatt on his hobby. He wrote about the horses which had now become the pride of the Chesterbrook stables: "Little is known of the origin of the hackney breed . . . defined in Johnson's Dictionary as 'a hired horse.' That he owes some of his good qualities to Arab crosses is probable. Where but from the Eastern horse could he get the broad forehead, the lofty carriage and high croup, the brisk cheerful temper, the extreme docility combined with resolute courage, that alike mark the true hackney and the Arabian horse?" In all, Cassatt wrote in a lively, knowledgeable style over 6,000 words about the hackney, concluding with praise of the breed "which comes to supply a long-felt want." Certainly it supplied a long-felt want for Cassatt, who never abandoned the hackney as he had the thoroughbred racer. He drove his hackneys himself in horse shows all over the country and until two years before his death always showed them in the annual classic at Madison Square Garden.

In the fall of 1892 he bought his great hackney stallion, Cadet, "the best horse in England," for $3,000. King Edward VII had won the Derby with Cadet's son, Field Marshall, and the line had great promise. Although Cadet was eight years old when Cassatt bought him, his form and manner were still impressive. When Cassatt first showed Cadet at the Chestnut Hill Horse Show in 1893, he took a blue ribbon, then went on to take first place honors in horse shows from Baltimore to Kansas City. Cadet became the sire of winners, all bred by Cassatt at Chesterbrook. Equally as famous was another of his English purchases, the hackney Little Wonder bought in 1888, for $5,000. These two hackneys became the stars of the Chesterbrook stable, but there were other fine blooded horses as well.

Philadelphia artist Thomas Eakins turned to Cassatt when he needed a model for his Civil War Memorial in Prospect Park, Brooklyn. Fruitlessly he searched for a horse which could serve as an inspiration for General U.

S. Grant's mount until a friend recommended Cassatt. He found his model at Chesterbrook. Cassatt's "Clinker" is forever immortalized in the Eakins sculpture in Brooklyn.

Three times a week at least, Aleck drove his prized tandem pair, Astra and Evening Star, Comet and Morning Star in his four-in-hand carriage from Haverford to Chesterbrook along the macadamized roads he had insisted be built for proper coaching drives in Lower Merion Township. In his tall gray silk hat and impeccable riding gear, he cut an impressive figure tooling along the unfrequented roads, an object of much admiration to the summer residents and local farmers.

Cassatt also rode to the hounds, was president of the Radnor Hunt, and host to a meet every season at Chesterbrook. His hunters were strong noble animals well able to carry his considerable weight, for as Aleck grew older his large frame became more massive, never obese, but heavy. His favorite horse, Fanny, which he rode until his death, had been bred from a strain of thoroughbred and Percheron to carry him comfortably.

Although Robert Cassatt had feared that Chesterbrook, with its extensive stables and crews of grooms and trainers, would be a mere rich man's toy, a needless drain on his son's fortune, it proved in fact to be an asset. After the first few years, Chesterbrook was always a money maker, due to Aleck's superior management skills. He kept a careful eye on the purses his horses won and held out for the maximum stud fees for the champion stallions. He insisted that the horses pay their way.

During the seventeen years of his retirement from the railroad, horses, their breeding, training, and racing fortunes, seemed to satisfy Cassatt's deepest needs. But in the spring of 1891, he accepted another responsibility. An international conference had finally endorsed the long planned intercontinental railway. President Benjamin Harrison, overriding political considerations, for Cassatt was a Democrat, appointed the former Pennsylvania officer to the commission which would superintend the railroad. When the commission, made up of representatives from both continents, met later that year, Cassatt was elected president, his qualifications far superior to that of the other delegates.

Two years later, in 1893, Democrat Grover Cleveland appointed Cassatt to the Board of Visitors at West Point, a signal honor for a non-military man, and a duty he took seriously even after his son left the Military Academy. During Edward's years at West Point, his father always spent New Year's Day and Easter at the Academy as well as the official visitors' fortnight in June. Cassatt must have had an affection for the military life. He avidly pursued a membership in the Society of the Cincinnati, that distinguished association of descendents of George Washington's officers. In the spring of 1891, he applied for membership in the order, citing his direct descent from his maternal great grandfather, James Johnston, ensign in the Fifth Regiment of the Pennsylvania Continental Line. His application, as the chief male descendent, was accepted. This ardor for the military seems all the more surprising when one remembers that Cassatt had made no effort to join the Union Army in his youth. He may have regretted that decision and now vicariously enjoyed the camadarie of arms through these associations.

In the early 90s the Cassatts traveled frequently—sailing back and forth to Europe to visit Aleck's family, going to the Hot Springs, to Florida, to South Carolina, as well as taking a memorable trip to Cuba, where, as Lois wrote in her diary, "We had a peep at the best society in the city of Havana." Lois reveled in the "best society" in Philadelphia, too. With her youngest child, Elsie, in a proper New York boarding school, Edward at West Point, and Katherine frequently away at fashionable resorts, she filled her time with purely social pursuits, balls, teas, the Emergency Aid, queening at Rittenhouse Square receptions. At home or abroad the Cassatts lived in regal style. President Roberts often lent them his private car No. 60 for their travels, adding to Lois' sense of consequence.

The ceaseless round of pleasure, journeying, entertaining, and being entertained seemed to satisfy Aleck as he entered middle age and contemplated the passing of the years which had brought him, if not all the prizes he sought, much fulfillment. But time was taking its toll. In April, 1891, after a painful illness, Lois' mother died in her Philadelphia home. The following winter, on December 5, Robert Cassatt suffered a fatal heart attack in Paris. Aleck would miss him, and Mary, who had seen a brother, sister, and father die, was left alone with her mother in France.

Aleck had now been retired for ten years, but efforts to lure him to positions of influence, in the railroad, in racing, and even in politics continued. His contemporaries could not understand his reluctance to become involved, his aloofness from all the seats of power. In the spring of 1892, he was urged by the Democratic Party to run for mayor of Philadelphia, a Republican stronghold. Edward, understanding his father's reluctance to enter such a rough and tumble arena, told his mother: "Papa writes me that he has decided not to accept the nomination for Mayor of Phila., and I am glad of it, as there is always so much newspaper talk connected with a campaign." Edward knew his diffident father hated publicity, and politics in the 90s offered little dignity.

The depression of 1893, largely caused by the continuing rate wars of the railroads, did not appreciably affect the fortunes of the Cassatt family. Aleck continued to show his hackneys, to travel, to live the luxurious life of a country squire. While Lois enjoyed the city social life, Aleck preferred to entertain at Chesterbrook. A highpoint of every spring during the 90s was the point to point race, preparations for which Lois found "annoying and most constant." In June, 1893, Edward graduated from West Point and returned home to await his cavalry appointment. Mrs. Cassatt sent her congratulations from Paris: "Your letter was very welcome telling us as it did that you were all well and had Eddie at home. He must feel as if he had reached paradise after West Point." He did and capped that delight by becoming engaged to Emily Phillips whom he had met at one of the summer dances in the nearby Bryn Mawr Hotel. As might be expected, Emily, whose parents lived in Holmesburg, New Jersey, was a ravishingly pretty girl. The wasp-waisted gowns of the period showed her striking figure to great advantage, and even the faded photographs of the day fail to mask her obvious charm. She had masses of dark hair and sparkling brown eyes, a real coquette, with delicate fine-boned features and a refined air. Lois, who would have looked askance at any choice of her wayward son, resented and disliked her son's fiancée from the beginning. Fortunately, the young couple began their new life far away from Lois' disapproving eye in Walla Walla, Washington, where Edward's cavalry regiment was stationed.

With his family growing up, Aleck now sought new outlets for his energy —travel and horses did not sufficiently challenge his restless nature. In the summer of 1894, he rented a yacht, the *Ramona,* and cruised up the eastern seaboard. As a young man, working for the Erie Railroad, he had spent many profitable hours piloting a small craft on Lake Erie. Now, he returned to his earlier enthusiasm. After all, yachting, like blooded horses, was a suitable sport for a Victorian millionaire. From June until September, 1894, the Cassatts cruised aboard the *Ramona.* When they returned after a three week layover in Bar Harbor to repair the yacht, they found a telegram from Edward announcing the birth of their first grandchild, Lois Buchanan Cassatt, on September 10, in Walla Walla.

1895 began inauspiciously and continued to bring increasing worry for the Cassatts. Emily arrived with little Lois, who had been born with a hip and foot defect which needed correction. This was Cassatt's first glimpse of the grandchild who would become such a joy and solace to him. He adored her, and none of his other grandchildren ever meant quite as much to him. The Philadelphia physicians advised an operation, but since this could not be performed until the baby was at least a year old, Emily took her back to Walla Walla.

During Emily's visit, the Reverend Buchanan, totally blind and incapacitated, died in his Pine Street house where he had been cared for by his spinster daughters, Henrietta, Harriet, and Annie. Lois sincerely mourned her father. He had been a thorn in the side of his children, demanding, critical, and sanctimonious, but the Buchanan sisters never acknowledged their father's less attractive qualities. Nothing evident in the Reverend Buchanan's manner or accomplishments explains his children's devotion but, typical Victorians, they dedicated themselves to him without question. For Aleck his passing could only have been a relief. Their relationship had never been close, in contrast to the mutual affection and admiration he had enjoyed with his own more worldly father. Yet Aleck had always been the most dutiful of son-in-laws, never disputing the Reverend

Buchanan's influence upon Lois and generously providing financial assistance when needed. In the summer of 1895, Aleck and Lois crossed the Atlantic for a final visit with his mother. She died in Paris that fall, leaving Mary alone, free at last from domestic demands. Now, both the Cassatt and the Buchanan elder generations had disappeared, although their influence remained.

In Europe Aleck chartered another yacht, the *Star of the Sea,* embarking from Southampton with his family for a cruise around Norway and Scotland. Pleased with sailing, Aleck decided to buy the yacht and rechristened it *Enterprise.* Lois, always a bit carping about her husband's extravagant gestures, was happy to leave the ship at Aberdeen with Aleck and take the train to London. The Cassatts traveled home by commercial steamer leaving a British crew of fifteen to bring the *Enterprise* across the Atlantic. The voyage was perilous, and the yacht almost foundered in the stormy seas. Without its mainsail, the *Enterprise* limped into Delaware Bay on faltering engines.

The Philadelphia newspapers described the *Enterprise* as "one of the most elaborately fitted vessels afloat." Its salon was furnished in bird's eye maple and walnut with a frescoed ceiling, and the interior fittings alone were rumored to cost $40,000. The purchase price exceeded $500,000, although Cassatt never revealed the exact amount. He, no doubt, agreed with J. P. Morgan that if you have to ask the price of owning and running a yacht, you can't afford one.

In the fall the Edward Cassatts, with little Lois, returned to Philadelphia for the dreaded operation on the baby's foot and hip. Eager to be in the East where the best surgeons were available, Edward had asked his father to use his influence in Washington for a post near home, and he was duly appointed assistant professor of languages at West Point, a position he was more than qualified to fill after his expensive European education. Emily remained in Philadelphia until Lois had recovered from her operation, and then they joined Edward at West Point. "So ended a very trying year in many ways," Lois Cassatt wrote in her diary.

The year had also been very trying for the fortunes of the Pennsylvania Railroad. Despite President Roberts judicious investments, conservative policies, and a far-sighted inauguration of improvements on the line, the railroad saw its income fall steadily although freight and passenger traffic increased. By 1895 the Pennsylvania's net income had shrunk from $9,000,000 to $7,000,000. To counteract the erosion, more stock was offered, but not as eagerly bought as in the past. Freight profit declined from 2.25 to 1.96 percent per mile, and dividends fell from eight to five percent. The Pennsylvania, still considered the greatest single industrial corporation in the nation, was standing still. Under President Roberts, progress had halted.

Aleck, occupied with his horses at Chesterbrook or in planning yet another journey, ignored the railroad's decline. In January, 1895, the Cassatts embarked on their most ambitious trip yet, a leisurely meander through Egypt and down the Nile. With them went their daughters Elsie and Katherine, who was now twenty-five and waiting patiently for her favorite beau, Dr. James Hutchinson, to make his way up the medical ladder. Katherine's health worried her father, and he hoped the tropical Egyptian heat would improve her condition. Fading photographs in the family album show Aleck reading, beside a stately, black gowned Lois, in a dahabeah drifting down the Nile. They reached the first cataract, but had to turn back "on account of the dervishes." Other photographs show Aleck, in a topee, his manner redolent with dignity astride a camel, impassively gazing at the Sphinx. No letters survive from this trip which extended from Cairo to Naples, where Elsie caught the measles from a German countess, and the family waited patiently during her convalescence. Although Lois rarely revealed any but the most cursory interest in the architecture, painting, or history of the countries they visited, for Aleck, distant climes and sights evidently held a real satisfaction and travel remained a favored recreation.

Back home in Philadelphia, the pattern of Cassatt life continued on its measured pace. The girls and Lois followed the social round, changing from town to country with the seasons. Edward and his young family remained at West Point, while Robert, now graduated from Harvard, went off to Altoona to learn about railroading as his father had before him, but without such fortunate results. He wrote to his mother in disgust about the railroad town: "I guess I can stand it for awhile. The noise and the dirt in the 'erecting shop' where I am, something extraordinary. . . ." Robert would soon abandon railroading, and Aleck would have to assist him in establishing a brokerage firm.

If neither of his sons showed any of the talent or firm determination to succeed in the world so evident in their father, Aleck himself was to blame. He had always been a compassionate father, paying their debts and making few demands upon them. Robert and Edward both depended financially on him. Earlier, Robert had informed Lois from Harvard in a typical letter: "I wrote to Pa the other day and gave him a full list of my financial affairs. He wrote me an awfully kind letter which made me much ashamed of myself." Not ashamed enough to alter his ways, however. Edward and Robert were charming, cultivated men with great social poise and easy manners, but they never saw the need to exert themselves in the competitive business world. Soft living seemed to have robbed them of their father's drive and genius. They saw no need for either. Papa would provide—and Papa did.

As the nineteenth century ended, Alexander Cassatt could contemplate with pride all that he had achieved. His personal fortune was secure and rising, while his reputation as a railroad man still commanded attention and respect. If his personal happiness in the family circle, offered no romantic excitement, it, at least, provided a tranquil shelter which he found satisfying. At fifty-eight Aleck could look forward, not to challenge, but to a comfortable progress toward old age. He preferred this measured pace.

Both his private and professional lives, however, were about to be disturbed. Early in 1897, George P. Roberts suffered a last attack from the valvular heart condition which had plagued him for years. He died in his Bala Cynwyd home, like Thomson and Scott before him, a victim of the pressures of his office. The Pennsylvania mourned him dutifully, but the directors needed a successor who could push the railroad vigorously into the new century.

The Reluctant President

On February 3, 1897 the directors of the Pennsylvania Railroad gathered around the massive circular table in the austere boardroom of the line's headquarters on Broad Street to elect a successor to Roberts. Cassatt attended the meeting, but he obviously had not considered himself as that successor: He had already given orders to the captain of the *Enterprise* to prepare for a lengthy cruise up the Atlantic seaboard.

Roberts had committed the railroad to a development plan which the new president would have to carry out. The Pennsylvania was already elevating its tracks in Elizabeth, New Jersey, and North Philadelphia where congestion had reached such a point that local traffic would soon be forced to a stop or into an inconvenient detour. Roberts had been spending, in a time of increasing business depression, $2,000,000 to reduce grades and curves, build a bridge from Philadelphia to Camden to replace the cumbersome ferry, and double tracking the entire Main Line to Pittsburgh. All these improvements had been introduced without seeking additional capital, an increasing drain on current expenses. The late president had seen fit to ignore the trend of ton-mile and passenger rates which was ever downward, now at the lowest ebb in the company's history. How would the Pennsylvania reverse the trend?

Conditions were ominous. The country was debating the gold standard. William Jennings Bryan, the perpetual populist, agitated for income tax and free silver. Agrarian discontent, fueled by the 1896 depression, forced the government to heed the high tariff advocates and contributed to the fall of industrial exports. Most serious was the continued decline in transportation revenue. The country's biggest employers, the railroads, were in trouble. Now was the time for a strong man who would not be afraid to expand and recapitalize the Pennsylvania. Timid half-measures would not work. But, even in death, Roberts' philosophy prevailed. Conservative men and management were his legacy. *The New York American* reported that Roberts had warned the Pennsylvania's board that Cassatt intended revolutionary changes for the Pennsylvania. Panic-stricken at Roberts' picture of a Cassatt-run railroad, the board chose a safe man: prudent, frail, hardworking Frank Thomson, nephew of the very different Edgar Thomson.

With his usual reticence Cassatt refused any comment on Thomson's election. Newspaper stories implied on one hand that Cassatt did not want to abandon the joys of retirement, and on the other that he would not take the chief office at the expense of his life-long friend. Thomson after all had spent the last fifteen years on the job, while Cassatt had been racing at Monmouth, sailing the Atlantic, drifting down the Nile, and idling in Paris with his family. Like all rumors both stories held some truth. Cassatt did not want to leave his enjoyable retirement, and he truly liked Thomson and thought he deserved the job.

Others were not so kind: *The New York American*, reporting Thomson's election, said, "He is by no means a genius." If not a man of unusual talent, Thomson was at least a solid railroad man, well-grounded in every aspect of the company's responsibilities. He had served his apprenticeship in the shops at Altoona and had helped Thomas A. Scott take charge of the nation's roads and telegraph wires during the Civil War. His expertise lay in maintenance, inaugurating a system of standard designs, a vital if not exciting contribution to railroad progress. Nothing in Thomson's career showed an ability to innovate policy or handle men dramatically. And railroad employees out on the lines, twenty-year veteran motormen, engineers, conductors, had not forgotten his intransigence during the Strike of 1877, when he chided Cassatt for worrying about the men's butter on their bread. *The Philadelphia Bulletin* summed up Thomson's tenure as chief of the Pennsylvania: "No condition arose during his presidency offering opportunity to test his ability at meeting any great departure in the railway policy of the country"—and Thomson was not the type of man to create one.

Certainly, the directors of the Pennsylvania must have realized that Thomson was "no genius," just as they must have known that the Pennsylvania badly needed one. Since 1885 when J. P. Morgan had extricated the Pennsylvania and the Central from their killing rivalry, the financial state of the railroads had improved under his skillful manipulation, but now events were causing concern even to the master financier. The vast increase in freight traffic was creating a management condition that the roads simply could not handle. Charles Francis Adams wrote: "The whole complicated system under which through or competitive railroad business is done, is

curiously vicious and extravagant and must be radically reformed. . . ."
Cassatt agreed, and moreover, unlike many of his contemporaries, he had
known how to reform it for two decades: Abolish the secret kickbacks and
preferential rates to shippers.

Why was Cassatt so unwilling to enter the battle for effective railroad
management in 1897 and then to reverse his decision a scant two years later?
As a member of the board which elected Thomson to the presidency, he was
privy to all the negotiations which preceded the vote. Modest, but not
unperceptive, he must have acknowledged to himself, if not to others, that
his own talents were far more suited for the position as chief officer than
were those of his friend. It is difficult to believe that he could not have won
the presidency if he had wanted it badly enough. What made him so
reluctant? He had retired from active racing. His sons were settled in their
careers, and his daughters, socially established, offered no problems. He
enjoyed his yacht, his travels, the Chesterbrook farm, but he had been
basking as a country squire for fifteen years. Could it have been his health,
which, now that he was approaching sixty, seemed to be failing?

Whatever Cassatt's feeling about Thomson's election, he expressed neither displeasure nor disappointment, in public or private. His long-standing
association with Thomson had continued during his retirement from the
railroad. The two men had shot grouse in Scotland, dined together in Paris,
and conferred in Philadelphia. Cassatt knew Thomson well and congratulated his friend with every sign of sincerity before returning to plan
another holiday, this time in Bar Harbor. In the fall, back in Rittenhouse
Square, Aleck's health caused disquiet. Lois wrote to her daughter, Katherine: "I am sorry to tell you that Papa is wretched." But by Christmas he
had regained his former vigor. "I am glad to say he seems on the mend now.
He has just walked around the square once. Dr. Sinkler gave him some
capsules which seem to act like a charm." In fact, Aleck had suffered a heart
attack which no doubt diminished his interest in railroad affairs, alleviating
any lingering disappointment he may have felt at Thomson's election.

During that winter, Robert, still complaining in Altoona, spent enough
time in Philadelphia to court and win Minnie Drexel Fell, daughter of a
socially prominent local family. The engagement afforded much satisfaction
to Lois and insured that Robert would move permanently to Philadelphia.
Unlike his father he did not want to take his bride to rough Altoona.

In the new year, 1898, Aleck again decided to run for Lower Merion
Township Supervisor, this time against steep opposition. A trolley car
company wanted to build a route through Bala Cynwyd, the lower portion
of the township, but refused to agree to Cassatt's terms that the roadway
on either side of the line be widened and proper grades and bridges be built.
Cassatt took his position to the voters through a letter in the local press:
"Where the residents of the township in any locality were in favor of
granting an electric railroad company the right to use the public highways

I should deem it my duty as a public officer to be governed by their wishes and should only require the railroad companies to conform to reasonable regulations. . . ."

The reasonable regulations, in Cassatt's view, included widening the main avenues to fifty feet to allow room for other transport than the trolley, which had to pass under the Bala turnpike by a bridge. Not all the residents of the township agreed with him. During February before the election, a heated dispute was aired in the local newspapers. The trolley interests saw no reason why the road should be extended beyond the thirty-three feet required by law and called for the defeat of Cassatt in the coming election as the most vital step in "moving this wealthy, populous, and magnificent" township toward a progressive future. Tempers were short and emotions high on both sides of the argument.

On February 15 at the polls, Cassatt headed the ballot for supervisor with 836 votes out of 2,200 cast for a slate of four. Cassatt, still a loyal Democrat in a heavily Republican township, had won re-election for the eighteenth time. *The Philadelphia Record* in reporting the outcome said: "Mr. Cassatt is a supervisor who has supervised. The roads in Lower Merion are models. Would there were more Cassatts in the country!"

As the seventeenth year of his retirement from the Pennsylvania opened, Cassatt's life seemed settled in a round of domestic and sporting pleasures. His health had improved and he found additional happiness in a visit from his sister, Mary, who returned to America on her first trip since the Franco-Prussian War. As usual the reunion was clouded by Lois' reaction. Mary stayed with Gardner and Jennie since Lois' welcome was so tempered. The artist enjoyed her visits in New York and Boston far more than she did Philadelphia where the local society was not enthusiastic about her talent. Mary never forgot this slight and with some justification held bitter memories of her former home. She returned to France in the summer of 1899, and *The Philadelphia Ledger* remarked provincially, "Mary Cassatt, sister of Mr. Cassatt president of the Pennsylvania Railroad, returned to Europe yesterday. She has been studying painting in France and owns the smallest Pekingese dog in the world."

On June 5, 1899, after little more than two years as president of the Pennsylvania, Frank Thomson died suddenly. His strength had been over-taxed by a trip to western Pennsylvania to inspect the Main Line of the railroad. Thomson was fifty-eight years old at his death and had devoted forty-one of those years to the railroad. His brief tenure in office had not halted the demoralization of the great trunk line, as his directors were well aware. In the minute announcing his death, they commented: "The forces which had been steadily disrupting the fabric of railway prosperity had become so controlling that disaster was imminent." The great trunk lines seemed bent on destroying each other. The directors concluded: "The strug-gle for competitive traffic had forced down the actual rates paid by shippers to a point where none but the strongest and best equipped lines could earn a profit." The Pennsylvania was among those strong and well-equipped lines, but even this giant was feeling the pressure of the shippers' extortion. "Agreements to maintain rates were not worth the paper upon which they were written," concluded the worried directors. Frank Thomson had given his life to the Pennsylvania, as had Scott and Roberts before him. But the sacrifice had not been enough.

Cassatt mourned his friend, well aware that the president's duties had shortened Thomson's life. Who would now willingly assume the burden, knowing the costs? In New York three rival railroad presidents, meeting for lunch in an uptown hotel, discussed the possibilities of Thomson's successor. Traditionally, the Pennsylvania president had been chosen from the ranks of the existing officers, which meant that the first vice president, John P. Green, a Philadelphia lawyer and Union Army veteran, should have had the inside track. But the railroad men discounted Green. He did not have the reputation or the ability to lead the Pennsylvania into the new age of transport. Cassatt was "the best man available for the place . . . the only man who knows all about every part of the Pennsylvania system. He is both a financier and operating man. No person understands better than he does the financial condition and policy of the Pennsylvania road, and no man is more familiar with the details of management." The clinching argument came from one of them—"He is a strong man." The Pennsylvania had not been run by a strong man since Thomas A. Scott laid down his burden in 1880. Twenty years later the emergency was acute. Only Cassatt would answer. Such was his reputation and the respect in which he was held by his peers that the seventeen years of retirement could have been but yesterday. Would he accept what the directors offered him after the June 9 meeting?

President of the Pennsylvania Railroad—probably no other position in the American business world in 1899 offered so much power and prestige. James Bryce, the British historian, believed that railroad presidents had "more power—that is more opportunity of making their will prevail—than perhaps anyone in political life except the President and the Speaker who, after all, hold theirs only for four years and two years, while the railroad monarch may keep his for life"—even if that life was shortened by the exercise of power. In 1899 the president of the Pennsylvania, the largest industrial employer in the nation, held a position comparable to the head of General Motors in today's technological society. Such an opportunity came to few men, and to none less willingly than to Cassatt.

When the nominating committee approached Cassatt with their offer, he was watching his horses run on the Chesterbrook track. His answer, "Gentlemen, I thank you for the honor, but I don't want it. I want to be left alone with my horses," may have been a figment of an imaginative reporter for *The New York American,* but there is no doubt that he did not welcome the invitation. The newspaper report revealed that the committee promised, cajoled, and argued, but Cassatt remained obdurate. Finally, the directors, according to the story, enlisted Lois' support. *The American* reporter believed that Lois persuaded Aleck because she had ambitions for her husband that "a squire's life was too narrow to encompass."

During his seventeen-year absence from the "burden," Cassatt had been objectively able to assess "more calmly than many of his fellow railroad executives the workings of the reckless and ruthless competition which seemed inevitably to destroy even the profitable Pennsylvania." What was more important he had also pondered how these perilous policies were influencing the American public to an ever increasing distrust of the railroads and of all corporations. Albro Martin, a recent railroad historian, believes that "Alexander J. Cassatt came late to the presidency . . . he had only a short time to make his mark and in his ambitions and in the growing demands on the railroad, the times and the leader found their classic coincidence."

Far from the seats of power in New York and Philadelphia, in the back alley of a Detroit machine shop, another man, years younger than Cassatt and from a far different background, was preparing his challenge to the railroad, one which would irrevocably alter the locomotive's monopoly of traffic. In June, 1899, the same month that Cassatt accepted the presidency of the Pennsylvania, Henry Ford produced his first operable motor car. Ford was a greater threat to the railroad than Carnegie or Rockefeller, a threat Cassatt, if he knew of it, failed to take seriously. Until the end of his life, he refused to accept the motor car as a serious invention, a cheaper and competitive transport which would one day virtually bring his locomotives to a halt along rotting tracks.

But in 1899 the railroad was still king of the roads, and the man with control of the Pennsylvania had almost unlimited power. Cassatt's election was hailed with relief by most railroad men around the country, even his rivals knew that he understood the problems of management, finance, and operation as no other railroad man did. They were eager to offer their congratulations. An officer of the Chicago, Milwaukee, and St. Paul, George W. Cross, expressed the prevailing opinion: "It is reported currently, among railroad managers here, that the PRR will be more aggressive. I know you have the strength and courage to lead her to the middle of the fight."

The congratulatory letters and wires came quickly—Henry Clay Frick, Cyrus Huntington, William K. Vanderbilt, George Gould, J. P. Morgan, every industrialist and railroad man of any importance hurried to tender his respects to the new president of the Pennsylvania Railroad. And with the congratulations came requests—to serve on boards, to find positions, to provide passes and private cars.

Of all these complimentary acknowledgements none, was more appreciated by Cassatt than a letter from his son Edward in San Francisco: "I am delighted to hear that Pa is doing so well in his health and that he is so interested in his work. Everybody out here is very much pleased with his election and they say so to me. The Army Officers without exception think him a very talented man in every respect."

On June 10 Cassatt took possession of the president's chair in the office on Broad Street. His first letter of the day was sent to the vice president of a southern railroad in answer to a note of condolence on Thomson's death: "Now you will have seen by the papers that I have been elected to the Presidency and you can readily understand that it was an office which I accepted with a great deal of reluctance. There, will, however, be some compensations for the labor and the responsibility which it will entail and one of them is bringing me in closer relations with my old railroad friends."

Some of those friends had a surprise awaiting them, one which they did not welcome. Cassatt's firm and unaltered determination about rebates called for immediate action. He knew that the Act of 1887 prevented pooling rates, but he also knew that the law had never been enforced. In 1885 the eastern roads had formed a traffic association to enforce rates within their territories, but this informal group had been outlawed by the Sherman Anti-Trust Act of 1890. At the time of Cassatt's election, the railroads were left without any protection against the rebating evil, vulnerable to the demands of the powerful shippers and unsupported by any federal regulatory act, despite the Interstate Commerce Commission.

Cassatt was convinced that "the general business of the country may be expected to increase in the future as the steel, iron and coal industries which form a large portion of your tonnage are entering a new era." Drastic measures were needed to protect the railroads from the shippers' blackmail. Cassatt's first move was to enlist the cooperation of Vanderbilt's New York Central, the Pennsylvania's strongest rival. To William K. Vanderbilt Cassatt proposed what came to be known as "the community of interest" plan. As Cassatt explained it to his wary board of directors: "To establish closer relations between managers of the trunk lines, it has seemed wise to your Board to acquire an interest in some of the railways reaching the seaboards and to unite with the other shareholders who control these properties in supporting a conservative policy. This will, it is hoped, result in securing reasonable and stable rates and do away with unjust discriminations that are the inevitable result of the course that has been heretofore pursued."

This frank statement meant that the Pennsylvania, with the New York Central, planned to buy a controlling percentage of the stock in the weaker trunk lines which would enable them to dictate rates to those shippers who had dominated them in the past through the divide and rule strategy. Cassatt's first target was the Chesapeake and Ohio, not an important trunk line in terms of the Pennsylvania's tonnage, but a large carrier of bituminous coal, and thus a factor in promoting Cassatt's "community of interest." The purchase of the C & O stock occurred late in 1899 and was immediately followed by a reorganization of that road's board placing four directors each from the Pennsylvania and Central in directorships. By 1901 the Pennsylvania had acquired 30,000 shares of C & O stock at a cost of over $5,500,000. The C & O was in the Pennsylvania's pocket.

The Baltimore and Ohio had a murky financial past and had gone into receivership in 1896. Three years later it was reorganized, but was still vulnerable to the Pennsylvania's overtures. In November, 1899, Cassatt began buying B & O stock winding up with 100,000 shares at a cost of over $8,000,000. Again, the Pennsylvania was able to force its men onto the B & O's board of directors enabling it to control policy and set rates. Through the B & O, Cassatt bought equally dominant shares in the Reading. Now the eastern trunk lines were controlled by one determined force with one set policy—that of lowering and stablizing rates. Cassatt's "community of interest" began operation. While Cassatt was busy on the east coast, the Central fulfilled its part of the bargain by securing controlling stock in the Lakeshore and Michigan Southern, the Michigan Central, the Cleveland, Cincinnati, Chicago, and St. Louis, and the Western, which ran through eastern Ohio to Peoria, Illinois, through all the vital coal, steel, and oil shipping areas.

By the end of 1902, Cassatt, with the final purchase of the Norfolk and Western, had spent over $110,000,000. This kind of creative and bold action required gigantic financing, the venturesome economic policy that George P. Roberts had so feared. His board meekly acquiesced—the directors were firmly under his thumb. Reports circulated about his methods. When George Roberts had needed additional financing he had approached his board, cap in hand, pleading for additional money. Not Cassatt—he told the board what they must do, and such was the respect in which he was held, so awed were the board by his management and success, that all measures were rubber stamped. The days of the querulous, complaining stockholders, questioning their officer's handling of finances were gone, never to return under Cassatt's presidency. Critics complained that he was a virtual dictator, but the railroad thrived and dividends increased. Cassatt had quelled insubordination in the company.

Naturally, these gigantic purchases cost a great deal of money. Cassatt increased the capital stock of the Pennsylvania by ten percent and was not about to stop there. At the beginning of Cassatt's presidency the total assets of the Pennsylvania stood at $280,000,000. By 1901 over half of this amount had been spent to secure the stock in the eastern trunk lines which formed Cassatt's "community of interest." This heavy drain on capital had meant some economies. The crack twenty-hour limited trains between New York and Chicago were cancelled temporarily. Cassatt was forced to accept an unprecedented four and one-half percent interest to borrow $35,000,000 on a short-term six-month loan from New York banks. In early 1901 stockholders were asked to authorize an increase of $100,000,000 in the capital stock of the company, and they eagerly subscribed to the shares, although they were priced $10 over the market price. Cassatt alone was responsible for what Albro Martin calls "spectacular equity financing." This economic feat was accomplished while the Pennsylvania's best customer, the United States Steel Corporation, was in profit trouble and when other railroads were also increasing their equity capitalizations. Yet, Cassatt never faltered. Ahead lay even more sensational financial demands on the dazzled stockholders.

Neither Cassatt nor the federal government seemed concerned that his actions to gain a virtual monopoly of the eastern trunk lines were in any way contrary to the spirit, if not the law, of the Sherman Anti-Trust Act. It is unlikely that he worried about this, if he was even aware that he was bending the law. Modern critics might question these business ethics, but Cassatt's associates accepted his purchases as a clever coup which saved the railroads from destruction. For a man who believed firmly in the right of government to regulate the railroads under federal law, his performance in pursuit of his "community of interest" concept is open to several interpretations, but it is impossible to deny that Cassatt believed that since the government was unable or unwilling to act against the shippers, he must do so himself.

By 1906 the Pennsylvania had sold the major share of its stock in the B & O, the C & O, and the Norfolk and Western. By then the job was done, rates had been stabilized, and the security of the trunk lines assured. Cassatt had acted ruthlessly, perhaps even illegally, but his "community of interest" plan had saved the railroads. Of course, it was not that simple. The shippers, who commanded millions of dollars in coal, oil, iron, and steel, did not submit meekly to Cassatt's tactics. They brought pressure of their own to bear in this conflict with the railroads. General of the battle was Andrew Carnegie who refused to entertain the "community of interest" for a moment, and as the largest shipper across the Pennsylvania lines was arrogantly certain that Cassatt's plan did not apply to Carnegie Steel. He lost no time in contacting Cassatt. The battle was joined.

Confrontation with Carnegie

Far from Philadelphia, behind the thick stone walls of his castle high above the Dornoch Firth in northern Scotland, Andrew Carnegie brooded over Cassatt's "community of interest" plan and what it meant to Pittsburgh and his steel mills. On October 9, 1900, he confided his fears to Charles M. Schwab, president of Carnegie Steel: "Mr. Cassatt's action is the most serious blow we have ever received, and it is a life and death struggle."

Struggle was still the breath of life to Carnegie, even now that he controlled millions of dollars, thousands of lives. Just the year before, he had challenged his one-time partner, Henry Clay Frick, to a test of power and won a Pyrrhic victory.

Frick was just beginning his phenomenal climb when Cassatt became superintendent of motive power and machinery in Altoona. Born on the Westmoreland farm of his maternal grandfather, Abraham Overholt, the whiskey maker, Frick had early shown that his chief interest lay in making money. Through a cousin, who had made an unwise investment in the coke business, Frick became involved in the operation, borrowing money to buy additional coke fields by mortgaging his improvident father's home, persuading Pittsburgh banker Judge Thomas Mellon to loan him $10,000 and also touching his affluent uncles for a loan. Frick had barely begun to build his coke empire in the late 1860s, but within twenty years he owned 1,100 ovens and 3,000 acres of coke land in western Pennsylvania cornering the market in time to capitalize on the production of steel which depended on coke for its manufacture. Carnegie quickly saw the advantage of securing a vital source of raw material for his steel works in nearby Braddock and wooed Frick with a partnership. The two formed an unholy alliance which would control the steel business for decades, but eventually their association faltered and collapsed. Frick, who had been a sickly child, small of stature and unprepossessing in appearance, had little of Cassatt's charm and generosity of spirit, but he did share the railroad executive's diffidence, reserve, and inclination for privacy. Unable to make friends easily, Frick, in his aloofness, admired Cassatt and transferred his allegiance from Carnegie to the president of The Pennsylvania.

Frick had been forced out of Carnegie Steel, and his executive chair was now occupied by thirty-eight year old Charlie Schwab whose allegiance to the chairman of the board was total. Carnegie's new fair-haired boy, charming, dashing, a salesman to his fingertips was far different from the retiring, diffident, gray Frick. Schwab appealed to J. P. Morgan who had never made any secret of his dislike of Carnegie. And Morgan would be the catalyst in this struggle between Cassatt and Carnegie, drawn into the fight because of his own steel interests, an integral part of any dramatic change in the financial structure of the country.

During the past few years, Carnegie had spent as much time in Scotland as in his Fifth Avenue office in New York, and he wanted to spend more time there. The center of his industrial life, however, was still in Pittsburgh. He felt deep nostalgic ties to the city, and although he rarely visited it, he had donated one of his libraries to the town which had brought him wealth and power. He felt no such ties to the Pennsylvania Railroad, although he had begun his career under Thomas A. Scott's aegis and had profited greatly from his connection with the road. On the contrary, Carnegie shared with many citizens of Pittsburgh a real dislike for the powerful railroad which had forced its will on the Steel City. In that same letter to Schwab, Carnegie had promised: "The deliverance of Pittsburgh is my next great work."

Delivering Pittsburgh from the thralldom of the Pennsylvania Railroad would not be easy. Carnegie knew the strength of his opponent, A. J. Cassatt. Again to Schwab he confided: "But I have great hopes, let me tell you, of our coming conference with him. He is a clever, able man, has a versatile brain. He has hastily assumed that he could make what rates he pleased through combination with competing lines. That the public will not stand."

It was not the public who complained, but Andrew Carnegie, who had rarely in the past showed much concern for that same public. The public cared only for the outcome of the fight. Cheaper rates, stable rates, would be passed along to them through lower prices for consumer goods. The public cared little whether Carnegie, Morgan, or Cassatt controlled rates. The end to the ruinous railroad wars could only work for its benefit.

His Scots stubborness thoroughly aroused, Carnegie decided to cut short his normal stay of several months at Skibo Castle and return to America before Christmas, prepared to battle Cassatt. The steel man had some justice on his side. Cassatt had informed him that rates would be raised one and a half mills per ton to Carnegie Steel as they would to all shippers. But the raise made the rate higher on the Pittsburgh lines than elsewhere, and Carnegie had no recourse because the Pennsylvania had a monopoly out of that city. He honestly believed that Cassatt's action was illegal. He intended to take his case to the people and enlist government support: "The Board of Trade in Britain controls the rates, and in every country in Europe railroad rates are regulated. So they will be with us unless these two reckless men are brought to their senses." When it suited him, Carnegie became a champion for the free enterprise system against "these two reckless men," Cassatt and William Vanderbilt, who were, of course, only trying to stabilize rates and do away with secret rebates.

On a cold day in early December, 1900, Carnegie met with Cassatt in the Pennsylvania president's Broad Street office in Philadelphia. The air outside was no chillier than the atmosphere in the large paneled room overlooking the train yards, the very heart of Cassatt's empire. Beneath him 238 trains arrived in the station daily, carrying freight and passengers from across half a continent. Lesser men than Carnegie, who was no stranger to the trappings of power, were impressed if not intimidated by the outward signs of the Pennsylvania president's authority. Four black porters guarded the entrance to the sanctum, and once beyond these sentinels the visitor had to pass William Patton, personal assistant to the president and a phalanx of assistants to the assistant. Members of the press, never welcome to Cassatt, found the environment awe-inspiring, as, perhaps, it was intended to be. *The Philadelphia Telegraph* believed: "The king upon his throne is not a more closely guarded man than he (Cassatt) is, and it is much easier to get an audience with the President of the United States than to gain admittance to the private office of Mr. Cassatt in Broad Street Station, Philadelphia."

Cassatt sat behind a large leather and mahogany desk which held a clean blotter, a telephone, and little else. In the corner of the vast forty by eighty foot room stood a globe which Cassatt could consult to trace the progress of his 8,000 miles of lines or contemplate one of his frequent trips abroad. Adjoining the office was a sumptuous bathroom and a dining room well stocked with expensive liquors and cigars for appropriate business lunches. Cassatt's working hours were short by modern standards, from nine until three o'clock. He managed to complete his correspondence, interviews, and financial dealings well within those hours. He never appeared harried or hurried, never took a briefcase full of papers home. He delegated authority quickly and expected his orders to be carried out. For all his mild manner toward subordinates his power was undisputed. Even Carnegie could not fail to be impressed. Much of the aura around Cassatt was designed for just that purpose.

Carnegie stood for steel, Cassatt for the railroads. It was as equally regal representatives that the two met that December day, each determined, each indomitable, each convinced that right was on his side. No notes for publication were kept of the private conference. Reports of what happened in the Broad Street office exist only in letters to colleagues and in newspaper speculations.

Carnegie began pleasntly. He greeted Cassatt with a smile and the assurance that there must be some mistake about those rates. After all, he reminded Cassatt, just three years ago Carnegie had made his peace with the Pennsylvania. Frank Thomson had agreed to pay the secret rebates in 1896 to Carnegie who supplied his railroad with $10,000,000 worth of business each year. The Scotsman felt that, at last, he was receiving as good a deal as his competitors on freight rates. Now Cassatt wanted to renege on the Thomson deal. Surely Cassatt's announcement cancelling these secret rebates was just for public consumption. The secret kickbacks would continue.

No mistake, Cassatt assured Carnegie calmly. His freight rates would be no different than those of any other shipper. Carnegie's smile turned to a glower. He cajoled, then threatened. If Cassatt would not agree to his terms, he would fight him all the way. Every resource of the Carnegie Steel Company would be marshalled to thwart the Pennsylvania. Moreover, with Gould's cooperation, he would build a line from Pittsburgh across the Allegheny Mountains to the seaboard which would destroy the primacy of Cassatt's road. Cassatt, unmoved, told the cocky little steelmaster that he had every right to do so, the continent was broad. He could do as he pleased except expect secret rebates on his freight from the Pennsylvania Railroad Company. Furious, all his old animosity toward the hated railroad returning, Carnegie stormed out of Cassatt's office. If Cassatt wanted a fight he would give him one.

In the season of "peace on earth good will toward men" that December, 1900, Carnegie had no charity in his heart. He quickly enlisted his forces, Schwab, Gould, and Rockefeller, a powerful triumvirate which would either force the Pennsylvania to give those rebates or force the railroad out of Pittsburgh. Of course, Rockefeller saw the rebates as a just tribute. He insisted in 1900, as he had in 1874, that refiners who complained about kickbacks did so, not from any legal or moral compunctions, but because they had failed to secure them for their own companies. If Cassatt had not forgotten his conflict with the oil magnate, Rockefeller remembered the railroad man just as unfavorably. Only Cassatt of all the railroad men had hastened to testify against the Standard before the federal government. As a Philadelphia reporter said, "Cassatt was not persona grata with the Rockefellers for various reasons." But in 1900 Rockefeller did not need to rely on the Pennsylvania Railroad to ship his oil. He now had pipelines to the seaboard and would reluctantly accept the cancellation of the rebates. His influence behind the scenes encouraged Gould and the Wabash to challenge the Pennsylvania.

Gould, on the other hand, was vulnerable. His Western Union Telegraph Company poles stretched across the Pennsylvania lines, on a right of way he had leased for years. Soon after his election to the presidency, Cassatt had been invited, as had his predecessors, to take a seat on the board of Gould's Telegraph Company. At first he had returned a tentative acceptance, but by the fall of 1899, he had seen that this directorship placed him in an ambiguous position. He wrote to the president of the Telegraph Company, General Thomas T. Eckert: "It has occurred to me that, in view of the pending negotiations for a new contract between our Companies, and because also of the various questions likely to arise in the future between us it may prove embarrassing to me to occupy the dual position. I feel, therefore, that I must ask you not to present my name to your Board." The old contract would expire on September 20, 1901, and already the companies were at loggerheads over the rental agreement.

Gould himself, as chairman of the board, was drawn into the discussions. He expressed his dismay at Cassatt's refusal, which boded ill for the contract renewal, in a personal telegram: "We all sincerely hope you will reconsider your decision . . . We have had the President of the Pennsylvania Railroad Company as a Director of our Company for the last five years and the association has been most satisfying and pleasant." It had ceased to be satisfying and pleasant when Cassatt had discovered that Gould had allied his Wabash railroad with Carnegie and was trying to bribe the Pittsburgh council to allow the Wabash to enter the city on equal terms with the Pennsylvania. Cassatt may have seen the justice of Gould's request, but as a practical businessman he could not sit back and allow another road to challenge the Pennsylvania where it earned its heaviest profits. Gould asked Carnegie for help in persuading the municipal officers to let his Wabash into the city. In return for Carnegie's cooperation, Gould would offer the steelmaster preferential rates well below those of the Pennsylvania. Standing in the way of the alliance were those telegraph poles, over 300 miles of wires along the Pennsylvania right of way, and now in jeopardy. Still, the railroad itself needed the wire service badly. In the end, Gould misjudged, the contract would be signed. He silkily assured Cassatt: "Relative to proposed contract we feel sure that we can sit down with you and in a very short time adjust any differences should they arise."

In no way was George Gould fitted to challenge Alexander Cassatt. He had recently inherited the huge fortune amassed by his late, forceful father, Jay Gould, but he did not also inherit that tycoon's dynamic character. Careless, impetuous, badly educated, self indulgent, prey to moods of great elation or great despondency, George Gould had never developed the temperament of a successful financier. He would have been better advised to stay at Georgian Court, his sprawling estate at Lakewood, New Jersey, to play polo and ride to the hounds. Gould looked his best astride a horse, slick, well groomed, and arrogant, the very picture of a New York socialite with his well tended black mustache and pomaded hair. In the marketplace his naivete and suspicious nature were easily manipulated by men of a harder mien.

Carnegie, no doubt, acknowledged Gould's deficiences, but thought they would be minimized by his control of forces vital to the fight against Cassatt. J. P. Morgan, the gray eminence behind all the country's financial manipulations, acute at sizing up men, realized that Gould had no chance of winning any battle against Cassatt and the Pennsylvania. Morgan feared little from Gould, but Carnegie was another matter. Much could be expected from the steelmaster, but none of it was likely to benefit the steel trust that Morgan was attempting to organize. A vital, behind-the-scenes general, Morgan, was a valuable ally of Cassatt's in the coming battle. The relationship between Cassatt and Morgan had always been close, socially as well as in business. During the next months that relationship would be cemented in personal meetings and correspondence. Morgan was privy to every plan in Cassatt's strategy to stabilize rates and keep the Pennsylvania paramount in Pittsburgh.

Gould lost no time in allocating the resources necessary to extend the Wabash from the Mississippi over the Alleghenies into Baltimore. Not even when a sixty-mile stretch over those troublesome mountains cost an unparalleled $380,000 a mile did Gould falter. Before he was finished it cost Gould $35,000,000 to link his Wabash to the Western Maryland road and complete the line to the seaboard. The challenge to the Pennsylvania would ruin Gould, but in 1900 he was riding the crest of the wave, bolstered by his alliance with Carnegie, eager to best Cassatt, and seeing as within his grasp his father's life-long dream—a Gould-owned, inter-continental railroad.

While Gould held the Wabash threat and the Western Union contract over Cassatt's head, Carnegie slyly continued to negotiate with the Pennsylvania over the rebates, reminding Cassatt that his company should honor the agreement made three years ago with Thomson. Carnegie believed he was acting reasonably. After all, it was to Cassatt's interest to favor steel shippers over grain shippers, for the former had the cheaper commodity to haul. Perhaps Cassatt, due to his seventeen-year absence from railroad affairs did not fully understand the situation, Carnegie implied in a rather snide letter to his adversary: "You have returned to harness after years of recreation and rushed into a policy which, being unsound, as I believe, you will soon abandon. I am looking forward with great interest to the new rates which you are to make early next week. No half way business will do any good."

Cassatt agreed, no half-way business *would* do any good. Instead of setting a 5.48 mill rate as Carnegie expected, Cassatt announced a hike to 6 mills per ton of traffic. Enraged, Carnegie let Cassatt know his displeasure: "I need all my philosophy every time I remember that we ship our products over your lines to Chicago and you assess 6 mills per ton, but when we get out of your grasp, railroads are delighted to take the same freight at just half what you extort. How you can see this to be politic, not to speak of fairness, I cannot perceive." There is no doubt that the Pennsylvania intended to keep its monopolistic grasp on Pittsburgh freight. But Cassatt also wanted to stablize rates for all roads, so that the destructive wars forcing railroads into bankruptcy would cease. Both men believed that they had right on their side. Carnegie could not accept that he did not, for the first time, have might also.

Carnegie might still have entertained hopes that Cassatt would modify his attitude after their conference and an exchange of letters, but Charlie Schwab had few illusions. He knew that Cassatt was determined to continue his "community of interest" plan while extorting the highest rates from Carnegie Steel. On May 15, 1901, Cassatt wrote to Schwab: "In reply to your favor of the 13th instant I beg to say that my understanding of the action taken at the meeting of the Traffic Officers as reported to you . . . is that the present rates are to continue throughout the season."

While the "community of interest" effort absorbed much of his time during the early years of his presidency, Cassatt spared many hours for other railroad matters. The welfare of his employees, the efficiency of his locomotives, the upgrading of track and the revenues and corporate structure of the company all received meticulous attention. In President Roberts' administration, the Pennsylvania had established a pension system for its employees, a paternalistic venture which the directors thought might ease relations between management and employees. During Cassatt's second year in office, the Pension Fund was firmly funded on his suggestions. The company pledged to spend $230,000 per year for the retirement pay of all men who at sixty-five or seventy had served for thirty years or were physically disabled by their service. During the first year of the Fund, 229 employees availed themselves of the allowances. Over $235,000 was paid, and Cassatt asked his board to increase the annual appropriation for the fund to $300,000.

Cassatt enthusiastically endorsed the Pension Fund for he had been concerned for the men on the line since his Altoona days. It must be conceded, however, that his attitude illustrated more of noblesse oblige than of a conviction of the rights of the working man. When his employees threatened to strike, or pressed too closely for control of their working conditions, or insisted on higher wages, his manner could be both lordly and inflexible. Cassatt wanted to give the men butter on their bread but in his own time and on his conditions. He remembered all too clearly standing on that hillside above the Pittsburgh yards in 1877 and watching thousands of dollars in rolling stock go up in flames. Such a holocaust must never happen again, and certainly not under his management. Just how indelibly that strike had been etched on his mind was revealed in a speech he made soon

after his election to the presidency in July of 1899. He proposed the organization of a private police force which would be able to cope with strikers,
a forerunner of the "goon squads" Henry Ford would use against his auto
workers in the 1930s. Obviously Cassatt was thinking about the Strike of
1877 when he made his proposal. In his files is a thick report from his general
manager of the lines west of Pittsburgh, L. F. Lorre, outlining the history
of the Brotherhood of Railway Trainmen and its activity during the seventeen years Cassatt had been absent from the management of the Pennsylvania. The report, which concluded that the Brotherhood "has been con-
spicuous from the beginning for its radical demands for labor legislation,"
met with Cassatt's approval. After studying the contents of the report,
Cassatt wrote Mr. Lorre: "The history of former strikes seems to show
conclusively that where the men have no real grievances, and where their
demands are resisted with firmness and decision, they cannot succeed in
seriously interrupting traffic for any considerable length of time."

Cassatt's intransigence against the just grievances of the underpaid trainmen can only inspire contempt today, but he was far less brutal than many
of his contemporaries, Pullman, Carnegie, and Gould, for example. On an
individual basis he showed compassion. His correspondence shows that he
often visited the families of men killed or injured on the job, listened
patiently to complaints, and attempted to understand the resentments of his
employees against management. There are several unexplained notations in
his letterbooks of contributions to what he called a "Conscience Fund." He
was not a cruel or arrogant man, but the concept of labor organizing to
bargain for better wages or working conditions was as much anathema to
him as to any capitalist of the 90s. Yet he was far from the black-hued villain
such muckrakers as Gustavus Myers would have us believe. Myers in his
exposé of great American fortunes, characterized Cassatt as a ruthless
plunderer for his endorsement of the Riot Indemnity Act of 1879: "With all
his unscrupulousness Jay Gould never had the face to do anything approaching in enormity the Riot Indemnity Bill of Cassatt. Yet when Cassatt
died the most lavish eulogies were everywhere published; he passed away
in the full attributes of superior respectability." Few observers went so far
as Myers. Even Ida Tarbell had praise for Cassatt, separating him from
robber barons such as Rockefeller, but what Lois Cassatt remembered as
"the most trying experience of his life" dogged Cassatt to the end.

During the summer of 1899, the Brotherhood of Trainmen showed signs
of erupting again. The trouble occurred on the New York Central, and
Cassatt hastened to give the president of that road his full support. On July
17, 1899 he wired S. R. Calloway: "We propose to stand firm against the
demand . . . for an advance in wages and I hope you will hold to the same
position. To yield now would be to invite trouble all along the line." During
these upheavals Cassatt revived his ideas for a railroad police force, but he
did not push the measure which came to naught. There were other ways

of dealing with the men. He wired the president of the Erie on July 22: "We shall make no advance in our wages. I am very glad to learn that you will not do so either. We have all the men we need at present rates." Brutal but effective, for if these men would not fall into line, there were others who needed the work. Cassatt had not earned the reputation of a brillant railroad manager by using timid methods either with lowly trainmen or with the mighty Carnegie.

But Cassatt could exercise great benevolence toward difficult employees. *The Baltimore Sun* repeated the story of his reluctance to rebuke an impudent trainman in public. One day Cassatt rode his usual train from Haverford to his Broad Street office. He noticed that the trainman, obviously new to the job and unknown to the president, failed to walk behind the train with a red flag during an unscheduled stop. Instead, the trainman, against all company rules, sat down on the rear platform and waited for the train to start. Cassatt, in a gentle voice, suggested to the trainman that this was not the proper procedure. The brakeman, not recognizing his critic and of a generally truculent mind, spit a stream of tobacco juice in Cassatt's general direction and sneered: "I don't know if it is any damned business of yours." "Certainly not, certainly not," Cassatt agreed and beat a hasty retreat to his seat. When he reached the station, he called the trainmaster into his office and reported the insubordinate. Of course, the trainmaster was horrified and hastened to assure the great man that the offender would be summarily dismissed. "No, you won't fire him," Cassatt replied. "But tell him not to be so disrespectful to people who ask for information in the future."

Petty vindictiveness was not in Cassatt's nature. On a personal level the president of the Pennsylvania could be tolerant, but his breadth of mind did not encompass the workers' right to question the decisions which emanated from the president's office. F. N. Barsdale, a contemporary journalist and close observer of Cassatt wrote about the Pennsylvania president's attitude toward his employees on July, 1901: "The disciplinary regulation of employees received very close attention at his hands. Their appearance and their manners in their relation to the public were defined, and while Mr. Cassatt was firm and determined in his relations with the army of men under his control, he was not dictatorial nor severe, and no official ever enjoyed in higher degree the confidence and respect of his subordinates. With equal facility the switch tender or the superintendent could get a hearing if he had anything to say." Cassatt dealt from strength, and while he was ready to listen to complaints from disgruntled employees and dissatisfied stockholders, he suffered no reins on his authority. He knew what was right for his railroad and proceeded unhampered by guilt or indecision.

While Cassatt's attitude toward his employees might be considered cavalier today, there is no denying that his leadership made the Pennsylvania, in the opinion of a modern railroad historian, "the center of the world for railroad construction engineers," in an era which tried his talents to the utmost.

Cassatt met the challenge of increased traffic and deterioration of the lines with a comprehensive plan for modernizing the road. Over $40,000 was allocated for new locomotives. To carry the additional freight traffic, four tracking of the Main Line was begun, a daring engineering feat for the new tracks would cross over the most difficult terrain imaginable. The new track would carry freight expeditiously and quickly, while passengers would continue to travel over the old line. By the end of 1900, there was "a broadway of steel" four tracks wide stretching from Jersey City to Harrisburg over which the new cars, built in the Altoona shops, could move with ease. Cassatt asked for and received $67,000,000 to complete the work within the next two years.

Cassatt did not stop there, additional tracks, grade and curvature reductions, the elimination of grade crossings were initiated all across the Main Line. Electrification of the New Jersey lines was introduced and the use of the automatic block signal became standard. In Pittsburgh ground was broken for a new terminal and station, a thirteen-story structure with an arched train shed 258 feet wide. In Philadelphia a revision of the approaches to Broad Street station and a new passenger depot in West Philadelphia were hurried to completion. Two new bridges spanned the Schuylkill River to accommodate relocated lines. In Washington, D.C., Cassatt became the moving force behind plans to build a giant modern station which would serve all lines coming into the nation's capital at a convenient location. With all these engineering innovations receiving Cassatt's attention, he still spared time for smaller details such as planting locust trees outside the Broad Street station, reducing the charge of ten cents to check a parcel, and overseeing the proper placement of vaults at the Pittsburgh depot. More important to the efficient management of the company was Cassatt's simplification of the corporate structure. The Annual Report for 1899 listed 126 divisions under the aegis of the Pennsylvania producing a multiplicity of legal and tax problems. Cassatt initiated consolidation of many of the smaller lines, simplifying bookkeeping and cutting costs considerably. These improvements—the new track, equipment, safety devices—and the consolidation immeasurably improved the operation of the Pennsylvania enabling it to enter a competitive era of expansion and challenge with greater strengths. Cassatt's fight with the Carnegie-Gould interests in Pittsburgh did not weaken his resolve to revitalize and extend the Pennsylvania. He never lost sight of his main objective—to manage the most impressive, efficient railroad in the world.

Cassatt's considerable success in driving his railroad into the new industrial age was not echoed in his private life. At a time when his full energy was demanded by the Pennsylvania's complex affairs, a family situation taxing all his sympathies and compassion rose to a climax. Edward had sailed for the Philippines in June, 1899 and remained there for almost a year with the Army of Occupation, suppressing the insurrection of natives who objected to being annexed by the United States. Edward felt that Manila would be uncomfortable and unsafe for his family, who temporarily settled near his parents in Haverford. Naturally, this long absence had its effect. Emily, unhappy under the close and censorious eye of her mother-in-law, traveled constantly, leaving little Lois in the excellent care of Miss Barrows, the English Nanny. On one of her many visits to the eastern watering spas, Emily met New York broker, George Batcheller, tall, brown-haired, cherubic, and charming. The friendship rapidly ripened into something closer, as Edward continued to insist that the Philippines was not the place for his wife and child.

Edward, did, however, recognize that the long absence was unhealthy. On March 16, 1900 he wrote to his father about "the advisability of my leaving the military service. This is no doubt a surprise to you and in fact it is a surprise to me that I should have come to consider the question at all." Service in the Phillippines was not to his taste, and he envisaged a bleak future with slow promotion. Moreover, he sensed what was happening to Emily: "I think also that it is a bad idea for me to be away from my family as much as I will have to be in the future, for the stations of the Cavalry will not be such that I should care to ask Emily to live in them, and even if I did, there is the question of the education of Baby which must be considered." Baby, indeed, was the question which concerned not only her father, but her grandfather, much as he believed his son's future lay in the Army.

Edward ended his disturbing letter by pleading for his father's advice, asking him to make the decision: "I should act immediately on receipt of your cable." Earlier, he had mentioned that if his father could secure him "a pleasant detail near home," he might reconsider. Aleck was only too willing to help. Within days of his son's letter, he had contacted the War Department in Washington. Elihu Root, the Secretary of War, was eager to placate the influential president of the Pennsylvania Railroad. Edward was recalled and promised the post, a real plum, of military attaché to the United States Embassy in London. By May, Edward was home planning to take his family to England that summer, but puzzled that Emily's reception lacked the ardor he expected. Emily continued to see her admirer, George Batcheller. On July 4, nonetheless, the Edward Cassatts and little Lois, with the faithful Miss Barrows in attendance, sailed for England.

A little less of Lois Cassatt's maternal interest would have been advisable at this critical juncture, but later that summer she sailed with Aleck to Europe. Ostensibly, it was a business trip to Germany—Aleck was searching for European funds to help recapitalize the Pennsylvania—but they found time to visit Mary in Paris with Edward, Emily, and little Lois in tow. Then, they went with the young Cassatts to London to help them settle into

12 Ennismore Gardens, near Hyde Park. The senior Cassatts returned to Philadelphia at the end of the summer. Aleck was wrenched by the farewell to his grandaughter and disturbed by the growing discord between his son and Emily.

Cassatt returned from London to face the obduracy of Carnegie and Gould in their determination to build the competing railroad across Pennsylvania. The fight was soon to be taken from Cassatt and Carnegie's hands into the capable grasp of J. P. Morgan. As the dark November days shortened, Morgan decided that he must act. While Carnegie and Gould's railroad inched painfully across the Alleghenies, both shippers and railroad men viewed the challenge to the Pennsylvania with alarm. They told Morgan: "Carnegie must be stopped." Morgan, his own steel interests in jeopardy, was convinced that Carnegie intended "to demoralize the railroads" as he had the steel industry which Morgan could not allow.

At this critical juncture, Charlie Schwab was the chief speaker at a dinner on December 12, 1900 at New York's University Club. Schwab spoke on the future of the steel industry, surprisingly portraying the very merger which Morgan contemplated. Both Morgan and Cassatt attended the dinner, but Carnegie was not among the guests. Did he know of his protégé's views? Was Schwab a stalking horse for Carnegie himself, who, now that the battle was joined, had second thoughts? Morgan knew that Carnegie's huge new steel plant on the shores of Lake Erie threatened his own National Tube Company. Carnegie produced eighty-five percent of all the steel in the country. Now Schwab was urging that his company expand into every aspect of steel manufacturing. Morgan's very idea, but he wanted to manage the steel trust, which Carnegie would never allow. Since Carnegie could not be forced from the market place, perhaps he could be bought? Morgan contacted Schwab. Would Carnegie sell?

Cassatt, of course, knew of Morgan's plan, but he saw little chance for its success. Carnegie showed little inclination to retire from the battle. The railroad continued to crawl across Pennsylvania. While Morgan plotted with Schwab in his New York financial den, Cassatt summoned his reinforcements. Carnegie's old friend, Wayne McVeagh, was now chief legal counsel to the Pennsylvania. Perhaps he could make the steelmaster see the folly of his fight against the Pennsylvania. On January 26, 1901 McVeagh wrote to Carnegie: "Now I cannot reconcile myself to the idea that two such men should differ about a plain proposition . . . You wish all you can properly get for your Co., Cassatt wishes all he can properly get for his Co., then there must be a common meeting point of these two interests, and you two men can find it if you desire to find it." McVeagh's simple view did not take into account that Cassatt refused to abandon his "community of interest" scheme to stabilize rates and Carnegie really did not want to accommodate his old employer and antagonist. Carnegie reacted emotionally and violently to what he felt was the Pennsylvania's age-old, unjust discrimination against Pittsburgh and his company which shipped the major portion of its manufacture from that city.

McVeagh doggedly continued to state the case for the Pennsylvania: "You fail to give proper weight to the fact that the rebates you were getting were not only unlawful but if he (Cassatt) had continued them after he knew all about them, he would have been committing a criminal offence, while you in taking them ran no risk whatever of that kind. . . ." McVeagh referred to the disregarded I.C.C. regulation forbidding secret rebates, more honored in the breach than in the observance. Tactfully, the Pennsylvania's chief counsel acknowledged Carnegie's point of view: "Don't suppose I don't appreciate your side of the case. I am perfectly sure you believe Pittsburgh as well as yourself badly treated. All I can say is that it is preposterous to assert that two such men as you and Mr. Cassatt both desiring to reach a basis productive of a fair proposition of advantage to both parties cannot do so. I know you can."

Preposterous, but neither Cassatt nor Carnegie would budge. Cassatt dared Carnegie to build his railroad, and Carnegie continued to feel a just grievance against the Pennsylvania for cancelling his rebates. Losers in the battle would not only be steel and railroad men, but the general public. Another depression could result, and Morgan would not let that happen. The country was even then slowly emerging from the debacle of 1893, brought on in part by railroad wars. Morgan summoned Schwab to New York in late January and asked him simply: "Would Carnegie sell now and how much would he ask?" The meeting in Morgan's library lasted till dawn. Reports of the conclave swept Wall Street where rumors abounded. How much did Carnegie know about what his lieutenant was doing? He wrote to another trusted associate, George Lauder, Jr.: "There is no substance to these reports anent a combination . . . Judge Reed here talking to the P. R. people . . . Gould with the Wabash system coming to Pittsburgh . . . I suggested it to him and he came to see me with his chief men and it is now closed. We get traffic contract at as low rates as prevail in any district of U. S. It seems almost too good to be true and I am not without fear that allied P. R. interests here and Morgan may frighten him from going to work. . . ."

Carnegie did not seem to welcome retirement to his Skibo castle from this evidence. He was exhilarated to think that Carnegie Steel with Gould's cooperation would show even greater profits than 1900's $40,000,000. Could he yield all this to the quiet world of golf and philanthropy? Yet, he was sixty-five, and his wife wanted him to retire. Morgan continued to press Schwab, who finally approached his mentor after a relaxing day on the Westchester Golf Club links. Carnegie agonized for hours. At last he scrawled on a piece of paper his price, $480,000,000. Schwab hurried to Morgan with the news. The financial king of America looked at the small piece of paper and said, "I accept this price." That was all there was to it, the largest deal in the country's industrial history. A few days later Morgan visited Carnegie in his 51st Street, New York mansion, and the two giants shook hands to seal the proposition. As he left, Morgan said: "Mr. Carnegie, I want to congratulate you on being the richest man in the world."

How much was Carnegie influenced by his desire to retire, or did he shrink from continuing the battle with Cassatt? Carnegie never revealed why he finally allowed Morgan to buy him out. He had the satisfaction of thinking that the Wall Street titan could not have beaten him in a competitive battle. He never had that satisfaction from Cassatt. Years later he said that Cassatt "was, in fact, a railroad imperialist, and his acts provoked the admiration of his arch enemies—for such he had professionally—and that was a high compliment." It was, indeed, and a compliment Carnegie never paid Gould, who was not consulted on the sale. Cassatt had the last word. As Morgan prepared to organize his trust, the United States Steel Company, he turned to Cassatt for advice on who would head the new organization. Should it be Schwab, who surely deserved consideration for his part in the merger? Or should it be the corporation lawyer and Illinois president of Morgan's Federal Steel Company? Cassatt wrote frankly to Morgan: "You probably know Judge Gary better than I do, but it may do no harm to say that I have a very high opinion of his character and ability. He is, I think, a broad-minded, able man, and eminently qualified to take the general direction of the Company." Cassatt accorded Schwab his due as a genius in practical mechanics and as a developer of economic methods, but, "it is of the greatest importance to have at its head a man of tact who will not provide antagonisms, and the ability and courage to resist them. I believe Judge Gary to be such a man." So did Morgan. Carnegie, as a condition of the sale to Morgan, had insisted that Schwab be named president of U. S. Steel, but he lasted only two years. Judge Gary was elected chairman of the board in 1903, and it was his hand that guided the giant trust to success.

Carnegie sailed for Europe on March 16, 1901. Despite their differences Cassatt and Carnegie remained in contact. Five years later Cassatt wrote a cordial note to his former adversary, "thank you very much for your life of Watt. I spent yesterday pouring over it and have been interested and instructed. Like most of the present generation I only knew the bare fact that Watt had built the first successful steam engine. I have you to thank for making the man known to me." Two such valiant fighters in the industrial forum could acknowledge each other's value. Gould was another story.

The Poles Come Tumbling Down

The Carnegie-Gould-Morgan negotiations may have been the prime topic of talk in the financial sanctums of Wall Street, but Cassatt did not dignify the rumors by any attention in his annual report to the stockholders of the Pennsylvania Railroad that March. Cassatt wired his assistant, William Patton, touring California, "Everything passed off smoothly at the Annual Meeting this morning." Everything always passed off smoothly at any annual meeting Cassatt conducted. He had requested and received his stockholders consent for additional capitalization of the company. No mention was made to the stockholders of the Carnegie-Gould threat to the Pennsylvania empire or to the in-fighting among the various tycoons involved. But the threat was very much on Cassatt's mind. The very morning of the annual meeting in 1901, he wrote to his third vice president, Joseph Wood, in Pittsburgh that "we have not yet been able to learn anything definite in relation to the Carnegie contract. Mr. Morgan is inquiring into the matter and is to communicate with us as soon as he learns anything. . . ."

Predictably, Morgan was not being quite open with Cassatt for by March 12 he had completed all but the final details of his monumental purchase. But then Morgan rarely shared the progress of his maneuvers with even his most trusted associates. On March 23, Cassatt was still worried over Carnegie's intrigues with Gould to bring the Wabash into Pittsburgh. On that date he wrote to Joseph Wood, his third vice president: "Last night an ordinance was introduced in Pittsburgh Council to give certain rights to the Pittsburgh and Carnegie Railroads." He must have known by then that Carnegie had abandoned Gould, for the steelmaster had left for Europe with Morgan's signed check for the sale. His departure was reported in the local newspapers. Cassatt had planned to go to Mexico, but postponed his trip because of the machinations of Gould and his Wabash.

Four days later Cassatt knew for certain that Carnegie had sold his steel company to Morgan, and he took immediate action. Without Carnegie's support, Cassatt thought that Gould would be forced to give up his plans to challenge the Pennsylvania in Pittsburgh. He was prepared to give Gould an alternative. Cassatt wired Hamilton McK. Twombley, of the New York Central, "Do you not think it would be well for you or Mr. Morgan to see M. Gould tomorrow and induce him to suspend any action looking toward tying up the Wabash and Missouri Pacific, and also as to the Pittsburgh extension, until we can have a conference with him?" Morgan, who had now put U. S. Steel firmly in his pocket, condescended to think about the Pennsylvania's problems. To him, the railroad was a minor pawn in his trust battle, but he intended to weld Cassatt firmly to his side. Cassatt met with Morgan, Twombley, and Cleveland financier Mark Hanna, who had President McKinley's ear, for a strategy session in New York. They decided to try and buy Gould off.

On April 1, his decision made, Cassatt left on his private car 60, for Pittsburgh, the first lap of a trip through the southwest to Mexico. No matter how pressing his business affairs, Cassatt rarely allowed them to interfere with his vacations. On the surface, he was all cordiality to Gould. That very day he suavely agreed to arrange the movement of Edwin Gould's private car along the Pennsylvania route, a courtesy he extended to many railroad officers, Congressmen, and financiers. Gould's brother, Edwin, would be no exception. As the Cassatt party set off on the Mexican jaunt, Morgan's U. S. Steel Company elected its officers. One of the members of the board was a Pennsylvania director and near neighbor of Cassatt's, Clement A. Griscom, who reported the new roster to the Pennsylvania president.

Apparently untroubled by the strategms of Gould to move his Wabash into Pittsburgh, Cassatt traveled leisurely from New Orleans to Mexico where his party was received with every honor by the Governor, to Lois' satisfaction. By the end of April, Cassatt had returned to Philadelphia and begun a series of meetings with Twombley, Morgan, and Schwab on rates for shipping the freight of United States Steel. Schwab took a hard line which Cassatt met with equal firmness. The rates would not be lowered. He urged Twombley to stand firm too. Friendly as he was with Morgan, Cassatt did not wholly trust the wily banker and would certainly not allow Morgan to dictate to him on railroad rates. The emergence of U. S. Steel had proved a mixed blessing to Cassatt.

The steel company's ownership of the short Bessemer line, built by Carnegie, to ship his steel from the Lake Erie plant, enabled the huge monopoly to compete with the trunk lines. Cassatt wanted U. S. Steel out of the railroad business. He could cope with Gould, but not while he was being undermined by Schwab and the steel interests. On May 16 Cassatt wrote to a Morgan partner, the urbane New Englander Robert Bacon: "It seems to me to be greatly to the interest of both parties that the Railroad Companies and the United Steel Corporation should work in harmony, but this will be impossible as long as the Bessemer and Lake Erie Railroad remains in the control of the Steel Corporation to be used as a club to enforce such rates as it may dictate." Cassatt was not about to let Morgan disrupt his community of interest plan to stabilize rates. He concluded in his letter to Bacon: "That line ought to be leased to the railroad companies. . . ."

Cassatt shared with most executives of his day the philosophy that what was good for his company superceded any other ethics. If the railroad prospered, then the public would be served, and the best method of assuring the success of his railroad was to eliminate unhealthy competition. While he flexed his muscles with Morgan, he continued to press Gould to sell his Wabash to the Pennsylvania, or at least that part of it which endangered Cassatt's profits in Pittsburgh. Gould, mindful that his Western Union contract with the Pennsylvania expired that fall, temporized, at first, and seemed willing to sell. Early in May Cassatt and Gould met in Twombley's New York office to discuss the terms. Hamilton McKnown Twombley, William K. Vanderbilt's son-in-law, a New Yorker of impeccable lineage, had become an officer of the New York Central upon marrying Florence Vanderbilt. He was privy to all Cassatt's negotiations with Gould and agreed fully with Cassatt's community of interest plan, which was proceeding so equitably under the domination of the two great eastern trunk lines. When it came to the final decision to sell his Wabash, Gould, typically, hesitated.

Cassatt, endeavoring to bring Gould to the point, wrote him on May 8: "I think you agreed fully with us in the general proposition that it was impolitic for the Eastern Trunk Line Companies to extend their systems West of their present termini, or for the Western systems to come further East, and having that in mind, you will remember you said you would sell your St. Louis-Toledo line and would name a price to Mr. Twombley early in the week following our meeting. I hope you have not changed your views, as I feel sure the policy indicated will conduce to harmony and bring better results all around." In other words, Cassatt offered a trade to Gould. If he would concentrate his efforts west of Pittsburgh, the New York Central and the Pennsylvania would not challenge him on that front. In exchange he must leave the eastern markets to them.

Gould, wavering, could not abandon the Pittsburgh, in which he had already invested too heavily, but he equally feared a long drawn out campaign against the Pennsylvania. Meanwhile, talk between the Pennsylvania and Western Union continued. In the fall of 1901, the twenty-year agreement between the two expired. Gould still hoped to renew it and vacillated before Cassatt's assertion of dominance in Pittsburgh. This was extremely irritating to Cassatt, who always knew what he wanted and drove straight toward it.

While the Gould scheme was in limbo, Cassatt decided to take his usual summer trip to Europe. He could not contemplate a longer absence from his granddaughter and was deeply concerned about Edward's marriage. During the winter of 1900–1901, Edward and Emily had reached an impasse. Mrs. Phillips, visiting her daughter in London that fall, had realized the disturbing state of the marriage. She wrote to her husband: "I found Emily looking awfully pale, so nervous and such a cough . . . Ed does not understand that she cannot go until she drops. Then this constant silly nagging. He means right but it is so wearing . . . He is most generous to her but you know that is not what she wants. . . ."

What she wanted was the warm, embracing affection that Aleck gave Lois, but Edward, although he loved his wife, was a critical, demanding husband. And, of course, there were other women who found the dashing military attaché attractive. His duties at the Embassy were light, leaving plenty of time for dalliance. The young Cassatts' life in London, gay, luxurious and very social, was enhanced by an allowance from Aleck. Mrs. Phillips wrote: "Pa. C. seems most generous to him." But Aleck's money could not ease the discord at 12 Ennismore Gardens—Emily continued to correspond with her comforting admirer, George Batchellor in New York.

In early spring 1901, while Cassatt was embroiled with Carnegie, Gould, and Morgan, Emily made her decision. Soon after Queen Victoria's funeral, she left London for Paris with her daughter Lois and the nurse. Ostensibly, she went to visit Mary, but she would never return to Edward. That spring she sailed for home leaving little Lois and her guardian, Miss Barrows, to join the senior Cassatts in Germany when they arrived in Europe that July. She explained her reasons for the separation to Mary Cassatt, who gave her every sympathy. Mary wrote to her on May 26 after Emily had arrived in Philadelphia: "You say you have not complained. I am afraid that has been a mistake, you ought to have complained and loudly . . . Ed is weak as most men. . . ."

Accepting that reconciliation between Edward and Emily was impossible, Aleck tried to secure the best arrangements for his grandchild. He insisted on a settlement which would leave the little girl in his care for six months of the year, since Edward's army duties prevented him from having Lois with him. He rented a house for Emily and Lois on 230 South 20th Street in Philadelphia, near his own Rittenhouse Square house. Lois, of course, took her son's part entirely. She had never liked Emily and now made no secret of her enmity. Emily naturally felt some bitterness toward her in-laws which Mary tried to alleviate: "You did your poor father-in-law an injustice. I am sure he feels the affair deeply." He did, but his innate fairness prevented him from treating Emily with anything but compassion. Lois never spoke to her daughter-in-law in the years which followed. But Aleck, tolerant and understanding, remained in touch with her for her own sake and for that of his beloved granddaughter. After three years Emily secured a divorce from Edward (the story made the front page of the *New York Times*) and married the loyal George Batchellor.

The tranquillity of his domestic circle, such a source of comfort and warmth to Aleck, was rudely shaken by Emily and Edward's break-up. Its affect on Aleck, who depended so heavily on his family for strength and relaxation from the competitive business struggle, was incalculable. Although Aleck himself enjoyed the companionship of beautiful women, his attentions never strayed beyond a permissable flirtation. Other, lesser men, might enjoy a back street affair but Aleck never seemed tempted to seek diversion with the women who would have been only too eager to attract the handsome, worldly president of the Pennsylvania Railroad. Only one story has survived as evidence of Aleck's interest in women other than his wife. On the railroad's route to New York was a tiny station, Islin, New Jersey. Cassatt ordered his trainmen always to make an unscheduled stop there if the engineer noticed a certain attractive matron waiting at the depot. The trainmen obeyed the president's orders punctiliously, even when prudence would have dictated otherwise. On one occasion Cassatt accompanied by his board of directors was traveling to New York for a conference when his private car neared Islin. The train stopped, and the privileged lady boarded. How embarassing to find herself the only female passenger in the midst of this distinguished company, and how unnerving to her proper admirer, the president of the Pennsylvania! But a discreet flirtation was far from the disruption of family life. Some of Cassatt's arrogant ruthlessness in his conduct of the Gould battle might be traced to his unhappiness with his son's marriage during the crucial years of 1901–1903.

By mid-May he had decided that Gould had no intention of selling the Wabash. He wrote to his general manager in Pittsburgh: "Although the matter is not finally determined and there is hope he may give up the project, it now looks as though Mr. Gould will go through with his extension into Pittsburgh. If he does, we ought to be prepared to strike back promptly, and I am to see Mr. Vanderbilt on Tuesday to determine joint action." Edward Harriman, the western railroad tycoon, had entered the lists against the Wabash chief, and Cassatt thought his rivalry might influence Gould. Cassatt enlisted the aid of his banking friend Schiff in the project, but by June 26 it was obvious that his strategy was unsuccessful. Cassatt informed Twombley that Schiff had failed to bring Gould to terms: "I think we may consider the whole thing off."

On July 16, when Cassatt sailed for Europe, the whole thing was definately off, and he had to look for new methods to deal with his rival. Aleck and Lois stayed at Claridge's in London for a week before visiting Paris and Hamburg. William Patton sent a series of cables about the Pennsylvania's earnings and the condition of the stock market. Gould seemed about to make another move. Patton wired Cassatt that the Wabash president had not acquired control of the Norfolk-Western stock, a rumor circulated by the newspapers, which had caused Cassatt much disquiet. The Norfolk-Western was an important feeder to the Pennsylvania and a line in which the president took a deep personal interest. He could not allow his foremost enemy to control it.

Cassatt was back at his desk in Broad Street by early September. As he girded for the coming campaign against Gould, shocking news came over the wires, and all business stopped. President McKinley had been assassinated in Buffalo by a crazed anarchist. Cassatt wired condolences to Mark Hanna and assured the Cleveland financier that the Pennsylvania would offer all facilities for the transport of the late President's casket to Washington. Cassatt himself superintended the complicated move of the six Pullman cars which made up the funeral cortege from the capital through Pittsburgh to its final stop in Canton, Ohio. And he did not neglect the new President, Theodore Roosevelt, who would prove to be such an ally in strengthening railroad regulation. On September 21, Cassatt arranged for the Roosevelt family to board a private car at Oyster Bay for the trip to Washington.

Meanwhile, Cassatt had not forgotten Gould's perfidy in Pittsburgh. Since the Wabash president wanted a fight to the finish, Cassatt delivered his expected coup. On September 20, 1901, the Pennsylvania Railroad terminated its contract with the Western Union, delivering the required six months notice: "The Telegraph Company shall at the termination of the contracts, or at any time thereafter, upon receiving written notice from the Railroad company, remove within six months from the receipt of said notice all of its poles and wires and leave the property of the Railroad Company in good condition and free from encumbrance thereof to the satisfaction of then general manager or other proper officer . . . and if not so removed the Railroad Company may remove them at the expense of the Telegraph Company."

Gould had received fair warning, but he did not take the threat seriously —a mistake. Cassatt had already shown what he could do once his wrath was aroused. Gould might have profited from the experience of one of Cassatt's Main Line neighbors. On the Paoli commuter line to Philadelphia, stood a small station, Upton, on the Villanova estate of Israel Morris, a very proper Philadelphian. Traditionally, the daily trains stopped at Upton whenever the trainmen noticed waiting passengers. One night Mr. Morris entertained a large group of city folk at a fancy dress party which continued into the dawn hours. The guests, still in their costumes, were driven to the station to catch the early morning train to town. To their surprise the train steamed right past them, not even slowing down upon the sight of the expectant revelers. The angry Mr. Morris rushed into the city on the first available transport and stormed into Cassatt's office to demand an explanation of such cavalier treatment. Morris insisted, in the full spate of his indignation, that such a contretemps never happen again. Unruffled, Cassatt promised Morris that certainly as long as the Upton station stood the train would never again fail to stop. He kept his word. Within 24 hours the Upton Station had been demolished. No train ever stopped there again. Nathaniel Burt, describing Cassatt's tenure as president of the Pennsylvania, remarked that no other railroad executive "was more ruthless if still respectable." Cassatt's power was absolute, unrivaled by any other Philadelphian. If Gould had learned of the Upton station incident, he might have been less sanguine about the fate of his Western Union poles.

With all hope of salvaging the Pennsylvania-Western Union alliance gone, Gould turned with renewed energy to the fight for Pittsburgh. By 1901 Cassatt's home town had become one of the foremost industrial cities in the world with a tonnage five times as great as either New York or London. Over 5,000 manufacturing establishments, with a production totaling $450,-000,000 a year, made the Steel City a lucrative prize for the Pennsylvania, a market Cassatt would not relinquish without a struggle. By the turn of the century production had become so intense that no railroad could carry the vast freight efficiently. Conditions worsened; transportation snarls dogged every manufacturer. Gould had his admirers, men who were eager to see the Pennsylvania challenged because they were worried about the fate of their products—coal, electrical machinery, iron and steel pipes, tinplate, glass, tableware, petroleum, pickles, white lead, and cork.

In the fall of 1901, the Pennsylvania, the only carrier out of the city, was handling 75,000 tons of freight daily, earning the railroad $165,000 a mile. But the strain of this carriage was telling. Pittsburgh shippers paid high freight rates and could not secure satisfactory service. Freight piled up at the terminal, packed into cars that could not be moved. Train crews worked beyond their limits, powerless to reduce the chaos. As the orders poured in from around the nation, thousands of workers in Pittsburgh were idle for weeks, waiting for materials rusting on the sidings within a few blocks of their destination, but unloaded and inaccessible. The owners of mills and factories laid off workers, cancelled orders, paid costly forfeits. No wonder the tycoons of Pittsburgh welcomed Gould. The Pennsylvania had been caught unprepared by the explosion of the Industrial Revolution, and the victims were the irate citizens of Pittsburgh.

To harass and frustrate Gould while the Pennsylvania attempted to correct the situation, the railroad transferred the immediate decision to the courts. The advance of the Gould line was opposed by the states of Ohio, West Virginia, and Pennsylvania, and their legal actions held up Gould's construction for months. The Supreme Court of Pennsylvania, influenced heavily by Cassatt and his board of directors, issued an injunction to stop the work within Pittsburgh, involving Gould in exasperating and expensive delay. Cassatt, in the meantime, continued with his own road's plans to widen the Pennsylvania's control of the Steel City with new tracks, terminals, and an impressive new station.

His correspondence during these months is studded with references to the work and his many trips west to investigate the snarled traffic situation. He well realized the effect of the tie-ups on the Pennsylvania's relations with the Pittsburgh manufacturers. On September 27, 1901, he wrote to Schwab: "I regret very much that we have not been able to supply you with all the cars you need. Notwithstanding the very large additions made to our equipment this year, and the fact that the movement is prompt and regular, we have never been so hard pressed to fill orders as at this time. I have given special directions that every effort be made to increase your supply."

After all, Schwab was Cassatt's biggest customer. He could not afford to ignore his pleas or let the steel president encourage Gould's railroad. During 1901 Cassatt spent over $5,000,000 for new equipment and over $17,-000,000 for improvement on the Main Line, including the four tracking of the road and the elevation of tracks. The new Pennsylvania station at Pittsburgh, rushed to completion, opened on October 1. Yet, it wasn't enough, as he confided to Mark Hanna that fall: "Notwithstanding the large number of cars we have built this year we never were so short of cars. We have discontinued sending empty cars to the Lakes for ore in order to help out at the mines. . . ." But by mid-October the condition had not measurably improved, and Schwab threatened to shut down his furnaces. Cassatt became, for him, quite frantic, and wired his fourth vice president, J. J. Turner, in Pittsburgh: "Can you do anything to help them, and what can I say to Mr. Schwab?" He rushed to Pittsburgh again, refusing an invitation to dine with a visiting Italian nobleman on the plea of business. Schwab had not exaggerated. Cassatt, appalled at the closing of the furnaces, which he saw for himself, stripped local stations of cars and dispatched them hurriedly to Pittsburgh to transport coke to the U. S. Steel Co., so that production could resume.

In the midst of this acute transportation crisis, Theodore Roosevelt requested Cassatt's presence at the White House to discuss the regulation of the railroads under the proposed Elkins Amendment to the Interstate Commerce Act. Cassatt had the temerity to wire the White House that he would not be able to cut short his trip. Stephen B. Elkins was a strange choice to sponsor reform legislation. The Senator from West Virginia had made a fortune in New Mexico land and east coast mining by exploiting his political office and marrying into money. Through his business interests, he had become vitally involved with railroads and considered himself an expert. He had close ties with the Pennsylvania, and a modern railroad historian, Gabriel Kolko, believes that the first draft of the Elkins Bill was written in Cassatt's office sometime in the fall of 1901, by the railroad's general counsel, James A. Logan.

Experts differ on the influence of railroad presidents in promoting regulation. Kolko states that Cassatt was in the vanguard of those wanting regulation—Cassatt considered his "community of interest" plan as an expedient until stabilization of rates could be more permanently fixed, and endorses the view that Cassatt helped write the Elkins Bill. John B. Thayer, an officer of the Pennsylvania, later denied that the bill was written by the railroad, but admitted that it "aided with suggestions." Thayer probably was not aware of how closely Cassatt and Elkins kept in touch over the progress of the legislation. Logan even told the press that he had written the bill, and Cassatt's letterbooks reveal frequent meetings between the Senator and the president of the Pennsylvania.

Gould, of course, was opposed to the Elkins Bill, as he intended to honor the Carnegie agreement for special rates to U. S. Steel. He continued with the Wabash, purchasing some small lines to extend his railroad. On November 9 Cassatt wrote to Samuel Spencer, president of the Southern Railway: "Judge Logan's draft was prepared after careful consideration of the whole question and after we had reached the conclusion that it was to the interest of the public that the Commission (ICC) should be clothed with the powers which the proposed amendment gives it. In my judgment it is much wiser and safer a grant than to allow the Commission broad powers over all rates affected by pools or contracts. . . ." Cassatt feared that if Congress did not adopt the Elkins Bill, more stringent measures, over which he would have no control, would be introduced to put teeth into the Interstate Commerce Commission.

He continued to press Elkins on the passage of the bill sending him a peremptory wire in January, 1902: "I am rather disappointed at your not having introduced that Bill. I thought your intention was to do so promptly. Is there any reason for further delay?" Elkins had delayed because other reformers had their own thoughts about regulating railroads. After a few more re-writings, the Elkins Bill was passed in February, 1903. Under its terms both receivers and givers of rebates could be prosecuted with resulting fines of up to $20,000. Cassatt was delighted with the bill. Gould and Rockefeller were not, but neither had the power to get it repealed. Gould continued to press his Wabash forward to the sea, undeterred by the legislation or by Cassatt's efforts to stop him.

By February, 1902, conditions between the Pennsylvania and Western Union had reached a crisis. The termination of the contract between the two companies the previous fall had caused the railroad considerable inconvenience. Without an effective wire service, the Pennsylvania had difficulty in dispatching and moving its cars. Gould continued to ignore the railroad's requests to pull down his wires. He was now totally involved with pushing the Wabash ahead, paying $5,000,000 for a right of way from the Monongahela River into his new station at Pittsburgh which cost $23,000,000 itself. By the spring of 1902, having bought the cooperation of the city council against Cassatt's strenuous efforts, it was evident that the Wabash would soon be shipping freight. Cassatt determined to play his final card. On June 25, 1902 Cassatt signed a contract with the Postal Telegraph Company, to provide the Pennsylvania with its services. He offered to buy the Western Union lines running along the Pennsylvania's tracks, but Gould ignored this, too. Gould's Pittsburgh line obsessed him to the detriment of all his other interests. In the west he was beseiged by Harriman, and his resources were rapidly being depleted.

Cassatt would not wait a moment longer. His enemy must be taught a lesson. He had served notice on Gould that he had a legal right to remove the Western Union poles. Gould responded by taking his case to court, asking for an injunction to prevent the railroad from this drastic action. On May 20, Cassatt learned that Judge Buffington, of the U. S. Circuit Court of Appeals, sitting in Pittsburgh, had denied Gould's request for an injunction. Now there was no legal bar to his action. That evening the order went out to take down the poles and wires from Pittsburgh across the mountains to Philadelphia, north from Baltimore through New Jersey to the banks of the Hudson. Crews stood by in the depressing eighty-seven degree heat waiting for the word which came at midnight. Section foremen learned that all the poles and wires must be down within twenty-four hours, and they bent to their task with a will.

Work gangs, mostly Italian laborers, attached ropes to each pole. The ropes were fastened to an engine which pulled a mechanical grappling hook, felling the poles as it moved slowly up the track, out of sooty Pittsburgh, across the green mountains and lush farmland of the state. Where the engine could not be used, gangs with cross-cut saws made short work of the poles, five minutes for each pole, felling them to lie along the line. No effort was made to remove the mass of lumber and twisted wire. A slight breeze blew up during that long day, relieving the gangs toiling under the hot sun. Spectators turned out all along the commuter route from Paoli to Philadelphia giving a holiday air to the scene. Whole families in station wagons and pretty young girls in brake carriages rode to the stations along the Paoli local line to watch the poles come tumbling down. At Bryn Mawr the college girls gathered to see the heavy crossarmed head of the poles topple and the wire clipped off the wooden uprights. As each pole hit the ground, a cry of "Sic Semper Tyrannis" was raised by the collegians. To residents of the Philadelphia area, the Pennsylvania was an omnipotent, righteous force, protecting its investments and their well being by this ruthless action. Over 1,500 miles of wire and 60,000 poles fell in that one day.

On the evening of May 22, Cassatt rode home on his usual four o'clock train to Haverford. His fellow commuters watched curiously as the president of the Pennsylvania Railroad impassively left the train and stepped over the fallen debris by the track into his waiting carriage. He showed no emotion and made no comment. Obviously, he was not impressed that with a single word he had destroyed $50,000 worth of property. Even the usually admiring Burgess and Kennedy, were appalled by what Gould's biographer, Richard O'Connor, called a "hot tempered and hard-headed" action. The railroad's official chroniclers believed that Cassatt's order produced "probably as drastic an act of eviction as has ever occurred in railroad history." J. P. Morgan said: "I don't like George Gould, but I don't like a man who destroys $50,000 of vested property."

Gould reacted predictably to the destruction of his Western Union equipment. Western Union's counsel charged the Pennsylvania with vandalism, but Charles M. Schaeffer, the Pennsylvania's superintendent, pointed out to the press that the railroad had tried to buy the poles, but that Gould had not even deigned to answer the offer. Moreover, the railroad had a legal right to remove the poles, and in fact, the wholesale destruction had saved Western Union both time and money, since the poles and wires were "too old to even bring a dollar in junk." Schaeffer insisted that the Pennsylvania was more sinned against than sinning: "If anyone should feel aggrieved in this matter it should be the Pennsylvania Railroad, not the Western Union. The Pennsylvania has lost in round numbers, $300,000 through this affair in the last six months." Schaeffer was referring to the disruption of railroad business through the termination of the contract with Western Union.

The railroad had lost $75,000 in annual rent revenue from the Western Union and now would be put to the expense of erecting new poles for its Postal Telegraph contract. This time the railroad would prevent a similar crisis by owning the poles and wires itself and leasing them to Postal Telegraph. Schaeffer remained the railroad's spokesman to press and public for Cassatt never gave press conferences. He considered the whole embrolgio so unworthy of comment that he did not even mention it in his annual report to the stockholders. The power of the Pennsylvania and its president could only be threatened by two critics, the United States government and Wall Street. Cassatt had already secured the allegiance of Roosevelt through his cooperation on railroad regulation. Now he moved quickly to answer Morgan and broaden his financial base in Wall Street.

Pennsylvania stock had been falling on the New York Exchange. To counteract this, Cassatt needed more capital. He contacted the Rockefellers, knowing that the Standard tycoon could force Gould into line and promote peace between the warring railroads. *The Philadelphia Bulletin* reported in late May, 1902, that the fight between Cassatt and Gould had really been an extension of a financial battle between the two Rockfeller brothers. John D. and his Standard supporting Gould in opposition to William and his brokerage firm, Koehn Loeb & Co., which was underwriting the Pennsylvania with a stock subscription of $75,000,000. By the beginning of June, Cassatt was in New York. According to *The Bulletin,* "The truce between the Pennsylvania and the Western Union is said to have been patched up several days ago as a result of a personal interview between John D. Rockefeller and A. J. Cassatt . . . Mr. Cassatt had become alarmed

over the big decline in Pennsylvania stock which threatened the new offering on the market. . . ." Again, as in most of the big deals between financial
giants at the turn of the century, no record was kept of the interview
between the two protagonists. How bitter it must have been for Cassatt to
negotiate with the oil tycoon who had forced him to surrender to the might
of the Standard over a quarter of a century ago. But accord was reached.
Within days the Pennsylvania syndicate reported that the underwriting
committment on the stock issue had been oversubscribed.

Gould insisted on taking his case to the courts, but here, as in the
stockmarket, Cassatt was again a winner. The Supreme Court upheld the
Pennsylvania's action against the Western Union in a decision rendered on
December 12, 1904. Gould was defeated in the courts, but he was hurt even
more by a stunning setback to his social and sporting pretensions. Within
weeks of the destruction of the Western Union poles and wires, Gould
arrived in Philadelphia with his polo team. In the past the railroad president
had been effusively welcomed by the city's socialites when he brought his
horses and players to the annual contest. His actress wife was a great
favorite among Philadelphians—in marked contrast to New York's four
hundred, who had never accepted the upstart Goulds. This time, he was met
by stony silence. No box seats were available for him at the Philadelphia
Country Club where the match took place; no dinner invitations were
offered; no places in the carriages of Philadelphians were available on the
polo grounds for the wayward Goulds. The pair had to watch the contest
from the sidelines. Shortly after the last chukker of the first game, Gould
withdrew his team and returned to New York. The social slight made page
one of the *New York Times:* "Society is a buzz with the affair, and by many
it is interpreted as a phase of the war of the Gould and Cassatt railway and
telegraph interests carried into the social circle . . . The responsibility for
it is said to rest with a number of persons living on the 'Main Line', who
perhaps suppose that it was a good means of currying favor with the
powerful Cassatts."

Certainly, the "powerful Cassatt" did not instigate the social shunning
of the Goulds. He did not need to stoop to such pettiness to assert his
authority. His action in arrogantly destroying the poles and wires reflects
little credit upon him, but there is no reason to suspect that he acquiesced
in his neighbors rudeness. Cassatt never allowed his business practices to
influence his social or family life. He was ruthless in opposition, but more
was at stake than a few thousand dollars worth of poles and wires. He felt
that Gould threatened the very foundation of his railroad, the Pittsburgh
freight business. And he was right, for he won his battle, but not the war.
Gould brought the Wabash into Pittsburgh the following year, capturing
a valuable percentage of the freight carriage. But Gould's victory had been
secured at a fatal cost. While he poured millions of dollars into the Wabash,
his dream of an intercontinental railroad fell to Edward Harriman. By 1907

George Gould had become "the sick man of Wall Street." Rockefeller interests took over the Wabash, while Harriman commanded the Missouri Pacific and the Southern Pacific. Even the Western Union eventually slipped from Gould's grasp. He retained enough of his fortune to continue his luxurious polo-playing life on his New Jersey estate, but he was never again an important factor in railroad life.

In time the Pennsylvania regained its ascendency in Pittsburgh, but Cassatt, ever one to cut his losses, spared little regret for the Wabash triumph. Now, every sinew of the Pennsylvania was taxed as its president prepared to storm the center of Manhattan, so long denied to him.

Moses on the Hudson

It was not a new idea. For more than a quarter of a century, Pennsylvania Railroad executives had looked longingly across the Hudson River toward Manhattan, but that long mile of water remained impregnable to the four hundred trains which daily entered the Jersey City terminal. Since 1871 when he had engineered the purchase of the United Railroads of New Jersey, Cassatt had realized what few Pennsylvania executives were willing to accept: The trading heart of the nation was centered in New York. If the Pennsylvania Railroad was to reap its share of the country's expanding industrial wealth, its executives could only ignore this financial fact of life to their peril.

The river barrier to his trains nagged at Cassatt for years. Each time he travelled to Manhattan—to secure financing unavailable in Philadelphia, to meet with the manipulators of American power, to dine at Delmonico's, to board a ship for Europe—he was faced again with that interminable ferry ride. On one of these journeys soon after his election to the presidency, his frustration reached a climax. On his return to Philadelphia he called his chief engineer, Colonel Charles W. Raymond, and complained: "I cannot bear with the fact that a river less than a mile wide separates this railroad from the greatest city in the western hemisphere." He couldn't bear it, and he wouldn't, not for another moment.

In the 70s, Cassatt had urged that his railroad bridge the Hudson. First the experts considered building a bridge across the north branch of the river, a frightening project which involved a span almost twice that of Brooklyn Bridge, an impossible undertaking in 1871. Each time the railroad considered constructing some kind of connection to Manhattan, a national business panic scared the timid, conservative heads of the Pennsylvania. But by 1900, three prohibitions had been removed: A favorable business condition had created a healthy climate for such a risk; tunnel construction methods had improved; and the use of electric power underground had been effectively tested.

Not content with reports from Europe on the engineering advances in tunnels and electrification, Cassatt investigated himself. During the summer of 1901 when he was in Paris visiting his sister Mary, he inspected the recently opened Orleans Railway Extension, which used the new electric power. He concluded that a New York tunnel was indeed possible and hurried home to put his plans in motion with little regard for engineering and financial obstacles.

On December 12, 1901, Cassatt announced his decision to the world: "The Pennsylvania Railroad Co., is now prepared to carry out its policy, long since adopted of extending its railroad into New York City, therein establishing a suitable passenger terminus for the accommodation of the public." Cassatt may have scorned personal publicity, refused to give press conferences, and preferred to keep his business plans private, but he was astute enough to realize that the press could be a potent force in selling the public on the benefits of his railroad breaching the water barrier into Manhattan.

In 1901 trains arriving at the western bank of the Hudson carried almost 100,000,000 passengers a year. Each one of these travelers had to alight at the Jersey City terminal, after a journey of 3,000 miles from California, or 110 miles from Philadelphia, to huddle impatiently and await the ferry passage into the city. A young Philadelphian, George B. Roberts, grandson of the Pennsylvania's former president, described those boyhood trips with a sense of adventure lacking in his elders: "Everybody got out of cars and climbed the dark, iron stairs to the open top deck, where there were benches in the sun and a fresh breeze from the harbor. Mother promised us a view of the Statue of Liberty and the Brooklyn Bridge and we began to climb on the life rafts and railings . . . At last the boat was loaded, a bell rang in the wheelhouse and the engines began to vibrate. Then, like a sick elephant, the most appalling blast came from the ship's whistle . . . we spent the rest of the voyage under the dim gas lamps of our drawing room . . . mother with cold compresses of cologne, a bottle of Poland water and a box of Petit Beurre bisquits." The ferry left every half hour throughout the day and night, but the thirty-minute journey was the least of it. If a family was travelling with a great deal of luggage, bound for the shipping docks and a trans-Atlantic voyage, with their own horses and carriage, perhaps, all this impedimenta had to be unloaded and reloaded again on the opposite bank, with tiresome delays. Until Cassatt's scheme was completed, no railroad train from New Jersey went into New York City. Passengers walked off the ferry, and then took a four-wheeled carriage into the center of Manhattan.

Cassatt himself, despite his august position as head of the Pennsylvania, endured the same delays and inconveniences as his most humble clients. For example, on September 6, 1901, William Patton wrote to the general manager of the road, about arrangements to transport Lois, Aleck, and their party to Haverford on their return from Europe that summer. "Will you please give directions to have special Car No. 60, in charge of porters, taken to Jersey City on train No. 70 this Friday night, to be held there to await the arrival of Mr. A. J. Cassatt, president, and party, who are returning from Europe on the White Star steamship "Celtic" due to arrive in New York sometime tomorrow (Saturday) or on Sunday. I will also be glad if you will arrange to have a special train, consisting of a combined coach and Car No. 60 ready to leave Jersey City on arrival of the party there and run through to Haverford, Pa., via the West Philadelphia yard." Not for Cassatt the boarding of an Amtrak train in New York and speeding into Philadelphia's Thirtieth Street Station as a returning traveler would today.

Car No. 60, the president's own Pullman, was typical, if not quite as elegant, of most private railroad cars owned by the nation's tycoons during the gilded age. As today's industrial magnate might equip a luxurious Rolls Royce or a Lear jet, the 90s man of substance furnished his private railroad car to reflect his status and importance. Frick, Vanderbilt, Gould, Harriman, Carnegie, Morgan, and Rockefeller would never have considered boarding a common train for their perambulations around the country. They demanded and received special courtesies for their railroad cars, which were, in fact, traveling palaces, each furnished as opulently as their mansions with bedrooms, drawing rooms, and complete kitchens presided over by a chef to concoct the multi-course meals so dear to Victorian palates.

Cassatt's car was more modest, but still impressive with its dark panelled walls, Tiffany lamps, red plush sofas and chairs. The main bedroom had an imposing brass bed, and the bathroom was a model of efficiency. Mr. Fletcher, the porter, and Mr. Green, the chef, were assigned to Car No. 60 and never relegated to duties on lesser Pullmans. At the massive dining room table covered with gleaming white napery, ten people could enjoy the spendid cuisine as the car sped along. In fact, Cassatt rarely traveled on a scheduled train except for commuting trips from Philadelphia to his Main Line home. Car No. 60 was always waiting and available for the president of the Pennsylvania Railroad.

Certainly the convenience of Cassatt and his 100,000,000 yearly passengers was a significant factor in the tunnel project, but of even greater importance, though not usually mentioned by the road's executives, was the delay in shipping freight across the Hudson. This cumbersome and involved process of unloading and reloading meant time and money to a competitive trunk line. Only the New York Central had a clear track into the city from the lucrative western markets. The Pennsylvania would challenge this advantage.

Cassatt further intended to encroach on his chief rival by pushing his line north and east, through the growing suburbs and into New England. His first move was to purchase the Long Island Railroad, kingpin of all suburban commuting traffic. During the 90s the population of New York had been rapidly expanding onto Long Island. By 1900 over 4,500,000 people lived within a twenty-mile radius of New York's City Hall, and most of these householders worked in Manhattan and had to be transported quickly and efficiently to their business. Many traveled on the Long Island Railroad and its fellow, the New York, New Haven, and Hartford. What a bonanza if the Pennsylvania could control this traffic!

Cassatt announced the acquisition of the Long Island Railroad to his board of directors at the annual meeting of March, 1901: "A purchase has also been made of a controlling interest in the stock of the Long Island Railroad Company, which owns the system of lines extending through that island, and reaches many flourishing towns and attractive seaside resorts." The price of that controlling interest—56.6 percent of stock—was over $6,500,000 financed through convertible bonds, a favorite Cassatt device. He did not stop there: "It is also in contemplation to use part of the Long Island Railroad to form a more convenient connection between your system and that of New York, New Haven and Hartford Railroad Company, over which a large traffic passes to and from New England points."

From the beginning of the tunnel scheme, Cassatt had intended to reach Boston, to challenge the Central not only in Manhattan but farther north, into Maine. Some of his interest in the New England traffic might have been stimulated by his purchase of land in Bar Harbor where he intended to build one of those sumptuous vacation "cottages." By an agreement with the New York, New Haven, and Hartford he would now be able, with hundreds of other Philadelphians, to ride directly from the Broad Street station through New Jersey and New York, via the New York Connecting Railroad, to reach his vacation home. But this was far in the future. In 1902 his chief concern was the Long Island Railroad, the first step toward realizing his tunnel scheme.

The LIIR, unlike the trunk lines, earned most of its $4,622,000 revenue from passenger traffic over its 372.35-mile route. The line passed from Montauk at the tip of the island to Long Island City, very much like the route it travels today. But in 1900 when the passengers reached Long Island City, they had to disembark and board a ferry to 34th Street. Cassatt's tunnels would change all that, too, and help Long Island become the first of New York's bedroom communities.

Because of his experience in Altoona, that huge complex of roundhouses and repair shops, Cassatt recognized the importance of a yard to serve his new extended line. He planned the Sunnyside yards outside Long Island City as a model of their kind. For the first time, all trains ran into the yard along a loop, pulling into a coach cleaning area at one end and departing from the other without recourse to the massive turntables used in Altoona.

Sunnyside yard covered 173 acres of land with fifty-three miles of track and provision for 1,387 cars. From Sunnyside tracks joined to the New York Connecting Railroad, which would join the New York, New Haven, and Hartford at Port Norris New York and cross the East River by the Hell Gate Bridge.

This grandiose extension of the Pennsylvania, however, lay several years in the future. In the meantime, Cassatt did not abandon the Pennsylvania's chief business, carrying freight and passengers along the Main Line. To round off the road's tracks west of Pittsburgh, he acquired the Western New York and Pennsylvania, a 585-mile line giving access to Buffalo and Rochester from the east and the west, a vital link in wresting business from the Central when the tunnel project was completed. In all, under Cassatt, the Pennsylvania controlled 6,032 miles east of Pittsburgh and 5,048 miles west of the Steel City for an aggregate of 11,080 miles, giving Cassatt's road a combined gross earning of $295,898,165.24, every dollar of which was needed for his adventurous expansion into New York.

Expenditures on such a scale never troubled Cassatt. In the first three years of his presidency, he authorized two huge issues of stock: the first in 1901 produced more than $50,000,000; the second in 1904 brought in more than $75,000,000. While this extraordinary financing was continuing, the road's business kept on growing as did its stock on the New York market. But its funded debt also increased by more than $100,000,000, a figure which would have caused Roberts sleepless nights, but which Cassatt viewed with equanimity, a necessary concomitant of a healthy company. The financial risks inherent in his invasion of New York City, the tunnel, the station, the subsidiary lines ultimately cost the Pennsylvania about $115,000,000, $15,-000,000 more than the original estimate.

Cassatt had the vision, saw the whole scope of the operation and what it could mean to the Pennsylvania, but the man on the scene carrying out his orders was Samuel Rea. It was Rea who went to England and France, to study intensively the results of electric traction and tunnel construction, who prepared the report which convinced Cassatt that nothing now prevented the Pennsylvania's breaching the Hudson and East Rivers. Rea, the grandson of an Irish immigrant, was a stocky, determined engineer with little formal schooling but vast experience on the lines west of Philadelphia, and he would eventually become president of the line.

Rea's report to Cassatt offered three schemes for entering the city. The first contemplated a tunnel from Jersey City to Manhattan across the north branch of the Hudson near the Battery and then across the East River to Brooklyn. The second proposed a line 31.5 miles long leaving the Pennsylvania line near Rahway, crossing Staten Island, passing under the Narrows to Brooklyn by a 3.5-mile tunnel, and then back across the East River by a bridge to a terminus at Madison Avenue. This second idea was less costly, but Cassatt would not count dollars and cents when the outcome promised rewards. The third proposal, favored by Rea, was a bridge across the

Hudson and a fourteen-line track into Sixth Avenue where a connection would be made with the Long Island by a tunnel under 42nd Street.

Cassatt studied Rea's report and then named a board of engineers to conduct a feasibility study. Included on the board were Gustav Lindenthal, a bridge expert who had wanted to attempt the entrance into New York for twenty years but had been discouraged by Roberts. Others were Charles Jacobs, the English tunnel authority, George Gibbs, a student of electric traction, Alfred Noble, who had supervised similar projects all over the world, and William H. Brown, chief engineer of the Pennsylvania. The committee was headed by Colonel Charles W. Raymond, Corps of Engineers, USA, to whom Cassatt had first confided his intention to cross that obstinate mile of water. Cassatt repeatedly told his board that the work was to be designed without regard to expense "as the governing factors must be safety, durability and proper accommodation of traffic."

Finally, the group produced a compromise which encompassed all these features and earned Cassatt's approval. Through trains for New York would leave Harrison, New Jersey, crossing over the old Pennsylvania tracks on a steel and concrete bridge. A double track, elevated line on embankments and bridges would extend across Hackensack Meadow on a high fill to Bergen Hill. At the western entrance to this hill, the tunnel would begin leading under the North River and then proceed into the Station between Seventh and Eighth Avenues at 31st to 33rd Streets. East of the terminus, four single-track tunnels would cross Manhattan through subsidiary tunnels under the East River to connect with the Long Island road. On the island itself, Sunnyside Yard would both store and service the locomotives.

Once the design was agreed upon and the financing secured, Cassatt moved quickly, opening an office in Manhattan at Broadway and Cedar Street which he visited several times a week. New Yorkers found Cassatt to be very different from his staid predecessors. *The New York Times,* quick to see the advantages to the city in his tunnel project, offered its readers a picture of the Moses in their midst: "A man of large stature, who gives instantly the impression that he is a man of affairs and of power, that he is occupied with great problems, and yet is alert and observant . . . seen coming up Cortlandt Street several times each week, making his way with great strides to the offices of the Pennsylvania Railroad Company at Broadway and Cedar Street." This was the man, the *Times* reminded its readers, who had forestalled the Vanderbilts by acquiring the Long Island Railroad and would now seize the trade of Manhattan. The Vanderbilts were of two minds about this titan, for by 1900 a large body of Pennsylvania stock was held by the leader of the clan, William, who had lost his own zest for railroad management and was content to leave the intricacies of engineering, traffic financing, and construction to a man who knew how to run railroads with ease, A. J. Cassatt.

If the officers of the New York Central were cold to their chief rival, other powers in the city were more enthusiastic, seeing Cassatt as the patron of New York business, who would lead it into a commanding position as the market place of the world. As a result of this engineering miracle, New York would have greatly increased real estate values, a surge in all kinds of trade, ease of suburban commuting, and quicker access to the great steamship terminals at Montauk Point, thus cutting a full day from the Atlantic crossing, vital to New York merchants who looked to Europe for customers, inspiration, and materials.

The New York Central executives had concrete evidence of Cassatt's intention to challenge their road on every line from New York to the Mississippi. On June 15, 1902, the Pennsylvania inaugurated a special run, a deluxe service of twenty hours from New York to Chicago aboard what would become the famed Broadway Limited. Seventy-five years later the Limited, although no longer running under the Pennsylvania's banner, still makes the historic trip. The Central's Twentieth Century Limited has long been banished. Passengers no longer receive five dollars if their arrival in Chicago is behind schedule, but a certain elegance still clings to the journey. On the train's anniversary run in 1977 few remembered that the Limited owed its birth to Cassatt.

Cassatt still had several thorny problems to solve before he ordered the first shovel of dirt turned for his tunnels. The aldermen of New York City and the legislators in Albany had little altruistic feeling about the long-range gain to the city and the state. They wanted a cut of the profits, and they were not willing to wait. No franchises would be authorized by these greedy lawmakers until they had been well bribed. Such a method of acquiring permission to build an intricate transportation system which would benefit the public as well as the Pennsylvania Railroad was abhorrent to Cassatt, against all of his deeply held principles.

He refused to consider bribery of the state and municipal officials for a minute. But to avoid this roadblock required more than determination. Once these gentlemen realized that Cassatt intended to build a $50,000,000 terminal in their backyard, they laid their plans accordingly. Corporations, even such prestigious and fairly honest firms as the Pennsylvania, suffered from the public distrust stirred up by muckrakers like Ida Tarbell and Lincoln Steffens. Corrupt politicians took advantage of this feeling to enlist the aid of the press. They would manipulate the public through the newspapers and cause such a row about the grasping, avaricious railroad that the public would rebel. Then, under cover of this manufactured rumpus, they could blackmail the Pennsylvania into paying their demands, even though what the railroad asked was legitimate and necessary for the public good. Before Cassatt's railroad could enter New York, he had to have the approval of these avaricious politicians.

As a first step, Cassatt cannily contacted the honest mayor-elect of New York, Seth Low, in the fall of 1901. With Low on his side, half the battle would be won. Low agreed to cooperate with Cassatt, but he made conditions, knowing full well the practices of his aldermen: "You must give me your word that you will not attempt to get by secret means what you cannot get in an open way." "Nothing could suit me better than that," Cassatt replied. "I give you my word and the word of my company. We shall make our fight above board, and our plans must go through on their merits, or not at all." Cassatt's word was not given lightly. Low respected his reputation, and a successful alliance against government corruption was sealed. The furious aldermen held up the terminal franchise for weeks. The mayor arranged a conference between the aldermen and the city's Rapid Transit Commission which worked out a modified franchise bill, but to no avail. The aldermen demanded their bribes, and they felt secure enough to procrastinate.

Cassatt was advised by many to pay the "paltry" $300,000 asked by the aldermen for the franchise, but he stubbornly refused to be blackmailed. And for once, time and the city's press were on the side of the giant corporation. The Pennsylvania, unlike the Central or Erie roads, never had a reputation for self-seeking aggrandizement. The public believed in the Pennsylvania, and so did the editors of New York's newspapers, who for the first time allied themselves with a corporation against the "people's choice," the aldermen. The mayor had assured the editors that Cassatt's proposal was an honest one, of great benefit to the public as well as to the railroad. The newspapers boldly and unanimously came to the support of a private corporation asking for public privileges. Day after day, week after week, the campaign continued.

In the end, the aldermen were forced to surrender. Cassatt won his franchise on October 9, 1902 without paying one cent of tribute. In Albany capitulation had occurred five months earlier. The New York legislature had been persuaded to amend the Rapid Transit Act to allow the Pennsylvania to close streets and raze five hundred buildings for construction.

In January, 1902, Cassatt outlined the progress of the work to Colonel Raymond and Gustav Lindenthal. Construction would proceed in four stages. The first section would extend the Pennsylvania tracks from Newark to the entrance of the tunnel under Bergen Hill. The second segment, "The North River Section," would double track a tunnel line between the western side of Bergen Hill and the west side of Ninth Avenue. Thirdly, they would build the passenger station between Ninth and Seventh Avenues. And finally, tracks would connect the station to the Long Island Railroad, "The East River Section." Cassatt concluded succinctly: "You are requested to formulate your own rules and regulations, and upon request, I shall be pleased to amplify these instructions." As was his usual policy, Cassatt chose competent, talented men and allowed them to do the job.

Nonetheless, he kept a close eye on the work. He contacted his old friend George Westinghouse, who had learned about an electrical accident in the

Paris Orleans Extension and another on a Liverpool line. Cassatt wanted Westinghouse's views on the possibility of such electrical mishaps in his tunnels. Then, there was the bill that James Logan wrote for the New York legislature which extended the Pennsylvania's franchise from the proposed seventy-five years to perpetuity. Cassatt took no chances. He might not be around to protect his railroad, but he would see to it that future generations could rely on the Pennsylvania to run its trains into New York.

Although he had told his committee to spare no necessary expense on the tunnel project, he insisted that featherbedding be eliminated. When Lindenthal wanted to lay some experimental track Cassatt vetoed the suggestion emphatically. He reminded the eminent engineer that he himself had a great deal of experience in replacing wooden ties with iron or steel: "I would not feel warranted in directing that a half mile of track be laid experimentally." The drawing board, not the roadbed was the place for experiments. He insisted that proper facilities for the police be included in the station; personally investigated several types of granite to be used in construction of the terminal; and reminded Rea that the building contracts should have clauses protecting the company from undue delays.

No single firm was awarded all of the contracts for the tunnel, but the first was given to the O'Rourke Construction Company, which began work on June 10, 1903. Their tubes consisted of a series of iron rings, placed at an interval of two and a half feet. Eleven segments and a key piece at the top completed the twenty-five-foot circumference; the entire ring weighed about fifteen tons. The cast iron plates, or sections of the ring, had flanges at right angles to the surface through which successive rings were bolted together. In an eight-hour day, five rings, or a distance of twelve and a half feet was completed without incident, slow, dogged, careful installation. Hydraulic rams, placed against the flanges every few inches around the tubes, were used to advance the huge shields with which the tunnels were bored. The shields, each weighing 194 tons, had nine doors through which came the rock, sand, and silt of the river bed. The pressing concern was to make the east and west bound shields meet exactly, and engineers calculated the problem closely, reporting each day on the previous day's progress.

The shields in the north tube under the Hudson River finally met on September 17, 1906, three years and three months after the first digging began. Each had traveled three thousand feet through a treacherous river bed, yet the meeting was perfect. One of the gravest problems connected with the tunnel construction was the uneven support given by various formations in the river bed which caused unpredictable stresses in the tubes. Some experts thought that these stresses resulted from the movement seaward of the waters of the river. Cassatt denied this, citing the old Hudson River tunnel, built twenty years earlier and abandoned, which had been carefully pumped out for a transit line. No movement had occurred in those twenty years: "The bed of the river is not at all bad material. There are a few feet of silt and ooze on top and below that clay hardening as the depth increases." He had gone down himself to inspect. Cassatt did not direct operations from the executive chair. He never left the more unattractive jobs to be explored by underlings if there was any doubt of the outcome.

The shields in the four East River tunnels came together at the same time as those of the Hudson. When all the tubes were placed end to end a 22-inch concrete lining was installed. On each side of the tunnel a three foot wide trench served as a walk and concealed conduits for telegraph, telephone, signal, and power wires. Where the two tracks emerged from the tunnel under the Hudson and reached the entrance to the station, they fanned out to encompass twenty-one tracks, a massive complex well able to handle all the Pennsylvania traffic.

Cassatt, with his engineering experience gained during more than forty years on the road, had no difficulty visualizing the tunnel structure and station. He had the dream and the blueprints, and before long a working model which was loaned to the St. Louis Exposition in 1904. His granddaughter remembers their trip to the Fair to see the model on display. The young guide who escorted them around the prototype painstakingly explained the more complicated features to the party. He did not recognize the gentle, white haired man, so elegantly dressed, who accompanied the blond curly headed child of eight. When the tour was over, Cassatt asked the guide if he could have an interview with the young man's superior. He wanted to commend the guide for his polite, knowledgeable tour. The guide asked who was requesting the interview. "A. J. Cassatt," came the quiet reply. The young man aghast at his temerity in instructing the president of the Pennsylvania Railroad on his own design for the New York tunnel was kindly reassured that he had done a fine job.

Cassatt insisted that the sandhogs burrowing ninety-seven feet below the water's surface be offered every safety measure. Two doctors were on duty around the clock, standing by the tunnel shafts ready for emergencies. The workmen were given hot meals, showers, and bonuses to press ahead on twenty-four hour shifts. Engineers, foremen, and skilled professionals who had dug tunnels in Egypt, England, and South Africa, led by a cadre of sixty Austrians, labored to conquer the most complicated tunneling maneuver in history. Experts insist that no project was ever carried out with more emphasis on strength, safety, and permanency than the New York tunnels, but accidents did happen. Fifteen men were hurt when a steam drill carelessly applied hit a stick of dynamite. One of the injured men later died in Bellevue Hospital. The soft ground on the Jersey side caved in, causing six coal cars to sink and injured many workers. A miner smothered agonizingly in quicksand.

Underwater excavation was dirty and dangerous. The sandhogs who labored beneath the North Hudson and East Rivers delved inch by inch in chambers filled with compressed air pumped to the surface. Blowouts did occur when the compressed air found a weakness in the roof of the tunnel and escaped with a violent rush. One blowout sucked four workmen from the tunnel and blew them through twenty feet of river silt forty feet into the air on the crest of a geyser. Only one of the men survived that terrifying experience. Still the men strained on, earning fantastic pay for their mole-like lives under the water. Over forty men were killed building Cassatt's tunnels.

The New York invasion may have been Cassatt's consuming passion, but he did not neglect the daily operation of the Main Line of the Pennsylvania. In one year, 1901, over $4,000,000 was spent extending the four track system and over $2,000,000 for new locomotives. The roadbeds and equipment of the Pennsylvania were the finest in the world, the best that science and money could produce, constantly upgraded and improved. The earnings of the great trunk line, over $149,000 per mile, easily supported these vast expenditures. The gross income of the Pennsylvania in 1901, the third year of Cassatt's presidency, increased over eighty percent, from $38,000,000 to $68,000,000 and would continue to grow throughout his tenure in office despite the incredible costs of the tunnel.

On April 24, 1902 Cassatt interviewed Charles F. McKim, the senior partner of McKim, Mead, and White, in his New York office. After some discussion he accepted the architect's bid on the $50,000,000 station. As the firm's head, McKim took charge of the Pennsylvania station, but Stanford White's indisputable hand can be seen in the design. On the day of the decisive meeting, Cassatt informed McKim, "Confirming the understanding had at our interview this morning I beg to say that your firm is appointed architects for the Terminal Station to be erected by the Pennsylvania Railroad Company between 7th and 8th Avenues and 31st and 33rd Streets, New York City; your compensation to be the usual commission of five per cent upon the cost of that part of the work placed in your charge, and is to include plans, specifications and supervision."

Cassatt also made it clear to McKim that the architect was only responsible under his $250,000 fee for the work "above the waiting room level." The retaining walls and foundations would be built by his own engineers. Amateurs would not be allowed to mess around with the main function of the New York station, transporting trains. Cassatt called upon his old friend George Westinghouse to install the electrical system, the lighting for the tunnels, and the heating and ventilation for passenger, freight, and tonnage service. Samuel Rea would act as liaison between Westinghouse, McKim, and the various contractors, but Cassatt's would be the deciding voice in any dispute. He may have delegated the work on his dream to experts, expressed his confidence in their abilities, and left them to get on with it, but he still controlled the grand design.

Before that design could arise, twenty-eight acres of ground had to be cleared, over five hundred buildings razed and 1,500 people displaced.

Thirty-Second Street between Seventh and Tenth Avenues, in the very heart of the city, was closed for months, so that miles of gas, fire, and water mains, telegraph, telephone, and electric wires could be removed before the construction began. The grave inconvenience suffered by New Yorkers aroused surprisingly little animosity: The Pennsylvania's subtle, low-keyed public relations campaign had promised them modern transportation, countless jobs, and additional income from the giant rising in their midst.

Two years after the bid was confirmed, on May 1, 1904, McKim, Mead, and White began construction of the 788-foot Doric colonnaded station. McKim and Cassatt had agreed on two ideals: The grandiose monument, modeled after the Roman Baths of Caracalla, which had fascinated Cassatt and depressed Lois, must not only encompass a great railway station but impress on every passenger that this was a monumental gateway to a metropolis which aspired to be the market place of the world. Neither utilitarian nor economic factors would be allowed to interfere. More than a mere railroad station, this was Cassatt's gesture of triumph developed from those days when he stood on the banks of the Hudson and yearned to transport his locomotives across the narrow barrier of water which impeded his access to the largest city in the country.

In its conception Pennsylvania Station defied imagination. Eventually, six city blocks would encompass the Doric monument, 799-feet deep and 788-feet long, over two and a half times the size of a football field. The Seventh Avenue facade was flanked by thirty-five foot columns, four feet six inches in diameter. Above the central colonnade, over sixty feet above the sidewalk, was a huge clock, seven feet across. Through this gateway would pass daily hundreds of thousands of passengers, intent on their destinations, rarely pausing to wonder at the granite palace which was simply a giant bridge atop twenty-one railroad tracks built to shuttle 1,200 trains through its sixteen miles of iron and steel.

The central entrance at Seventh Avenue led to a main waiting room through an arcade over 225-feet long, flanked by shops to serve the passengers' needs. Beyond, the general waiting room dwarfed the reception halls of many emperors—soaring 150 feet high, overlooked by huge semicircular windows sixty-six feet wide at their base. Only the Roman baths had larger roofed-in areas treated in such a manner. Baggage rooms, ticket offices, telephone and telegraph facilities were arranged, so that the passenger could proceed from one to another with a minimum of inconvenience. Here, the passenger was king, a vital, respected element, not just a number on a computer to be shuffled uncaringly from station to station on a sterile iron horse.

Up the thirty-nine foot grand stairway of Italian marble, he would travel to the central waiting room, the heart of the great station. Beyond, lay the concourse, a covered assembly point extending the entire width, four hundred feet, of the station under Thirty-First and Thirty-Third Streets. The concourse served as a mere vestibule to the tracks, roofed by a lofty dome of iron and glass forming intersecting arched vaults. For the first time in the history of American railroading, complete separation of incoming and outgoing traffic was achieved, allowing the passenger to avoid congestion by leaving the building through any of the exits onto four adjoining avenues.

Enormous quantities of stone, iron, glass, and steel were used to build Pennsylvania Station. A total of 550,000 cubic feet of Milford pink granite, transported in 1,140 freight cars from the Massachusetts quarry, formed the ornamentation. Some 15,000,000 bricks, 27,000 tons of steel, and 150,000 cubic yards of concrete went painstakingly into the slow construction. To light the station even the 500 arcs and 20,000 incandescents often failed to penetrate the misty gloom which gave the cavernous palace of transportation an unique aura of excitement.

Figures alone fail to create the intoxicating air of mystery which surrounded the station. Through the Seventh Avenue facade, up that grand stairway into the huge waiting room streamed the train travelers of the world. For many Americans some of the most dramatic events of their lives occurred there, memories forever connected with its soaring space, hurrying, indifferent crowds, in winter's twilight, summer's deadening heat, through two World Wars and countless crises both national and personal. Standing foursquare amid sprawling, demonic New York, Pennsylvania Station was a symbol of Philadelphia, as contradictory and superior as the Quaker City itself, thumbing its nose at the crass materialism of its rival.

Cassatt conceived the tunnels, the trackage, that enormous pile of pink granite, glass, and stone as the ultimate railroad station, superseding all others, a tribute to his mighty 11,000-mile road. He did not live to see it completed, but as long as it stood, until 1963, it represented the final monument to this man who knew how to run a railroad as no one else did. Four years, four months, and a week after the first earth was displaced, trains began a scheduled run from the station. The first train out was the Perth Amboy local at 12:01 A.M. on November 27, 1910.

By then the creator of the tunnel, Cassatt, had been dead for almost four years. But from 1900 when he began negotiations for the purchase of the Long Island Railroad, through the wearying months of the franchise fights, the tragic deaths of the workmen, the endless complaints, revisions, obstructions, Cassatt had never lost his vision. Like Moses on the banks of the Red Sea, he calmly awaited the parting of the New York waters to allow his Pennsylvania Railroad into the promised land.

The Bull Moose Roars

By 1904, when Theodore Roosevelt, grinning his way into the hearts of the people, won the presidency in his own right, the railroads had become the ogres of American life. Roosevelt might not know much about economics or understand the problems inherent in an industry which had grown out of control, but he was adept at taking the national pulse, at knowing which causes stirred the minds and hearts of the voters. And no single facet of his country's business aroused such wrath as the railroads.

Since 1900 the anger had been smoldering among a wide spectrum of the people. The farmers, through their Granges, demanded control of railroads which had changed from allies who shipped their grain to new markets, to enemies who threatened their existence through esculating rates which they were helpless to control. Shippers of steel, grain, and manufactured products alike complained of discrimination, bad service, and disdain for their needs. Investors wearied of the graft and rebate wars, unchecked by the Elkins Bill, which affected their profits. Passengers, the forgotten clients of the transportation giant, feared for their lives and limbs aboard locomotives which careened unheedingly across the countryside. Ten thousand Americans were killed every year and another 80,000 injured while the managers of the roads callously continued to manipulate their stock. The workers whose average weekly wage rarely exceeded $25 were enraged at the huge fortunes acquired by the railroad tycoons who paraded their ornate mansions, their spanking horses and carriages, the jewels on their pampered women. The trunk line officers' control of local and state politics, their power over Senators, Congressmen, even Presidents, had been received the sullenly by the public, but a new prairie populism had arisen, abetted by

eastern radicals, which clamoured for regulation. Control the railroads—
the nation demanded, and Roosevelt heard the cry.

At first he seemed less than eager to wield his celebrated big stick against
these obvious "malefactors of great wealth." Many of his trusted lieutenants
were captives of the railroads. His party, largely conservative, favored
unchecked railroad expansion. He waited until the indignation had reached
fever pitch before acting. In his message to Congress of December, 1904, just
after his election, he proposed new social and economic legislation which
would redress the balance between corporate greed and the public weal, but
with reservations: "Increased supervision is the only alternative to the
increase of the present evils on the one hand or a still more radical policy
on the other." Obviously, the radical policy was much to be feared.

Cassatt had sensed this mood and the need for action well before Roosevelt, in fact as early as 1901. But his "Community of Interest" plan, his effort
to force the railroads to regulate themselves by discarding secret rebates to
such shippers as Standard Oil and U. S. Steel, had rebounded. Unfortunately, many Americans believed it was just another ploy to enable the
Pennsylvania to control its rivals. The Elkins Bill, which Cassatt had helped
to write and pass against formidable opposition from his peers, had proved
a slender reed. Congress and the courts failed to prosecute offenders against
the law even when evidence of wrong-doing was blatant. Roosevelt himself
from 1901–1904 was reluctant to proceed against the obvious culprits and
even protected them when they asked his cooperation. After all, some were
his friends and supporters, and he had yet to be elected to the Presidency.

Paul Morton, Roosevelt's Secretary of the Navy and a former vice president of the Atchison, Topeka, and the Santa Fe, was a patent example.
Morton had been an officer of the western line when it had granted unlawful
rebates. When the case broke after Roosevelt's election, Morton resigned,
but the President publicly defended the cabinet offiicer. No judgment was
brought against the Santa Fe. International Harvester, that great farming
combine, should have been fined for accepting rebates, but Roosevelt's
Attorney General, William H. Moody, interceded, and the case was
dropped. The "railroad Senators," Foraker of Ohio, Aldrich of Rhode
Island, Elkins of West Virginia, and Spooner of Wisconsin, were all against
strict regulation of the railroads. In sum, until 1904 Roosevelt honored the
ideal but not the law. Once his power was secure, however, he felt safe to
oppose some of the most potent forces in his own party and requested a
stronger law against the railroads.

Contrary to popular belief, not all railroad men were resisting efforts to
strengthen the Elkins Law. Samuel Spencer, of the Southern, was one such,
Charles S. Mellen, of the New Haven was another. But it was to the most
influential of all, A. J. Cassatt, that Roosevelt turned for advice on his
pending bill. Cassatt was no stranger to intimate Presidential conclaves over
railroad problems. A month after Roosevelt succeeded to office, Cassatt had

written a long memorandum to the President on the flaws in the Interstate Commerce Law.

Cassatt listed procedures which he believed would strengthen the law. First, the ICC should have the authority to direct a rate change after investigating a complaint and allowing the carrier to appeal as far as the Supreme Court if necessary. Second, the orders of the court should be speedily enacted. Third, if the evidence justified it, the ICC should be empowered to examine the books of the offending road. (This last suggestion was too much for many, including Roosevelt.) Fourth, criminal prosecution should be abandoned in favor of heavy fines. Finally, Cassatt came out strongly for the railroads' own effort to regularize rates, pooling, until now illegal under the Sherman Anti-Trust Act, and the basis of his own "Community of Interest" plan. Pooling had never proved effective, but he was unwilling to abandon it.

Almost every "railroad Senator" and trunk line president were against Cassatt's suggestions, and Roosevelt himself felt that the scheme was too radical. Realizing that some stringent measures were needed, Cassatt tried repeatedly to bring his fellow presidents into line. In January, 1902, he wrote to Stuyvesant Fish, president of the Illinois Central: "We are so far apart in our views on this question that I fear nothing would be gained by its further discussion by us." Sharply, for Cassatt, he took Fish to task for the latter's stand against the ICC: "I do not understand your reference to a bargain believed to have been made between certain officers who had violated the law, and members of the Interstate Commerce Commission, or persons acting for them. None of the railroad managers of the country, so far as I know, has expressed himself in favor of granting any additional powers to the Commission except myself, and I beg to assure you that there is no agreement of any kind between me and the members of the Commission; indeed, I can hardly suppose you intended to suggest there was."

Cassatt bridled at any imputation of personal impropriety. He reminded Fish: "I cannot accept the responsibility of acting as trustee of all the railroads in the United States, which you seek to place upon me, nor can I admit that our influence is so prepondering, as you seem to suppose." But if Fish was wrong about Cassatt conniving with the ICC, he was absolutely right in suspecting that few other railroad presidents enjoyed the respect and prestige which Cassatt inspired in his peers and the public. Fish kept trying to persuade Cassatt to join the legion fighting regulation until the president of the Pennsylvania refused to discuss it. He also refused to attend a meeting of railroad chiefs with Roosevelt later in the month: "I very much fear that in view of the diametrically opposite views which we hold, nothing would be accomplished by such a meeting." In those days Cassatt was far ahead of Roosevelt in regulating railroads.

In the succeeding two years, with the Elkins Bill fulfilling some of his demands—although it failed to allow the ICC to fix rates—Cassatt was occupied with his New York tunnel scheme and the day-to-day running of the Pennsylvania.

Cassatt now showed the effects of the burdens of his position. His hair and moustache had turned white. Less time for exercise had added pounds to his large but dignified frame. He seemed indomitable, but he tired more easily. The job was taking its toll, and family affairs had added to his many business worries, although he never allowed those to interfere with the tranquility of his domestic life. He rarely discussed with Lois his enormous responsibilities. His children were another matter, however, and they did nothing to lighten his exacting duties as president of the Pennsylvania. There was now no chance of his elder son's marriage surviving, and his younger son, although safely and happily wed to Minnie Drexel Fell, had failed to find a compatible career.

In July, 1903 his new summer home, Four Acres, at Bar Harbor, was finished, down to the last Dresden cup and Waterford goblet. A lavish mock Tudor "cottage," the sprawling complex with stables, gate house, and dock had servants' quarters for sixteen maids and four men. The Cassatts with a full retinue, including little Lois and her nurse and Elsie (Mrs. Plunkett Stewart), who was expecting her first child, arrived to spend the summer. Just a month before, Katherine, Aleck's favorite, and the last to leave home, had married her long-time suitor, Dr. James P. Hutchinson, who had finally been successful enough in his profession to support a wife in a manner worthy of a Cassatt.

At her marriage Katherine was thirty-two and already suffering from a goiter disease still undiagnosed. The Hutchinsons, following their June 8 Philadelphia wedding, spent the summer in Europe and joined her parents in September in time for the birth of Elsie Stewart's son, Cassatt. During that winter, after the family had returned to town, Lois first noticed her daughter's failing health. By Christmas both Aleck and Lois realized that Katherine's condition was deteriorating. At first, Lois thought that her daughter had a nervous malady. In March Aleck decided to take Katherine, his granddaughter, and Lois to Aiken, S.C. for a change of air. At sixty-six he had outlived any previous Pennsylvania president, and his responsibilities increased with each month. Aiken helped him, but his daughter continued to flag, which added to his already heavy cares. A man of temperate habits, a country lover well disciplined in both mind and body, Cassatt was finding the strain of his family and business taxing at last. Emily Cassatt's divorce had reached its final stages, a situation which the Buchanans also found "tedious," and they advised Lois to follow her inclination to have nothing to do with "the Mother." But Aleck, worried about his beloved grandchild, did not adopt their attitude. He wrote punctiliously to Emily about her daughter's welfare, her entrance into Miss Spence's school in New York, her music and language lessons, thanking Emily for allowing him to have "Baby" in Aiken. The eleven-year-old seemed to ease his troubles. Her companionship was, as always, a delight and a source of relaxation.

On April 11, 1905, after yet another abortive trip to Aiken with her father, Katherine Hutchinson died. Ironically, a cure for her goiter problem was discovered within months of her death. Aleck took her death hard. Lois wrote many years later in her diary: "Her loss to us and her husband was irreparable, and I feel now that your father was never able to get over the shock of her death." Within a month of Katherine's funeral Emily Cassatt married George Batchellor, thus ending any faint hope of a reconciliation with Edward and a reuniting of the family. The marriage to George was a happy one, lasting over forty-five years. Most important to Aleck, the marriage did not separate him from his grandaughter who continued to make her home, six months of the year, with the Cassatts. Katherine's death and Edward's divorce darkened 1905, among the most taxing of Aleck's forty-year railroad career, and although he met adversity with outward calm and strength, the emotional drain was heavy.

Neither of these personal tragedies influenced Aleck's inspired direction of the Pennsylvania Railroad. At no time, before or since, had the trunk line been run with such efficiency or at such a profit. Both tonnage and mileage showed an exceptional increase in volume, the largest in the history of the company while dividends rose to a record seven percent. After meeting all the liabilities for the year, the expenditures on the tunnel, the increased taxes, and the steady price rise of all materials purchased for the road, there was a surplus income of over $11,000,000. The gross earnings on the Main Line had expanded by $2,000,000, while the net income of the entire company had grown by $10,000,000. Such astonishing gains were made during major improvements throughout the system and accompanied a ten percent hike in wages. Cassatt's imaginative financing and creative management brought the Pennsylvania to the peak of its profit and power.

When Roosevelt began his effort to regulate the railroads, Cassatt directed over 120,000 employees, more than one third as many as then worked for the federal government. The Pennsylvania's income equalled nearly one-half of the national revenue from all sources. There was much that Roosevelt could have learned from Cassatt, who was more than willing to advise the President, but the ebullient Teddy was determined to ride the crest of the national hatred for the railroads. In the exhiliration of leading the popular outcry, he made no distinction between a Cassatt and a Gould. They were both "malefactors of great wealth."

When Roosevelt announced to Congress in December, 1904 that he intended to enact legislation to control the railroads, he had no idea what that control would embody. At first, as he told the editor of *Outlook,* all he cared about was the battle. He announced: "I shall fight," but the battle plan was missing. In his speech to Congress, Roosevelt said: "I am of the opinion that at present it would be undesirable, if not impractical, finally to clothe the

Commission with general authority to fix rates." A month later he had changed his mind and informed business leaders in Philadelphia, at the Union League Club, of his reversal. He demanded a bill to give some "tribunal" authority to fix rates. Cassatt, of course, was at that Union League dinner and in close contact with the White House over the proposed bill, the Townsend-Esch Act. The measure allowed the ICC to declare a freight or passenger rate unjust and fix a substitute which would go into effect in thirty days, subject to court appeal.

Cassatt, one of the few men to favor the bill, did not believe that it went far enough. In February, 1905, he wrote to Spencer, of the Southern, a memorandum of a recent conference they had both attended at the White House. He called attention to the weakness in the Townsend-Esch Act: It did not really reconstitute the ICC, but only allowed the President to replace uncooperative commissioners. Most important, Cassatt objected to a special "tribunal." The Circuit Courts were better equipped to handle complaints of secret rebating. He had also persuaded Roosevelt that water traffic should be covered by the law.

Roosevelt seemed to heed Cassatt's suggestions, but he was beseiged on all sides by Republicans who opposed any bill at all, much less the Townsend-Esch Act. Cassatt, mindful of the impact of personal influence, tried to talk many of his fellow presidents around. In a long letter to E. P. Ripley, head of the embroiled Atchison, Topeka, and Santa Fe, he elaborated on the salient points of the Act, especially the clause permitting pooling. Cassatt was not as fond of pooling as were his fellow presidents, since he felt that it led to abuses, but he conceded that "conditions do exist in certain sections of the country which would make such a right useful." He warned Ripley that the public was demanding a strict bill. If this bill foundered, then another would be required, for the time had come for "the power to supervise rates in some governmental body." Since the Elkins Bill had relieved rebating somewhat, most railroad leaders were not as enthusiastic as Cassatt for federal interference, but the public felt far differently and Cassatt knew it.

Cassatt accepted the inevitable, but Roosevelt hesitated, reluctant to face the storm he had stirred up. The Townsend-Esch Bill passed the more liberal House in February, 1905 by a wide margin, 326 to 17, but the Senate, controlled by Republicans in bondage to the railroads, stalled the bill indefinately. Now, the President was having second thoughts: "When I say a square deal, I mean square deal—exactly as much a square deal for the rich man as for the poor man; but no more." He asked Congress for another bill, "not only in the interest of the public but in the interest of the honest railroad man and honest shipper alike ... This legislation should be enacted in a spirit as remote as possible from hysteria and rancor." This was a far cry from his earlier diatribes: "The railroads have been crazy in their hostility," and "I shall fight."

By the fall of 1905, Cassatt realized that the Townsend bill was pigeon-holed. Now, he made a gesture of his own. Every annual report of the Pennsylvania Railroad since 1880 had advocated the free pass, one of the gravest abuses connected with train travel. Throughout his professional life, Cassatt had been beseiged for free passes, from distant connections of the Buchanans, from journalists, from favored shippers, from anyone with a tenuous railroad connection. In the forty-seven letterbooks of Cassatt's presidential correspondence, an inordinate amount of space is devoted to requests for this favor.

Politicians were the greatest offenders, regarding the free pass as an inherent privilege of their position. In each state as January 1 approached, railroads sent annual passes to the Governors and all state officials; in the smallest hamlets mayors and party leaders received their tokens of the railroad's esteem. On the floor of the Pennsylvania state legislature in Harrisburg, a representative of the Pennsylvania Railroad had a desk. His business there was to issue passes for certain favored constituents and through this largesse keep an eye on the lawmakers who might pass bills unfavorable to railroad interests. Cassatt might argue against the practice, but had felt up to now that he had had no choice but to continue it.

By 1900 the ability of a state legislator to get trip passes for his constituents was among his most potent patronage methods. Naturally, the practice was abused. "A political boss who has obtained and used for the purpose of debauching his followers a bushel or more of passes is not likely to be indifferent to the expressed wish of the railroad company for some new kind of crook in legislation, or the suppression of bills which ought not to be suppressed," warned the *Philadelphia North American,* a newspaper dedicated to attacks against the railroad.

But the days had passed when Thomas A. Scott could manipulate the state legislature with the bribery of the free pass and other favors. During Roosevelt's first year in office, railroad presidents whether liberal or conservative in philosophy, had accepted Cassatt's view. The benefits of the pass system were more than outweighed by the animosity it aroused. The free pass was no longer a useful tool. It was doubtful if any legislator was influenced by a bribe he considered simply a just tribute to his power. Money talked where ideas failed. Cassatt produced statistics to show that free passes meant a difference of $1,000,000 a year to the gross earnings of his road. Other presidents were also quick to learn the obvious lesson. Cassatt's friend, L. F. Loree, head of the Delaware and Hudson, insisted that passes had ceased to be regarded by politicians as an occasion for gratitude, much less for reciprocal favors. It had only become possible to offend by refusing them.

On December 15, 1905, while the passions aroused by Roosevelt were at their height, Cassatt issued a directive "that the issue of passes and free tickets of all kinds be discontinued from and after 1st January next." A day later the heads of the Philadelphia and Reading, the Central Railroad of New Jersey, and the New York Central followed suit. Again, Cassatt had led in cleaning the railroads' house. *The New York Sun,* a conservative newspaper opposed to much railroad legislation, revealed the inequities of the Southern Pacific in California. Lincoln Steffens, Ray Stannard Baker, Henry Beach Needham all attacked the railroads and related shippers. In the spring of 1906, while the railroad bill was still being debated in the Senate, Upton Sinclair exposed the scandal of the meat packing industry in his novel *The Jungle.* Chicago's Armour & Company, the largest meat packing firm in the country, offered the railroads enough business to control rates, another mammoth shipper in league with the hated trunk lines. While capitalizing on this explosive publicity, Roosevelt remained above what he called "the lunatic fringe," the "man with the muckrake in his hand." But the revelations increased public indignation, and Roosevelt used this opportunity to press his reforms.

In January 1906, Peter Hepburn, Congressman from Iowa, a state bitterly against the railroads, introduced a new regulatory bill in the House. Cassatt was now not alone in urging its passage. Many of his colleagues had lined up behind the bill, though many continued to oppose it. Most of the managers insisted on a broad judicial review clause, giving the courts wide latitude to judge the roads' performance on rebates. Cassatt put his arguments before the President in a letter sent during the House debate. He pleaded "our right to have orders of the Commission reviewed by the courts as to their reasonableness and justness . . . I respectfully submit that we have a right to expect that a Bill would be framed which would be just to the railroads as well as to the public . . . In common justice to the Railroads the Bill should go further and give the Courts power to suspend an order pending a hearing, the railroads giving bonds to endemnify the shippers in case the order of the Commission shall be affirmed." Roosevelt agreed with Cassatt but pointed out that Philander Knox, his former Attorney General, and now a Senator from Pennsylvania, refused to consider such an amendment. Knox advocated broad judicial review which would allow the railroads more latitude. He was joined by Aldrich and Foraker. Cassatt brought his influence to bear on Knox for a more lenient attitude, but was not wholly successful.

Ironically, a latter-day muckraker, Gustavus Myers, believed that Cassatt had placed Knox in the Senate to do his railroad's bidding. Myers quoted a story in *Colliers* which reported that after Republican Senator Matthew Quay's death in 1904, the bosses gathered in Cassatt's Rittenhouse Square house to name a new Senator. While Cassatt entertained the men over port and walnuts, so the story went, Governor Samuel W. Pennypacker, who would make the appointment, was escorted into the garden by Boise Penrose, the senior Senator, to look at the moon. While the two state politicos were gazing at the night, Penrose told the Governor, "It's

Knox." And Knox it was. Myers commented wryly that "some minor interest is lent by the fact that Cassatt was a Democrat." Myers believed the story, which was revealed after Cassatt's death, and insisted that "its accuracy was not disputed, and no denials were made," specious reasoning when the man who could deny it was dead. If Knox was a captive of the Pennsylvania, he did not act like one during the debate on the Hepburn Bill. If Cassatt had any hand in naming him to the Senate, he backed the wrong man, an error of judgment of which he was rarely guilty.

The Hepburn Bill, outlawing the free pass, giving the Commission the power to fix a definite rate, to prescribe and enforce a uniform system of accounts, and to oversee not only railroads but sleeping cars, private cars, express companies, terminal lines, and pipelines, passed the House by a decisive vote of 346 to 7 in February. Once again, however, its passage by the Senate was another affair. The opposition to the bill included almost every powerful Republican Senator. Even Elkins, sponsor of the earlier bill, and a railroad tycoon himself, refused to sponsor the bill as he should have as chairman of the Senate Committee on Interstate Commerce. Nelson W. Aldrich, a Rockefeller son-in-law, and the Republican party whip, as well as Henry Cabot Lodge, Roosevelt's friend and staunch ally, were also cool to the Hepburn Bill. Foraker, of Ohio, was adament against it. They were a daunting cabal.

To embarrass the President, and in the hope that it would kill the measure, Elkins, Foraker, and Aldrich arranged that a Democrat, "Pitchfork" Ben Tillman, of South Carolina, would lend his name to the Hepburn Bill in the Senate. The fire-eating Carolinian had earned Roosevelt's dislike by engaging in a brawl on the Senate floor when Roosevelt as Vice President was presiding, and the two did not speak. How could a man who was not speaking to the President sponsor his bill? But a friend of the quarreling pair arranged a partial rapproachment. Tillman, while protesting about Roosevelt's bad faith, presented the bill. Roosevelt had been forced by the conservative railroad Senators to ally with the despised Democrats, but even that was better than siding with the junior Senator from Wisconsin, Robert La Follette, who advocated a radical amendment to the Hepburn Bill. He demanded that the Senate introduce a scientific, rate-making standard based on evaluation of railroad property, a design so revolutionary that it seemed no railroad man could ever countenance it. But Cassatt was not averse to the proposal. In all, fifty amendments were offered to the Hepburn Bill during the debate on the floor, and as the winter lengthened into spring, it seemed that Roosevelt's demands for a square deal on the railroad question would not be met. During that long winter Roosevelt relied on Cassatt for advice, recognizing his dedication to railroad reforms. Tillman, who was unwilling to acknowledge Cassatt as an ally, took exception to his frequent visits to the White House.

In March, while the debate on the Hepburn Bill still raged in the Senate, the ICC began an investigation of "railroad discriminations and monopolies in coal and oil," initiated by the outcry against Standard Oil but aimed at the anthracite combine organized by J. P. Morgan which also involved the Pennsylvania. The newspapers headlined the graft revealed by the ICC counsel who moved his headquarters to Philadelphia and began a vigorous and very public investigation into the Pennsylvania railroad. Cassatt, wearied by a year of haggling with friends and enemies over the Hepburn Bill and by personal tragedy needed to escape from the pressure. Then, too, there was the French loan, a delicate negotiation, which only he, with his many European contacts, could successfully bring to fruition. He needed a vacation, but he could not run away. On April 9 he wrote to Martin A. Knapp, Chairman of the House ICC Committee: "If the Commission desires to examine me in connection with the investigation now being made of the coal and oil carrying railroads, I would be very much obliged if you could arrange to have me called some day this month, as I propose sailing for Europe on the ninth of May, and although I shall return the latter part of June, I expect to be at my office only for a few days, after which I shall go to Bar Harbour."

The ICC counsel, William Glasgow, assured him that there would be ample time for his trip. As evidence of his good faith, Cassatt supplied Glasgow with a detailed statement on the railroad's coal holdings, including a list of stockholders and the declared dividends. That memorandum would return to haunt him. He prepared for his trip certain both that he had satisfied the immediate requests of the ICC and that his own affairs would reveal no taint. Cassatt's fortune was safely invested in banks, trusts, and railroads. He had sold his coal holdings before assuming the presidency.

On May 9 Cassatt sailed for London aboard the *Baltic* with his wife and granddaughter. Lois wrote: "I was so rejoiced that he could go and enjoy a complete rest. We had a very comfortable voyage and arrived in London at the Berkeley Hotel well and in good spirits." On May 18, while the Cassatts were in England, the Senate passed the Hepburn Bill, 71 to 3, with only Foraker and two states' rights Democrats in opposition. The final victory had been assured when Roosevelt allowed his conservative friends to include a broad judicial review provision in the statute. In fact, the new act only refined the Elkins Act and did not radically depart from it. The bill broadened the jurisdiction of the Commission which was enlarged from five to seven members, and the time for notice of the rate change extended from ten to thirty days, both provisions which Cassatt had favored. Fines for breaking the law were set at three times the sum of the unlawful rebate, and a prison sentence, a maximum of two years, was restored. Section 15 dealt with rates. Upon complaint of a shipper or a railroad, the ICC "could determine and prescribe what will be the just and reasonable rate. . . ." No criteria for court action were mentioned, which meant that the broad judicial review advocates had won hands down. La Follette was pleased that Section 20 imposed a standard book-keeping system on the railroads, although it did not allow the ICC to evaluate their property.

It was Section 1, "the commodity clause," which was to cause Cassatt the most uncomfortable and saddening weeks of his professional life. The clause, aimed at the anthracite roads, forbade a line to transport goods, exception for timber and its own property, in which it had a direct or indirect interest. Despite his obvious reliance upon and respect for Cassatt as the chief among "the decent railroad men" who had called for regulation, Roosevelt did nothing to protect him when the crusading counsel of the ICC decided to investigate the Pennsylvania.

On May 16, the day after the Cassatts arrived in London, the *Paris Herald* reported, in Lois' words, "the outrageous action of the commission in Philadelphia and criticism upon your father, as well as false statements in regard to some of the officers of the Pennsylvania Railroad." But were they false? The May 18 *Public Ledger* was headlined "Railroads Admit Discrimination." Favoritism in the distribution of cars to certain coal operators was the charge and worse was to come—actual payment by these same operators to some officials of the railroad. Lois, of course, bristled at any imputation of wrong-doing in her husband's conduct of his affairs. But she had never understood them. Aleck had always sheltered her from the indignities of the market place. She might, however, have been warned by a letter from her son, Robert, the previous summer. Robert Cassatt, now head of the family firm, had suggested: "Tell Pa I am working on a consolidation of coal interests in the Latrobe field which will include three of our companies ... All this is not very interesting to you, I suppose, but I thought Pa would like to hear of it." Pa did, but he had no idea that his son's coal interests would reflect on his own integrity.

Lois was inclined to blame Roosevelt for the whole affair. Such matters were always black or white to her. Her diary reveals that her husband was "much annoyed by the attitude of the president in the matter of the railroads, and especially by his interstate commerce work. . . ." She failed to appreciate that Roosevelt's attempts to secure regulation of the roads had spared no one. Cassatt would be a victim of the President's determination to parlay the public bitterness against some railroad managers into a personal popularity contest. In a passion of anger against her husband's critics, Lois wanted to return to Philadelphia immediately, so that Aleck could confront his accusers in Philadelphia's Federal Building: "As soon as I saw [the newspaper article] I told your father there was but one thing for us to do and that was to return home at once, as I knew he would wish to help his friends and I felt the charges made could only be answered by him personally."

What were the charges? That Cassatt and other officers had used their position to withhold cars from coal operators whose mines rivaled those owned by the Pennsylvania and their friends; that other coal owners, in gratitude, had paid for favors with stock and money, enriching these transportation robbers. "Railroad Officers Admit Big Gifts," ran the May 17 *Ledger* headline. That same day the reporters learned that Robert Cassatt would testify before the investigating commission. Lois was frantic. But Cassatt, with his usual objectivity and calm, waited to hear from his deputy, Captain John P. Green, acting as president of the company in his absence. Green, a veteran of Sherman's "March to the Sea," had a cheery disposition and a true soldier's sense of discipline, but he failed to inspire the confidence which Cassatt commanded so easily. He admitted too little, too late, and then temporized, waiting until Cassatt could gather matters into his own more capable hands.

On May 19, after it was learned that both Robert Pitcairn and William A. Patton, Cassatt's own personal assistants, had been subpoened, Green admitted to reporters the truth of some of the allegations. He tried to downplay the scandal by saying that the revelations were a "surprise" to him. Green's statements received short shrift, for he was not the real target. *The Ledger* on May 19 revealed "Men Near Cassatt Hold Many Shares in Coal Companies." Pitcairn, recently retired from the company, had been a Cassatt man since the 1877 Railway Strike. Just the day before Cassatt had left for Europe, he had written his former aide: "I cannot let the occasion pass without expressing the regret which I feel at the severance of the pleasant official relations which have existed between us for many years." Pitcairn deserved his loyalty, as even more did Patton, whose whole professional life had been devoted to smoothing Cassatt's path. Patton and Pitcairn—the ICC investigation was striking close to the respected head of the Pennsylvania.

Even in this personal crisis, Patton tried to protect his chief from unpleasantness. On May 22, the very day he admitted to the committee that he owned $307,000 worth of coal stock in the tainted companies, he wired Cassatt, "All well. Hope you will not allow sensational newspaper reports to interfere with your vacation. Your name has never been mentioned and there has been no intimation by Commission of their desire to have your testimony. Your offer to testify is well understood by public." Patton had tried to minimize the outcry. He protested to Glasgow that his stock had come to him legitimately, through judicious investment encouraged by former Pennsylvania presidents, which was in no sense illegal.

Cassatt's refusal to grant press interviews, his imperviousness to publicity now served him badly. The newspapers, eager to capitalize on the scandal involving the powerful head of the Pennsylvania, kept up the pressure. Cassatt offered to come home immediately, but both Patton and Green assured him that it was not necessary. He had to go to Paris for a brief visit with Mary and to secure the French loan of $50,000,000 which was so vital to improving the Main Line and financing the tunnel. On May 24 the Cassatts arrived in Paris to be greeted by more unfavorable publicity. Now, even Green and Patton were concerned. That evening Cassatt received a cable which Lois remembered "made your father decide to sail for home on Friday" (May 25). They boarded the fast Hamburg line vessel, *Amerika,* at Cherbourg and arrived in New York on Sunday, June 3.

The newspaper campaign did not abate. While he hurried across the Atlantic, one front-page cartoon showed the beset Green waiting anxiously while a balloon above the tossing waves had Cassatt promising, "Hold the fort, I'm coming." He left the *Amerika* by pilot ship and rushed to the Jersey terminal where his private car, sent by Patton, was waiting to whisk him home. On the dock hordes of reporters greeted him. They had one over-riding question: "Would he resign?" For the first time in his life, he was forced to heed the clamoring of the press. They were not satisfied with the terse Marconigram he had sent from the ship to the Associated Press: "No foundation for rumor that I intend resigning. Am returning to take part in investigation by Board of charges against officers."

A huge collective sigh of relief must have swept through the offices of the Pennsylvania on Broad Street when the wire was printed. Cassatt would rescue the company from what he believed to be a concerted effort on the part of the federal government and his erstwhile friend Roosevelt to capture popularity by trying the Pennsylvania Railroad on the front pages of the newspapers. *The New York Sun* agreed. That organ of big business accused Roosevelt of just that action: "After a Railroad President, Roosevelt Hopes to Convict One or More. Thinks the Example Thus Set Would Be a Wholesome Check on Rebaters."

Roosevelt, in his ebullient effort to become a trust buster, had conveniently forgotten what he owed Cassatt, the real champion of railroad regulation. While Cassatt sailed homeward, while the ICC attacked Cassatt and the Pennsylvania, John P. Thayer, a vice president of the road, was called to Cleveland, to testify about the company's rebates to Standard Oil. Cassatt's humiliation at the hands of Rockefeller in 1874 was not enough. Now it would all be raked up for a press circus. Even Carnegie added his mite, sanctimoniously above the fight in his secure new image as a benevolent philanthropist. He informed the newspapers that he had never accepted rebates from the Pennsylvania even when they were offered and had never interviewed Cassatt. It seemed that the king was falling.

On Sunday evening Cassatt boarded his train for Philadelphia, leaving his wife and granddaughter to be escorted home by William Patton. Only Robert Cassatt accompanied his father to the city, and he served only as Job's comforter. Cassatt & Company had mammoth coal holdings. As Cassatt traveled, his thoughts must have been bitter. Was he after forty years of railroad management, a pioneer in every aspect of the profession he had mastered so successfully, with his tunnel dream in sight, his "Community of Interest" plan translated into federal law, to be denied the respect which he had every right to expect. Had he abandoned his quiet life as a country squire for this?

End of the Line

A few minutes before 8:30 on a hot humid Monday morning, June 4, 1896, A. J. Cassatt's carriage drew up at the Haverford station. With his fellow commuters, he boarded his usual city train, accompanied by an equally grave William Patton. In the train sheds of Philadelphia's Broad Street Station, the normal clanging activity signaled that Cassatt's railroad continued on schedule. None of the uneasy quiet of the executive suite which greeted the chief's arrival permeated the yards where locomotives and freight cars racketed back and forth. No welcome committee had gathered to receive the beleaguered president, noted a *Bulletin* reporter, waiting outside the offices. Cassatt, outwardly as impassive as ever, was ushered into his suite by the black porter guarding the sanctum. The door closed, and whatever anguish and dismay awaited Cassatt behind that mammoth mahogany and leather desk was not witnessed by the outside world. "If President A. J. Cassatt did any personal investigating of the charges of graft against the Pennsylvania Railroad officials at his office this morning, the public was not taken into his confidence," *The Bulletin* reported.

But A. J. Cassatt did do some investigating, and immediately. He first summoned the railroad's counsel, Francis I. Gowen, for a progress report and was closeted with the lawyer for an hour and a half. Later, each top executive, beginning with Captain Green, was summoned to state his case. They came and went quietly, *The Bulletin* announced. No hint reached the reporters' ears as to the probable date of Cassatt's appearance before the ICC investigating committee which had reconvened that morning a few blocks away in the Federal Building. The newsmen were all struck by the change in the atmosphere, not only at Broad Street, but in the Federal

Building as well. That Cassatt had arrived and had matters in hand affected the attitude of the ICC committee. The proceedings lost much of the "Star Chamber" quality which had so delighted the sensationalists.

Rumors abounded in the city's financial district and out along the 11,000 miles of the Pennsylvania system: Cassatt had rushed back from Europe on the demand of Congressman Knapp; the ICC committee had subpoenaed him; his own family were involved in the Berwind-White and Keystone Coal Companies which had received favored treatment from Cassatt's railroad; Cassatt would resign and be succeeded by George F. Baer of the Reading. Reporters thronged the outer offices of the Pennsylvania, speculating, inventing, clamoring for an explanation. Finally, Cassatt emerged late in the day to issue his first and only official statement.

He had returned from Europe, he said, because he had learned "that charges had been made against certain officials of the acceptance of bribes from coal operators . . . The Board would investigate all such charges exhaustively, and if any officer or employee should be found guilty of corrupt practices he would be summarily dealt with. . . ." But, Cassatt warned, the railroad "would not sacrifice faithful and efficient officers to a manufactured and mistaken public opinion." Loyalty was a Cassatt trademark. In the past that quality had enabled him to accept the dubious actions of a Scott or a Roberts. He would not desert his associates now, no matter how misguided their deeds or intentions. He would not be badgered or panicked into making unwarranted concessions to the popular clamor. Not exactly Vanderbilt's "public be damned" attitude, but a firm resolve that publicity, however damaging, would not stampede him into careless actions.

The calm, reasoned statement reminded the press that it, too, had a responsibility. If the heedless attacks continued, the Pennsylvania would be forced to suspend its planned improvements on the line, and a country-wide depression could follow a failure of confidence in the railroad. He called attention to his railroad's past performance, his support of the Elkins Bill, the two-year fight to end secret rebates, the management's "taking the company out of politics and abolishing the free pass." He insisted, in answer to charges of favoritism, "That all shippers are on an absolute equality, paying full tariff rates." The only favoritism possible could be exercised through the distribution of coal cars, and for that, too, there was an excuse: "There has always been a shortage of coal cars . . . and in recent years this condition has been aggravated by the increase in the production of coal, notwithstanding the very large increase the Company made to its equipment. This has given rise to many complaints." Some of these complaints were justified. Cassatt remembered only too well Charlie Schwab's demands and the snarled traffic in Pittsburgh when Cassatt had been forced to rush to that city to supervise personally the movement of 40,000 freight cars. Despite herculean efforts the rise in production meant that the situation would probably become worse, and the public should be prepared.

He did admit, a conclusion he had reached through the revelations of scandal in the press, that Pennsylvania officers in the future should not own stock in coal companies. But he had no criticism of their former holdings. In the past both Thomson and Scott had encouraged their employees to buy coal stock as an incentive to the nascent industry along the railroad's lines. Cassatt, here, was on dubious ground, and he knew it: "The subject was troublesome and complicated but it would do no good, but harm, to adopt unworkable and unenforceable regulations." He promised that his board would handle the affair pragmatically, but gave no indication how.

Cassatt was wise enough not to attack the investigating committee and admitted that "there might be instances of misconduct," which the Company itself would root out and punish. Throughout the statement Cassatt made no attempt to answer any of the personal attacks against him. He referred only to "the Company" or "the management," never to "me." He maintained, against criticism to the contrary, that "the Company's affairs were honestly conducted in the interest of the shareholders and with full recognition of its duty to the public."

Naturally, he defended his company, believed in its integrity, and took umbrage at the attacks against it. He chided his fellow citizens for their lack of loyalty to the railroad, ignoring Philadelphia's decades of suffering beneath the yoke of the Pennsylvania's monopoly. After all, the railroad had been founded to bring wealth and prestige to the city, and Cassatt felt that it had done that and more: "The management deserved better treatment than it had received from the press and particularly from the press of the Company's home state. It had rendered an immense service to the public and to the cause of honesty and decency in the conduct of the transportation industry." In this argument he was on firmer ground. For compared to the Central, Erie, and Union Pacific, the Pennsylvania was indeed a model of propriety. He mentioned again the Elkins Bill and the company's cooperation with lawmakers who had now attacked him, the friend of regulation. Roosevelt's posture in the whole affair was not overlooked, although Cassatt never mentioned him by name. The press, in its current hostility to the railroads in general, "was only following the lead of some heads of the two great political parties who were trying to outbid each other for popular support by attacking large vested interests indiscriminately."

Large vested interests—and the railroads were the largest of these—had certainly aroused the public's ire. Cassatt was too knowledgeable not to know this. He quarreled only with the "indiscriminate" war against the Pennsylvania. His opinion of the popular press and its willingness, in search of circulation, to be manipulated by the politicians had never been high, and in his present difficulties he found the press' attitude unforgiveable. Both the press and politicians were now his enemies. Even Senator Philander Knox, believed by many to be a captive of the Pennsylvania, chose this time to rail against the abolition of the free pass, solemnized in the Hepburn Bill.

In answer to the tumult, Cassatt himself decided to manipulate the very newspapermen who were threatening the good name of his Company. While still abroad he had instructed Captain Green to appoint a committee of Pennsylvania directors to make an in-house investigation of their own, hoping by this stratagem to turn the public wrath from his door. To a certain extent his ploy succeeded. The committee was chaired by a distinguished Philadelphian, C. Stewart Patterson, who promised to delve into every stock holding of every executive in the Company. Cassatt himself led the way by revealing the source of his own wealth in railroads, trusts, banks, railroad supply houses, with not any coal stock among them. He had divested himself of all these suspect stocks upon assuming the presidency. His own hands were clean. Of his son Robert and William Patton there was still suspicion, which his statement did not remove. Cassatt did inform the committee that he was prepared to take the stand at any time in defense of his own integrity and management. He awaited a call which never came.

Four days after his father's statement, Robert Cassatt appeared voluntarily before the committee to discuss Cassatt & Company's embroilment in the coal graft. He protested against dubbing the Keystone Coal Company, in which his firm owned one quarter of the stock, "a Cassatt concern." But he had trouble explaining why the Keystone, which shipped only 875 tons a day, had access to railroad cars for 1,000 tons while less fortunate companies waited in vain for transport. The Keystone was one problem, not satisfactorily solved, but the Berwind-White was another, and Mr. Berwind, too, hurried home from Europe to deny favoritism charges before the ICC.

In the next few days, it seemed that Cassatt's obdurate stand, his refusal to resign, the announcement of the company's investigation, and his own reputation had deflected much of the censure. Then on June 6 another storm broke. Joseph Boyer, chief clerk to the superintendent of motive power at Altoona, the position once held by Patton, admitted that he had accepted gifts from certain coal companies amounting to more than $45,000 in cash and 11,000 shares of stock. On a salary of $2,700 a year, he had become a wealthy man. Boyer's job enabled him to buy millions of tons of fuel a year for the Pennsylvania from any company he wished. He had been unable to resist the graft opportunities. His testimony created a fresh furor. The next day, Joseph Aiken, chief clerk of the Monongahela division, confessed that he had augumented his $125-a-month salary by "purchase" of $50,000 worth of coal stock now worth double that amount. He insisted that his holdings were not "incompatible" with his position in the railroad company. His tone, under questioning by the ICC counsel, was arrogant and insolent, and the old animosities were rekindled.

Various coal company presidents rushed to the stand to testify that the Pennsylvania had almost forced them out of business through discrimination in the matter of car distribution. Only Edward Berwind remained firm.

Asked by reporters as he docked in New York whether he had been favored to the detriment of smaller companies, he denied the allegation. No Pennsylvania officer was a member of the Berwind-White board. The company had not benefited from special treatment. On the contrary, the suave Berwind said: "If anything our company had suffered at the hands of the Pennsylvania through lack of cars."

On June 8 Cassatt fired both Boyer and Aiken (*The Bulletin:* "Mr. Cassatt Hews Off Another Head"). The two clerks, both minor culprits, were the only Pennsylvania employees to lose their jobs as a result of the ICC investigations. The worst was over, and the company could feel it had been lightly treated. The ICC counsel, Glasgow, did not summon Cassatt, to his amazement and the public's. Was Cassatt's power and reputation such that Glasgow was afraid to subpoena him? Or was he satisfied with Cassatt's statement, the announcement of his holdings, and the thorough house-cleaning promised by Patterson's probe? Patton suffered no reprisals, retaining all his coal stock. Cassatt would have defended him to the last, but there is no doubt that his trusted associate's involvement deserved more scrutiny. Certainly, the investigation had revealed improprieties. Although a few hapless officials were punished, and Cassatt himself proved guiltless, the reputation of the Pennsylvania had suffered—and during the presidency of A. J. Cassatt. By mid-June the ICC committee had turned its attention to the New York Central.

Cassatt continued to press Patterson for a full exploration of the company's interest in coal companies and other suspect manufacturing, but he felt he had the job well in hand, the immediate outcry silenced. He wrote to a Wall Street friend, George R. Morse: "While there has been gross unfairness and exaggeration in the published reports before the Commission, enough has been disclosed to show there must be a thorough house-cleaning. This the Board has already undertaken in a most vigorous way and I am sure that the shareholders and the public will be satisfied with the results." The shareholders, whose dividends suffered little from the exposé, may have been satisfied, but the victimized public continued to despise the railroads. And the scandal continued to haunt Cassatt.

On June 16 Cassatt hired an independent audit company to examine the company's books, directed Patterson to send out a letter demanding that every employee reveal his personal holdings, and made a meticulous explanation of his own former coal interests. He even insisted that a minor station agent resign his connection with a coal company. He explained his decision to Patterson, with a touch of bewilderment that such an edict was necessary: "While in many instances employees of coal companies have from motives of convenience and economy been appointed agents at stations, especially where the principal business of the station was that of the establishment with which they were connected . . . yet it is no doubt desirable that the duties of an agent should be performed by a deputy."

When he remembered Thomas Scott's free-wheeling direction of the Pennsylvania, he must have sighed for the days of non-interference by public, press, and government, although he had been among the first to see its need. He directed the purchasing department to be independent of all other departments, vital to effective reform. Repeatedly, he reminded Patterson that any area of the railroad which could possibly be accused of conflict of interest should be cleansed of all taint of corruption. An official owning warehouse stock, known to the management and never previously discouraged, must resign his directorship: "I think, for several reasons, it is undesirable that officers should continue to hold such stocks or be officially connected with such companies." Christmas gifts were to be discouraged. Even the New York tunnel contracts were scrutinized. Cassatt informed Patterson that he had learned of rumors accusing the Pennsylvania of favoritism in awarding construction and supply contracts. He did not believe them, but promised to delve deeper and report any evidence to Patterson. A steam-towing superintendent was forced to surrender his stock in a dry-dock concern because this subsidiary of the Pennsylvania could be suspected of wrong-doing. So it went throughout June. Once Cassatt had decided that the Pennsylvania needed to be purged, he spared no effort.

Long inimical to the press, Cassatt during this crisis authorized an interview which appeared in *Pearson's Magazine* that same month. James Creelman, the writer, praised Cassatt for his reform of the rebate system, for his fight against the New York alderman, for his championship of government regulation of railroads. He traced Cassatt's long struggle against secret rates and asked: Could this man be personally corrupt? "There is something unspeakably sinister and unfair in the vultrine instinct which scents only the evil, and persistently ignores the good in the constructive business life of America; and it is this silence . . . which marks the present mob-like campaign of abuse as light-headed and temporary in a nation ordinarily distinguished for its average commonsense and sober justice." The writer took his readers to task for not honoring Cassatt's struggle against the illegal rebates. Instead, Cassatt had endured "currish insults," Creelman complained. He hoped that history would vindicate this oppressed president of the Pennsylvania. Eventually, he believed: "The average honesty of American businessmen today will compare favorably with any period in the history of the country . . .," a dubious judgment. He refused to think that the American people can long be startled from their customary sanity "by shouting and scribbling class-agitators."

Current economists and historians are inclined to agree with Creelman that the charges against the "malefactors of great wealth," the Morgans, Vanderbilts, and Rockefellers, have been exaggerated. In truth the country owes much of its industrial leadership to these titans. There is some evidence that the outcry against the Pennsylvania was inspired by balked politicans and headline-hungry journalists, but there are also enough data to suggest that the Pennsylvania, like other railroads, had engaged in illegal practices. Cassatt found the Pennsylvania involved in politics and did his best to extricate it. *The New York Times,* in its august editorial pages, said: "In the later years of Mr. Cassatt's career he openly advocated and practiced the doctrine that the true policy of a public service corporation was to deal candidly, fairly, and honorably with the public, to seek no advantages by secret or corrupt means, to rely on informed public opinion, and to use all honorable means to keep the public informed of what it had the right to know. It is not unkind to him to say that the corporation with which he was so intimately and influentially connected had not always lived up to this doctrine and that indirectly at least he may be accountable in part for its failure." It was ironic that the country's most passionate advocate of government regulation, its most progressive and far-sighted railroad manager should be singled out for persecution. Experts agree that under Cassatt's aegis no railroad in the United States, perhaps in the world, was so well directed, so efficient, so safe and profitable for both stockholders and public. But the Pennsylvania had proved vulnerable, and the nation delighted in the humiliation of the proud railroad and of the imperious man who ran it.

But there were also many who remained loyal. From Jacob H. Schiff, New York banker and old friend, Cassatt received not only sympathy but good advice which he adopted: "What you say in relation to the importance of our making a statement of our financial requirements is entirely in accord with my views. It has been in our minds for some time past and we will proceed at once to prepare a draft. . . ." Cassatt alone among railroad presidents had agreed with the radical LaFollette that the government should be allowed to examine any road's books. And Cassatt had much to reveal with pride. The previous year the Pennsylvania's 44,000 stockholders had shared a net profit of $73,969,249, more than any other American railroad. Of the $192,000,000 spent in improvements to the Main Line and for the New York tunnel scheme, $70,000,000, had been secured from annual revenue. The stupendous tunnel project had far from bankrupted the Pennsylvania, as some critics had feared, but had been furthered by the growing prosperity of the whole system.

A week after answering Schiff's letter, Cassatt cabled Captain Green en route to Europe, that the French bankers had subscribed the full amount of the requested loan, $50,000,000. Green would visit the Paris bankers and confirm the details which Cassatt had failed to complete because of his hurried trip home. Cassatt had weathered a rough passage, probably the stormiest of his professional career, to bring his company safely through the shoals. But at what a cost!

He still expected to be called before the Commission, although he had received no subpoena, and was tempted to appear voluntarily. "I do not want to give anyone a chance to say I have avoided going before the

Commission," he wrote to Green in London. Inexplicably, the ICC counsel and the newspapers no longer seemed interested in Cassatt. He noted: "There has been a complete change in the tone of the press; in fact very little attention is being paid to the proceedings before the Commission." The reporters had turned to other, more assailable subjects.

Saddened, aged, and far from well, Cassatt in those sulfurous late June days, had some slight satisfaction in announcing the French loan and in the progress of the north and south tubes under the Hudson River, soon to be joined. By the beginning of July, he could anticipate a holiday from his cares and a restoration of his health at Bar Harbor. His former ally and betrayer, Roosevelt also prepared to leave for the summer White House at Oyster Bay. Not a word had been sent to Cassatt by the President during his recent trials. But he had no compunction about asking for special accommodation from the Pennsylvania Railroad. One of Cassatt's last chores before leaving Philadelphia was to arrange for the President's trip—but this time without a free pass. The letter explaining the details of the Roosevelt trip concluded "and render a bill for the service made out against the Executive Office, Washington, D.C."

On July 5 Private Car 60 steamed out of Haverford Station at 7:35 A.M. bound for Boston, Maine, and the Mount Desert Ferry. Aboard were Aleck, Lois, Elsie Stewart and her children, Cassatt and Katherine, and twelve-year old Lois Cassatt. Young Cassatt Stewart was suffering from a bad cold which proved to be the forerunner of whooping cough. No sooner had the party settled into Four Acres at Bar Harbor than all the children came down with the disease. And Cassatt, ever the devoted grandfather, helped with the small patients.

He continued to keep in close touch with his office, his full attention now centered on the New York construction. His dearest wish was to preside over the official ceremony opening the tunnel link. The ICC might have finished with the Pennsylvania, but Patterson's probe persisted. On July 21 Cassatt wrote to his general manager, W. W. Atterbury, that he had just received the names of employees who had not answered the questionnaire sent out concerning financial holdings: "Please write to all of those who are not thus marked informing them that a prompt answer is expected. I have attended to the others." Woe to those recalcitrant officials who had drawn their chief's censure. He managed to further deflect the public wrath by choosing this time to announce a reduction of fares by two and a half cents a mile. Harriman's Union Pacific had claimed credit for introducing all steel construction for its passenger trains, a requirement Cassatt had introduced previously. He was irritated by the western magnate's unwarranted claim: "We ought to get a little advertising from what we have done. I think a statement had better be given through the Press Bureau." He had learned the hard way that public relations played a necessary if annoying role in running a railroad. By the end of July, Cassatt's correspondence from Bar

Harbor ceased. He, too, had caught the whooping cough, a serious disease for a tired man with a heart condition in his sixty-seventh year.

Lois realized the threat to her husband: "It was so severe that I feared he might die in one of the spasms of coughing. I took the precaution of having a nurse in the house all the time, and finally got a young physician to sleep in the house as the worse spells were only in the nighttime." Lois had every reason to worry. In 1894, the Philadelphia doctors had warned her that her husband's heart malady was very grave and might kill him at any moment. Throughout the summer he remained ill and could not attend the tunnel ceremonies. But by September he had recovered sufficiently to resume some gentle exercise. He walked from Four Acres to the club every day and went sailing in his sloop *Scud,* which had replaced the *Enterprise.* He again attended to business and received Edward Harriman on a brief visit.

Harriman, about to be investigated by the ICC, wanted Cassatt's advice on how to handle the Commission's questions. He had much less of a case, due to his manipulation of his western railroad funds. Not one of Cassatt's favorite colleagues, Harriman, with his brusque manner and ruthless attempts to monopolize rail traffic through stock manipulation, had antagonized the Pennsylvania chief. Although still convalescent, Cassatt agreed to see him. Harriman arrived at Four Acres early in the morning after the long trip from Boston in the ferry to the Cassatt private dock. He remained closeted with his host for some time and then took his leave. Lois Cassatt, coming downstairs just before luncheon, reproached her husband for not inviting their visitor to share the meal. Cassatt testily replied: "No Harriman will lunch at my house." Business was one thing, but he did not consider Harriman worthy of his hospitality.

As Aleck's health improved, he sailed daily in his sloop and determined to take part in the last race of the season in mid-September, although Lois felt it might be too much for him. He piloted the *Scud* with his usual skill, coming across the finish line in good order against high winds and a spitting rain. Triumphant but tired, he would not admit that the race had taxed his strength.

After this summer holiday more tiring than soothing, Cassatt returned to Haverford and immediately took up the burdens of his office. In November the family moved into their Rittenhouse Square house, and still he drove to Broad Street every day although his wife and associates noticed how much the effort cost him. Obviously, the rugged frame and iron will which had served him so well were faltering. Patterson had completed his investigation of the company's employees, and his report, sent to all the stockholders, eased Cassatt's mind: "The Committee find, as the final result of its examination of the whole subject (whether officers of the road charged with furnishing cars to shippers were interested as owners of the coal carried) . . . that with few exceptions the officers and employees of the companies constituting the Pennsylvania Railroad system have been faithful to their duty." Patterson and Cassatt, both aware that the report could be termed a whitewash, had concluded: "As a matter of policy, it has been determined that it is to the interest of the Company that none of its officers or employees shall have any ownership, direct or indirect, in any company, or any interest in any firm or with any individual owning or operating mines located on your system or dealing in coal produced therefrom . . . The necessary measures have been taken to force compliance with this regulation."

If only it could rest there. Cassatt had dealt fairly and firmly, he believed, with the threat to his railroad, but the time of trial had been fatal. As his sixty-eighth birthday approached, it was evident that he had suffered a mortal blow. His family rallied around him—Robert visiting his father every day and Edward coming from Fort Myers to spend a three-week leave in Rittenhouse Square. After December 8 Aleck no longer even attempted the trip to Broad Street, and Patton brought the most pressing work to the house. Everyone hoped that the domestic quiet, so removed from the confusion of the executive suite, would allow him to rest and regain his health. Lois noticed that he was not responding to the enforced isolation, but in fact, grew more and more feeble. She dreaded the onset of a long and painful illness with her husband permanently invalided. For the first time the family dinner at Christmas was cancelled, although Aleck gave out the gifts to the children around the tree that afternoon. Only his favorite grandchild remained for the evening meal when, as Lois sadly remembered, "for the first time he did not put on his dress suit for dinner."

The day after Christmas he remained in bed until afternoon, and on the twenty-seventh he did not leave his room. Still, Patton brought the correspondence to the house to be signed. The final letter in book No. 95 was a reply to a complaint against a porter on the ferry boat *Brunswick* which carried Pennsylvania passengers across the Hudson river to New York. He promised to "give the subject of your complaint a thorough investigation and communicate further." Elsie Stewart came to spend the night of the twenty-seventh, intending to go to the opera, but decided to remain in the house when she saw her father. Lois insisted she go as "it might arouse his suspicions" as to how ill they believed him to be. She returned before the last act and remained by her father's bedside.

On December 28, a dreary, dour day, Lois called in a second nurse to help her cope with the patient through the long night ahead. That morning the doctor found Aleck weaker and advised him not to try to get up.

But at noon, he became restless and told Lois to call his valet, Joseph, to help him up. With his usual consideration, he waited for the valet to finish his luncheon. Joseph then helped his master to the bathroom and back into the bedroom. Aleck told Lois he felt tired and would rest a bit before going downstairs. He lay on the bed, and then suddenly said with a frightened voice, "I'm going to faint." She called the nurse, and they gave him the medicine which in previous alarms had never failed to rouse him, but there was little response. He sighed, looked at his wife, put his hand to his heart, and died. It was one o'clock.

Four years after Cassatt's death James McCrea presided over the ceremonies inaugurating the opening of Pennsylvania Station. "We are here today to honor the memory of the late president of the Pennsylvania Railroad Company, Mr. A. J. Cassatt," Samuel Rea intoned. By his side stood Edward Cassatt, who unveiled the bronze statue designed by Alexander Weiner in the niche prepared at the foot of the grand stairway. The inscription on that statue, which would be passed by millions of unheeding passengers for over fifty years, read "Alexander Johnston Cassatt, President of the Pennsylvania Railroad, 1899–1906, 'Whose Foresight, Courage and Ability Achieved the Extension of the Pennsylvania System into New York City.' " McCrea said that hot August day in 1910 that, "As the years roll round, the greater will be the tribute to Mr. Cassatt's genius."

But that prophecy has not been fulfilled. The name that once ranked with that of Carnegie, Rockefeller and Vanderbilt, has sunk into obscurity with the railroad he ran to perfection. Within fifty-three years, the very statue which marked his contribution came under the wrecker's hammer. That same year, as his portrait by Sargent reproached them from the walls of the director's room, the officers of his once proud road merged with its arch rival, The New York Central, and together they rode down the road to scandal and insolvency. Today, neither the New York Central nor the Pennsylvania exist, sunk into those anonymous corporate structures, Con-Rail and Am-Trak, run by the very federal government whose cooperation had once been sought by Cassatt.

Who remembers Cassatt? Not the men who followed him in executive office, driving his empire into bankruptcy, disgrace, and oblivion. Where once the Pennsylvania and its competitors ruled the transportation world, trucks, motor cars, and airplanes have captured the imagination and devotion of a mobile America. Besieged by government regulations, labor feather-bedding, greedy manipulators, the Pennsylvania has lumbered into history. With it has gone the man who gave it its proudest hour.

For Alexander Johnston Cassatt the end of the line was not reached that rainy December day when he died, but on a cold midnight fifty-seven years later when the last red Pennsylvania passenger train steamed out of the Thirtieth Street Station in Philadelphia. It moved down the track, its red tail lights gleaming, riding into the past and taking with it the final memories of the man who ran the railroad.

Bibliographical Note

Even at its apogee, the Pennsylvania Railroad discouraged examination of its operational methods. Traditional Philadelphia reticence combined with a nineteenth-century business philosophy to prevent executives from cooperating with any author interested either in the lives of the officers or in the organization and running of the company. In later years the Pennsylvania's confused affairs intensified its directors' tendencies toward secrecy.

Although this biography does not pretend to be the story of the Pennsylvania, considerable railroad history is involved. My chief source on Cassatt's tenure as president was the presidential letterbooks which encompassed all his professional correspondence from 1899–1906. Several bales of unfiled letters to him in the Pennsylvania warehouse were also studied. The authorized history of the company by Burgess and Kennedy was a useful starting point, but it is strongly prejudiced in favor of the company's view, particularly on the strike of 1877. Burgess and Kennedy barely mention the I.C.C. investigation which clouded the final months of Cassatt's life. Certainly, new studies of the Pennsylvania are badly needed, and when the records are finally released by the bankrupt corporation or by Con Rail, scholars may have the opportunity to examine them.

For Cassatt, the man, Mrs. John B. Thayer's family letters formed the basis of the research. Without these letters it would have been impossible to glimpse the personality behind the official figure. She also recalled many illuminating stories of her grandfather. The family letters are now the property of her heirs and are unavailable to scholars.

The day-to-day operation of the railroad, the reaction of the public and of the state and federal governments were largely taken from the newspapers. I have not made a separate notation of these accounts, but a study of the relevant years of *The New York Times, The Philadelphia Bulletin, The Philadelphia Record, The Philadelphia Public Ledger,* etc., would be useful to any railroad student interested in pursuing the matter. I have also consulted various railroad journals.

Listed below are some of the other valuable sources which have enabled me to understand the business climate, so different from our own, which provided a background for the Cassatt life.

Adams, Charles Francis, Jr. *Railroads: The Origins and Problems.* New York, 1878.

Allen, Frederick Lewis. *The Great Pierpont Morgan.* New York, 1949.

Alexander, Edwin P. *The Pennsylvania Railroad: A Pictorial History.* New York, 1947.

Anonymous. *Alexander Johnston Cassatt.* Privately printed. Philadelphia, 1913.

Amory, Cleveland. *The Last Resorts.* New York, 1951.

Baker, Ray Stannard. "Railroads on Trial: How Railroads Make Public Opinion." *McClure's Magazine.* March, 1906. pp. 535–549.

Baldwin, Leland D. *Pittsburgh The Story of a City.* University of Pittsburg Press, 1937.

Baltzell, E. Digby. *Philadelphia Gentlemen.* Free Press, Glencoe, Ill., 1958.

Barksdale, F. N. "Alexander J. Cassatt." *World's Work.* July, 1901. pp. 972–977.

Beard, Charles A. and Mary. *The Rise of American Civilization.* 2 vols. New York, 1934.

Blair County's First Hundred Years, 1846–1946. Blair County Historical Society, Hollidaysburg, Pa., 1945.

Bruce, Robert V. *1877: Year of Violence.* Indianapolis, 1959.

Burgess, George H. and Kennedy, Miles C. *Centennial History of the Pennsylvania Railroad Company 1846–1946.* Philadelphia, 1949.

Burt, Nathaniel. *The Perennial Philadelphians.* Boston, Toronto, 1963.

Carnegie, Andrew. *Papers.* Library of Congress.

Carson, Julia M. H. *Mary Cassatt.* New York, 1966.

Carson, Robert B. *Main Line to Oblivion.* Port Washington, N.Y., 1971.

Cassatt, Alexander Johnston. *Letterbooks.* No. 48–No. 95. June 10, 1899–December 28, 1906. Penn Central Transportation Company, Philadelphia. Unpublished.

———"The Hackney." *Harper's Weekly.* April 9, 1892. pp. 346–348.

———*Miscellaneous Correspondence.* Penn Central Transportation Company, Philadelphia. Unpublished.

Cassatt, Lois Buchanan. *Diary.* Philadelphia, c. 1915. Unpublished.

Cassatt, Robert Simpson. *Family Record.* Unpublished.

Cochran, Thomas C. *Railroad Leaders 1845–1890.* Cambridge, Mass., O953.

Collier, Peter and Horowitz, David. *The Rockefellers: An American Dynasty.* New York, 1976.

Cowan, John L. "Freeing a City from a Railroad's Control." *World's Work.* Jan., 1905. pp. 5712–5722.

Creelman, James. "All Is Not Damned." *Pearson's Magazine.* June, 1906. pp. 543–554.

Daughen, Joseph R. and Binzen, Peter. *The Wreck of the Penn Central.* Boston, 1971.

Depew, Chauncey M. *My Memories of Eighty Years.* New York, 1922.

Farrow, Barbara Alyce. *The History of Bryn Mawr.* Bryn Mawr, Pa., 1962.

Faulkner, Herbert Underwood. *The Quest for Social Justice.* New York, 1946.

Fellmeth, Robert. *The Interstate Commerce Commission.* Ralph Nadar's Group Study Report. New York, 1970.

Fiftieth Anniversary of the Incorporation of the Pennsylvania Railroad 1846–1896. Philadelphia, April 13, 1896.

Fisher, Sidney George. *A Philadelphia Perspective.* Nicholas Wainwright, ed. Philadelphia, 1967.

Flynn, John T. *Men of Wealth.* New York, 1941.

Hacker, Louis M. *The World of Andrew Carnegie 1865–1901.* Philadelphia and New York, 1968.

Hale, Nancy. *Mary Cassatt.* Garden City, N. Y., 1975.

Hendrick, Burton J., *The Life of Andrew Carnegie.* 2 vols. Garden City, N. Y., 1932.

Hofstadter, Richard. *The Age of Reform.* New York, 1955.

Holbrook, Stewart H. *The Age of the Moguls.* Garden City, N. Y., 1953.

———*The Story of American Railroads.* New York, 1947.

Hoyt, Edwin P. *The Vanderbilts and Their Fortunes.* New York, 1962.

Hubbard, Freeman H. *Railroad Avenue.* New York, 1945.

Hudson, James F. *The Railways and the Republic.* New York, 1886.

Hungerford, Edward. *Men and Iron.* New York, 1938.

Jeffries, Thomas C. "The Pennsylvania Railroad System." *Manufacturers Trust Co. Bulletin.* New York, Nov. 27, 1921.

Josephson, Matthew. *The Robber Barons: The Great American Capitalists 1861–1901.* New York, 1934.

Klein, Philip Shriver. *President James Buchanan.* Pennsylvania State University Press, 1962.

Knox, Philander. *Papers.* Library of Congress.

Kolko, Gabriel. *Railroads and Regulation 1877–1916.* Princeton University Press, 1965.

Lorant, Stefan. *The Life and Times of Theodore Roosevelt.* New York, 1959.

Lyon, Peter. *To Hell in a Day Coach.* Philadelphia and New York, 1966.

Martin, Albro. *Enterprise Denied: Origins of the Decline Of American Railroads, 1897–1917.* Columbia University Press, 1971.

——"The Troubled Subject of Railroad Regulation in the Gilded Age—A Reappraisal." *The Journal of American History.* September, 1974. pp. 339–371.

Massey, George V. *Remarks.* Philadelphia. December 16, 1911.

Mawson, H. P. "Leaders on the Turf." *Harper's Weekly.* May 31, 1890. pp. 434–435.

McKown, Robin. *The World of Mary Cassatt.* New York, 1972.

Moody, John. *The Railroad Builders.* Yale University Press, 1919.

Mowry, George E. *The Era of Theodore Roosevelt 1900–1912.* New York, 1958.

Nevins, Allan. *John D. Rockefeller: The Heroic Age of American Enterprise.* New York, 1940.

The New York Improvement and Tunnel Extension of the Pennsylvania Railroad. Philadelphia, October, 1910.

O'Connor, Richard. *Gould's Millions.* Garden City, 1962.

New York, Philadelphia and Norfolk Railroad. *Annual Reports, 1885–1895.* Cape Charles, Va.

Oliver, Smith Hempstone. *The First Quarter-Century of Steam Locomotives in North America.* Smithsonian Institution Bulletin 210. Washington, D.C., 1956.

"One Hundred Years in Philadelphia 1847–1947." *The Philadelphia Bulletin,* 1947.

Pennsylvania Railroad Company Annual Reports. Philadelphia, 1864–1882, 1898–1906.

Pennsylvania Senate and House of Representatives. "Report of the Committee Appointed to Investigate the Railroad Riots of July, 1877." Harrisburg, Pa., May 23, 1878.

Pringle, Henry F. *Theodore Roosevelt.* New York, 1931.

"The Railroad Situation in the United States." *Railway Times.* January 26, 1907.

Ripley, William Z., ed. *Railway Problems.* New York, 1907.

——*Railroads, Rates and Regulations.* New York, 1913.

Roberts, George B. *Letterbooks, 1873–1897.* Unpublished. In possession of Bayard Roberts, Philadelphia.

Roosevelt, Theodore. *An Autobiography.* New York, 1920.

——*Letters.* Elting E. Morison, ed. 8 vols. Cambridge, Mass., 1951–54.

Schotter, H. W. *The Growth and Development of the Pennsylvania Railroad Company.* Philadelphia, 1927.

Sharfman, Leo I. *Railway Regulation.* Chicago, 1915.

Snyder, Carl. "American 'Captains of Industry'." Offprint *American Monthly Review of Reviews.*

Southerland, Thomas C. Jr., and McCkeery, William. *The Way to Go: The Coming Revival of U. S. Rail Passenger Service.* New York, 1973.

Spearman, Frank H. *The Strategy of Great Railroads.* New York, 1904.

Stevers, Martin D. *Steel Rails: The Epic of the Railroads.* New York, 1933.

Stover, John F. *American Railroads.* University of Chicago Press, 1961.

——*The Life and Decline of the American Railroad.* New York, 1970

Sullivan, Mark. *Our Times.* 6 vols. New York, 1971.

Sweet, Frederick A. *Miss Mary Cassatt: Impressionist from Pennsylvania.* University of Oklahoma Press, 1967.

Tarbell, Ida. M. *The History of the Standard Oil Company.* David M. Chalmers, ed. New York, 1966.

Taylor, George R. and Neu, Irene D. *The American Railroad Network 1861–1890.* Harvard University Press, 1956.

Thayer, Mrs. John B. *Correspondence. Scrapbooks.* Unpublished.

Townshend, J. W. *The Old Main Line.* Philadelphia, 1922.

United States Senate, Select Committee on Interstate Commerce. *Report.* Senate Report No. 46. 49th Cong., 1st Sess. Jan. 18, 1886.

United States Interstate Commerce Reports. Vol. XI, XII. Rochester, N. Y., 1906, 1907.

Wall, Joseph Frazier. *Andrew Carnegie.* New York, 1970.

Ward, James A. "J. Edgar Thomson and Thomas A. Scott: A Symbolic Partnership." *Pennsylvania Magazine of History and Biography.* January, 1976. pp. 37–65.

Wilcox, David. "Proposed Interstate Commerce Legislation." *Railway World.* February 3, 1905. pp. 87–90.

Winkler, John K. *Morgan the Magnificent.* New York, 1936.

Wilson, Ellen. *American Painter in Paris: A Life of Mary Cassatt.* New York, 1971.

Wilson, William Bender. *History of the Pennsylvania Railroad Company.* 2 vols. Philadelphia, 1895.

Wood, Jerome H. Jr. "Philadelphia, a Very Personal City." *Mankind.* December, 1974. pp. 8–18.

"Workin' on the Railroad." Richard Reinhardt, ed. Palo Alto, Cal., 1970.

Index of Names